THE PROGRESSIVE ERA

THE PROGRESSIVE ERA

Lewis L. Gould
Editor

SYRACUSE UNIVERSITY PRESS   1974

First edition

Library of Congress Cataloging in Publication Data

Gould, Lewis L.
  The progressive era.

  Includes bibliographical references.
  1. Progressivism (United States politics)—Addresses,
essays, lectures. I. Title.
E743.G67   1974   320.9'73'091   73-20793
ISBN 0-8156-2163-9
ISBN 0-8156-2164-7 (pbk.)

Manufactured in the United States of America

PREFACE

Several years ago the editor invited a group of younger historians to take a fresh look at some of the significant problems relating to the period of reform in the early twentieth century known as the Progressive Era. This book is the result of their labors. The editor chose the topics, but the opinions and conclusions are those of the authors.

The contributors have endeavored to combine coverage of important events and individuals with analytic treatments of the major questions of public policy and social reform in the Progressive Era. They have not exhausted all the issues and controversies of these seminal two decades, but they hope that their essays will give some indication of the vigor, exuberance, and creativity of the time.

As a collection, moreover, these essays display a more positive attitude toward the achievements of this period than might have been the case even a few years earlier. While aware of the failings and lapses of Americans in these years, the authors collectively recognize the difficulties of securing reform in any era and the intractability of many of the problems with which progressive reformers had to deal. In light of such obstacles, the breadth of accomplishment appears substantial and impressive.

LEWIS L. GOULD

Austin, Texas
Fall, 1973

CONTENTS

ILLUSTRATIONS

THE PROGRESSIVE ERA

INTRODUCTION

The Progressive Era

LEWIS L. GOULD

Between the end of the depression of the 1890s and the conclusion of World War I, the United States passed through the Progressive Era, a period of social change and political ferment. In response to diverse pressures of industrialization, urban growth, and ethnic tension, American society embarked on a myriad of reform movements that, taken together, set the terms for debate on public policy for the succeeding half century. Fascinated with reform and its agents, historians have made the first two decades of the twentieth century one of the most scrutinized periods in the national past. Yet their careful investigations have revealed as much complexity as clarity about the larger significance of the era.

The reform impulse that pervaded American life after 1901 had clear roots in the turbulence of the 1890s. The depression that lasted from 1893 to 1897 dramatized the social problems of the country and raised the troublesome prospect of more violent upheavals if reform did not occur. In such a setting advocates of change found an audience. Religious spokesmen for the Social Gospel, drawing on the analysis and fervor of Henry George, pushed churches into the community, contributed a cadre of workers to settlement houses and other urban reform causes, and helped to impart a characteristic moral tone to the era. By challenging older doctrines of governmental inaction, academic insurgents exposed many upper-middle-class students to social ills and shaped an intellectual rationale for political innovation. Most important, citizens' groups, angry at poor public facilities, tax favoritism, and corruption, waged local campaigns against business privileges and excesses that laid the basis for municipal and state reform in the next decade.

Other forces joined with economic adversity and social discontent to

1

launch the Progressive Era. The proliferation of national magazines gave investigative journalists and critics of the status quo a medium for their revelations, and worked to create a constituency for reform ideas. Debate about the nation's expansionist adventure heightened the mood of self-examination that the depression began. The intensity of electoral warfare in the middle of the 1890s left voters weary of strident partisanship and receptive to arguments that less politics would mean better government. Finally, growing fears about the acceleration of economic consolidation and "trustification" aroused qualms about diminishing opportunity for the small entrepreneur whom Woodrow Wilson called "the man on the make."

By the turn of the century proponents of reform had defined a rough agenda of significant problems. Among these the question of business consolidation and government regulation of corporations dominated. In the seven years after 1897 trusts and large-scale industries multiplied. Combinations and mergers in key businesses like railroads, iron and steel, tobacco, and sugar concentrated power in small groups of managers and owners. Creation of such giants as United States Steel and International Harvester were striking examples of a trend that, by the end of Theodore Roosevelt's presidency, enabled 1 percent of American companies to turn out nearly 45 percent of the nation's manufactured goods. Smaller businessmen and middle-class professionals, often expressing the grievances of less favored regions, spearheaded an emerging effort to tame business giants through strengthened regulatory legislation.

As apprehensions about large-scale enterprise mounted, the public became increasingly aware of its role as a consuming as well as a producing force in industrial society. Rising prices made citizens sensitive to the "high cost of living" during the decade after 1900 and focused animosities on such apparently inflationary policies as the protective tariff. The quality of consumer products also drew attention. Muckraking journalists exposed the dangers of unsafe or ineffective medicines, unsanitary conditions in plants handling meat and other fresh commodities, and the health hazards of impure or adulterated foods.

At the same time evidence of corporate influence in the political process raised questions about the ability of public institutions to function fairly in the presence of corrupt temptations from industrial coffers. Congressional committees and state legislatures conducted celebrated investigations of national insurance companies, investment bankers, and business pressure groups that disclosed the impact of corporate lobbying and campaign donations on lawmakers and government officials. The "Money Trust," Wall Street, or "Invisible Government" were, for many reform-minded Americans, the dangerous offspring of an unrestrained business community.

Social injustices were an equally disturbing legacy of the country's industrial surge. In contrast to the successful 5 percent who owned nearly half of the property, more than one-third of the nation's seventy-six million people in 1900 subsisted below the poverty line. Social legislation now taken for granted was absent, as reformers had to overcome older notions that poverty was the responsibility of its victims. In the absence of laws to prevent child labor, more than a million and a half children under sixteen worked long hours in wretched conditions. For their parents a working week in excess of sixty hours was common. Wages were pitifully low and industrial accidents killed or crippled hundreds of thousands annually. Labor unions, hampered by conservative leaders in the American Federation of Labor and restrictions on their ability to organize, bargain, and strike, could do little to alleviate these inequities.

The condition of the nation's cities rivaled economic bigness as a matter of public concern in progressive America. Rapid growth, obsolescing governmental machinery, and populations in flux created intense pressures on the institutions and leaders of urban areas. Between 1880 and 1910 the number of Americans living in cities rose from fifteen million to forty-five million. In another ten years the number of urban inhabitants exceeded the total of rural residents for the first time in American history. Individual cities felt the resulting impact even more directly as immigrants from Europe and defectors from the countryside swelled the population of such metropolises as New York, Chicago, Boston, and Philadelphia. The burgeoning populace clamored for services—streetcars, sewers, sidewalks, electric lights, and housing. In the process of meeting the demand, corporations secured lucrative contracts from city governments, and often, as in the case of traction magnate Charles T. Yerkes of Chicago, gave less than satisfactory performance in return. Critics concentrated on the business-government nexus as a major source of urban weakness and found responsive audiences for proposals to take politics out of city affairs.

Ethnocultural considerations gave another dimension to progressive emphasis on the city. Urban political machines and the bosses who ran them relied on the votes of new immigrants and cohesive national groups to stay in power. Since there were few adequate public agencies to ease the immigrant's transition to American life, the bosses supplied rudimentary social services to their electoral legions. Some reformers recognized this fact, but most did not. They complained instead about the corrupt practices that fueled the machines, deplored the impact of "foreign" influences on national mores, and sponsored measures to strip the bosses and their supporters of power in favor of the middle class.

The expansion of industry and the growth of cities in the late nineteenth century made the conservation of natural resources and the quality of the environment significant issues in the Progressive Era. Americans faced polluted rivers in urban areas, breakdowns in the handling of garbage, and deterioration of the atmosphere. Engineers and city planners joined organized citizens in campaigns to improve sewage and garbage collection. This coalition also tried to control emission of industrial waste and other pollutants into the air, and to provide parks and other recreational areas for city dwellers. If they did not question the premises of economic growth that led to the society's ecological problems, Americans sought to control the effects of these problems on their lives.

More pervasive than the diverse drives against environmental abuses was the movement to conserve and protect the country's natural wealth in forests, minerals, and river systems. The conservation spirit took several forms. The dominant theme was orderly use of existing resources to insure that the economy would always have the necessary raw materials. Advocates of this view looked to scientific techniques and cooperation with large corporations to develop a coherent policy of government regulation. Another group saw irrigation and land policy as devices to revive agrarian society and reverse the trend to an urban America. Finally there were those who wished to preserve natural areas in their original state as esthetic and cultural buffers against the pressures of modern life.

An intense interest in political reform permeated all the policy issues of the Progressive Era. On every level of government Americans debated procedural alterations that had, as their stated purpose, to make political machinery more democratic or more effective. Structural changes reflected the period's fascination with efficiency, rationalty, and expertise. The commission form of city government replaced elected aldermen from distinct wards with officials assigned to a specific department and in theory responsive to the larger interests of all residents. Regulatory agencies like the Interstate Commerce Commission or the Federal Trade Commission, staffed with men knowledgeable about the industry they were to supervise, sought to achieve orderly operation of the marketplace free from the pressures of patronage and partisanship. For many students of American institutions the application of scientific procedures of management and control seemed a fruitful answer to the apparently corrupt, haphazard, and costly mechanisms of government left over from the Gilded Age.

An emphasis on making the political process more open and responsive to citizen action paralleled the campaign for structural improvements. Direct primaries and the direct election of senators sought a greater public voice in the selection of candidates and national office-holders and a corresponding reduction in the power of organized parties. The initiative allowed voters to propose legislation; the referendum enabled them to express an opinion on public issues; and the recall provided machinery for the removal of officials whom the voters deemed unsatisfactory. Women's suffrage was designed to expand the electorate and incorporate the views of certain members of a sex long denied an active part in governmental affairs.

The essays in this book will examine the various ways in which Americans of the Progressive Era dealt with such issues as the economy, the city, the environment, and political reform. In analyzing this period, it is useful to remember the similarities between its problems and the concerns of present-day United States. But it is also necessary to stress the very important differences of content, style, and mood that separate these years from contemporary America.

The condition of national politics provides a good case in point. The Republican party dominated the scene as a result of its success in the 1890s; the Democrats were split over sectional and ideological quarrels and struggled to escape perpetual minority status; the Socialists hoped to move beyond pockets of strength in a few cities and states to challenge the two major organizations. Although partisanship was declining from the intensity of the Gilded Age, the nation was far more occupied with political questions than would be the case six decades later. A tolerance for lengthy oratory lingered and an audience persisted for full coverage of party maneuvers in the press. Political affiliation could still make a social difference. Republicanism in the South was disreputable, and in certain parts of the North Democrats enjoyed only slightly more elevated status.

The GOP came to supremacy in the elections of 1894 and 1896, and it remained the majority party even during the years when Woodrow Wilson interrupted its hold on the White House. Though it spoke for and endorsed the work of the nation's capitalists, the Republicans were not simply the agents of "Big Business." In the 1890s the party's advocacy of governmental action to promote economic growth impressed a broad coalition of prosperous farmers, urban workers, and businessmen as a plausible alternative to Democratic depression. The return of prosperity under William McKinley established the GOP as the champion of effective government and a general diffusion of economic benefits through policies like the protective tariff. Combined with its reputation for having preserved the Union and a sound currency, these assets gave the party confidence and cohesion at the turn of the century.

In the Progressive Era these Republican strengths became sources of weakness and discord that culminated in the trauma of 1912. As the effects of industrialization spread, the party's endorsement of an encouragement of economic expansion no longer seemed a sufficient answer to charges that Republicans favored business at the expense of other groups. The main pillar of party orthodoxy, the tariff, came under fire as a weapon of special privilege and monopoly. Diverse interest groups asked the government to regulate corporate behavior, redress economic imbalances, and administer social justice to the less fortunate. During the administrations of Theodore Roosevelt and William Howard Taft, Republicans disagreed angrily over the extent to which the government should oversee the economy and society and over the proper role of the president in pursuing social change. For the GOP in this period the great question was whether to remain the party of moderate innovation under the leadership of a figure like Roosevelt or to allow the pressures of the status quo to become a rationale for conservatism.

The Democrats, meanwhile, were still more the party of Andrew Jackson and Grover Cleveland than of Franklin Roosevelt and Harry Truman. Association with the depression of the 1890s left the party a beleaguered minority in every section but the states of the Solid South. The dominant traditions of the Democracy remained localism, negativism, and racism. Many party members clung to the belief that no man could disavow state rights and be a Democrat. Northern Democrats serving urban and labor constituencies had little common ground with Southern colleagues obsessed with the race problem. As a result it was very difficult to develop a coherent policy on major issues or to mount effective presidential campaigns in 1904 and 1908. A heritage of ineptitude and the memory of hard times kept the party on the defensive during the first ten years of the century.

While the Republicans ruled from 1897 to 1913, the Democrats moved slowly away from the older doctrines of inaction. During the Cleveland years state parties had taken steps to regulate corporations and to mitigate the effects of the depression, and William Jennings Bryan spoke forcefully for a more activist posture in 1896 and after. By 1912 there was sufficient ambiguity in the party's legacy to capitalize on Republican division and put Woodrow Wilson in the White House. Wilson exploited this flexibility effectively in his first term to enact a wide array of reforms and build a coalition that won him four more years in the presidency in 1916. The Democrats did not resolve all their internal contradictions, as Wilson's second term and the 1920s demonstrated, but in the Progressive Era they began the slow process of erecting the base on which Franklin Roosevelt would construct the New Deal majorities.

A vigorous and expanding Socialist movement also marked the first decade and a half of the Progressive Era. Socialist mayors won election in cities in Massachusetts, Wisconsin, and other industrial states; party members sat in state legislatures, and a handful went to the House of Representatives. The perennial presidential candidate of the Socialist Party, Eugene V. Debs, saw his vote increase from 94,000 in 1900 to nearly 900,000 in 1912. A variety of daily and weekly newspapers carried socialism's message into all sections of the nation. Ranging from the militance of the Industrial Workers of the World to the more political aims of Debs, socialism was a genuine third force on the American political landscape before internal bickering, the First World War, and government repression sapped its vitality.

Just as the domestic political scene in the period differed significantly from contemporary alignments, foreign-policy problems were far less imposing for American society than would be the case after the 1930s. The Spanish-American War and its aftermath had brought new world responsibilities, and Presidents Roosevelt, Taft, and Wilson devised policies with important historical implications. In the Caribbean the United States exerted its influence to secure the Panama Canal and a dominant position over the nearby countries. American diplomacy in Asia attempted to protect the Philippines and perhaps gain access to the China trade while avoiding confrontations with powers like Russia and especially Japan. But geographic isolation and a concern with internal questions kept most Americans occupied. The Progressive Era before 1914 had few experiences that resembled the omnipresent crises of the world after the Second World War. A sense of security and confidence lingered until the shocks accompanying the outbreak of war in Europe and American entry two and a half years later.

These divergences do not exhaust the problems of evaluating the work of the generation of Americans who gave the Progressive Era its name. There is a general consensus among historians on the range of problems that the nation confronted in the twenty years after the death of William McKinley. Similar agreement exists about the specific details of the solutions proposed to resolve them. What troubles students of the period is the meaning of the questions and the quality of the answers. Was it an "age of reform" or a period of cosmetic alterations that left the basic weaknesses of the country untouched? Were the progressives forward-looking, socially constructive agents of needed change, or elitist, cautious instruments of capitalism whose mild improvements prevented a more drastic transformation of the United States? Did the rhetoric of democracy and broader participation mask an effort to exclude ethnic and racial minorities from participating in the political process?

Scholars have also disagreed about who the progressives were, and have not been able to produce a generally accepted definition that encompasses all the groups and programs that appeared in the period. Studies that placed white, Protestant, middle-class professionals at the heart of progressivism's political thrust lost significance when investigations of nonreform leaders revealed corresponding ethnic, religious, and occupational characteristics. Movements with tolerable progressive credentials have been found in the agrarian South, among machine politicians in the city, within technical and professional groups, the military, the arts, as well as in the more familiar political environs of middle-class America. In the least precise sense progressives were any Americans who advocated amelioration of the social order, a formulation that gives such conservatives as William Howard Taft and Henry Cabot Lodge a tenuous claim on reform membership. So diverse have been the various manifestations of the reform spirit that one observer has labeled the term "Progressive Movement" as of doubtful validity because of the vagueness of the two words that compose it.

Equally intense controversies persist about the dominant impulse of reformist Americans. In the last decade and a half attention has shifted away from older divisions between virtuous progressives and sinister conservatives to more complex alignments among competing economic, political, and regional interest groups. Some historians use the presence of business leaders within the reform equation, for instance, to show that the progressive surge was as interested in heading off more drastic change as it was in improving society. Others find the interaction of these contending forces, with their emphasis on order, science, and efficiency, a more intellectually satisfying way of accounting for the rise of a bureaucratic, technological American society in the last sixty years. Critics of that society, however, have of late returned to the original premises of the early progressives to underscore their concern with citizens as consumers, their attacks on business evils, and their faith in democratic procedures.

Scholars have proposed divergent answers to these interpretive questions about the Progressive Era because the period itself is so full of contradictions and paradoxes. What gives the first twenty years of the century their perennial fascination is the intriguing interplay of modern and traditional ideas about the direction of American society. It is possible to locate in these two decades many of the themes that have shaped subsequent national history—government regulation of economic power, the application of scientific ideas to social problems, a concern for the quality and preservation of the environment, and reform of political institutions to make government more effective. But simultaneously Americans in the Progressive Era retained strong allegiance to values that contemporary society has to a large degree discarded—a faith in the perfectibility of mankind, optimism and a sense of progress, and a belief in general moral standards.

The Progressive Era delicately balanced confidence and doubt. Individuals hoped that scientific and technological advances would improve the conditions of life sufficiently to produce a more enlightened humanity. At the same time this faith in environmentalism was tempered with a reluctance to abandon traditional ethical principles as they applied to fallible human behavior. Americans in this period were able to live with the contradictions between their hopes about human progress and their apprehensions about social unrest. For many artists, social scientists, and participants in public affairs, the resulting tension released creative energies and contributed to a sense of liberation and possibility in the years just before World War I.

An appraisal of the Progressive Era must also emphasize the obstacles that confronted proponents of social change. A majority of the population probably supported, at one time or another, one or more of the individual causes that historians associate with progressivism. But there was never a solid consensus behind the whole range of reform ideas, and vigorous critics contested every step in the march of change. An underestimation of the degree of opposition to innovation oversimplifies the public policy battles of the age. The heyday of reform was also relatively brief. At its longest, allowing for the years of preparation and the last period of decline, it extended from 1897 to 1921. Few historians would accept this whole range without qualification. Allowing for shrinkage at both ends, a single decade, from 1906 to the start of the war, encompasses the significant years of progressive achievement.

It is also important to recognize that *progressive* was not simply a synonym for *socially desirable* as the current generation of scholars and students would define it. Confronted with the effects of industrialism and urbanization, many Americans endorsed reforms as a means of restoring older verities and recapturing a lost sense of community. They did this, in the case of such causes as prohibition and immigration restriction, through programs now unpalatable to the modern observer. Useful changes like women's suffrage or electoral reform often sprang from an effort to curb the power of ethnic or minority groups in the society whose life-style and values deviated from existing norms. Finally, reformers, like their political enemies, overlooked the plight of black citizens and excluded that festering problem from the roster of change.

On balance, then, how well did American society in the Progressive Era meet and resolve its social problems? As the 1920s opened, glaring ills remained. Corporate power had not been checked, the cities still had ethnocultural frictions and structural weaknesses, the problems of the environment and conservation would perplex succeeding generations, and the cluster of political innovations had not brought all the hoped-for improvements in the institutions of government. There was reason for discouragement among weary progressives during the presidencies of Warren G. Harding and Calvin Coolidge.

Such judgments were too harsh. It is not necessary to accept every manifestation of the reform push to agree that this period of self-examination and renewal made a basically healthy contribution to the nation's history. If the regulatory agencies, direct primaries, municipal reforms, and conservation legislation did not remove all the inequities of the new industrial society, they softened its impact on numerous citizens and established the principle of government's responsibility for the general welfare of the various elements of the social order. If one accepts the legitimacy of democratic capitalism in the United States, the work of the Progressive Era demonstrated the society's ability to ameliorate itself without revolution. This process lacks the glamour of confrontation and violence, but subsequent generations of Americans have found the example of gradual, measured reform the most important legacy of the Progressive Era.

1

THE ORIGINS
OF PROGRESSIVISM

STANLEY P. CAINE

Progressivism began with the breaking of chains of intellectual and religious thought that bound Americans in the late nineteenth century to precepts and assumptions that militated against reform. So long as men believed that the enormous gap between rich and poor was the natural result of an inexorable process of selection ordaining that some would succeed but others must fail, dogma hemmed in those who sought change. Until men reexamined their belief that the granting of privileges by government to corporations was good for the country, but help for working men and the needy would endanger the American system, reformers had few tools to use in forging a new society. But when, at last, the rigid bonds of tradition and dogma were broken, the advocates of constructive change could act effectively.

A most unlikely gladiator struck the most powerful early blow to the encrusted system of belief. Henry George was the epitome of the improvident man, half-educated, utterly impractical, and persistently in need. (He had to borrow clothes to marry in. Later he begged to keep his family alive.) In 1879, however, he wrote a book that helped trigger a process leading to the Progressive Era. In *Progress and Poverty,* George focused on the paradox of a country growing in wealth at the same time as poverty increased. "The 'tramp' comes with the locomotive, and almshouses and prisons are as surely the marks of 'material progress' as are costly dwellings, rich warehouses, and magnificent churches," he declared.[1] Through 563 pages George insisted that there was no necessity for such suffering, no reason for such ostentation. Writing in tones of outrage, George demanded that men disabuse themselves of ideas of inevitability. "The laws of the universe . . . do not deny the natural aspirations of the human heart," he asserted. "The progress of society might be . . . toward equality, not toward inequality." Poverty was abnormal, contrary to natural law. Injustices caused depressions; purging the system of inequities would eliminate economic want. Quoting a Stoic emperor, he declared that men were made " 'for cooperation—like feet, like hands, like eyelids, like the rows of the upper and lower teeth.' "

What made George's message so striking, and so palatable to many, was his insistence that justice and harmony could be achieved without the horror of revolution or the abandonment of capitalism. Confident that "great changes can best be brought about by old forms," he attacked laws that granted special privileges to a few. Although critical of patent laws, protective tariffs, and municipal franchise statutes, he especially condemned American land and tax laws. They encouraged privileged individuals to monopolize land and reap the unearned fruits of its appreciated value. Society gave land its greater value by creating greater demand. To reward those who inhibited the productive use of land by society helped create the social and economic chasms that characterized late nineteenth-century America.

If government taxed all the appreciated land value not created by actual improvement of land itself, selfish individuals would be deprived of ill-gotten gains, millions of acres of unimproved land would become available for those who wanted it for productive purposes, and the society itself would reap the benefits of the value it had created. Since this "single tax" would raise sufficient revenue to permit the abandonment of all other taxes, manufacturers and workers, the really productive members of society, would be free to enjoy the full fruits of their enterprise.[2]

George's dream of a harmonious, cooperative society, achieved by removing privilege, had enormous appeal. *Progress and Poverty* became one of the largest selling nonfiction works in American history, and George became an international celebrity. By 1890 over one hundred Single Tax Clubs had been formed. The depression of the 1890s increased even further the appeal of his message. "Tens of thousands of industrial laborers had read *Progress and Poverty* who never before looked between the covers of an economics book," asserted progressive economist Richard Ely.[3]

George's work was especially influential with leading Protestant thinkers. A deeply religious man, George suffused his work with the condition that man must turn to God for the strength to bring about needed changes. Although verging on utopianism in the sense that he seemed to propose a rather simple solution for complex problems, George never insisted, like Karl Marx and others, that historical necessity was on his side. The problem of poverty *could* be solved if men, with God's help, brought about the needed changes. Solutions to economic problems depended upon Christian men working the will of God. "The struggle of good with evil was to Henry George the process that reduces economics and religion to common terms."[4]

George's call for activism on behalf of the needy and downtrodden impressed many churchmen who were struggling to redefine the role of religion in urban industrial America. The desertion of working men from Protestant churches in the late nineteenth century was the most striking evidence of what many perceived as a crisis in American religion. Some accepted the defections. Henry Ward Beecher, pastor of a well-to-do New York City church, spoke for the smug when he declared: "Our churches are largely for the mutual insurance of prosperous families, and not for the upbuilding of the great under-class of humanity."[5] But many others, shocked by labor upheavals that rocked the very foundations of the country, charged that the churches had lost the worker's allegiance because they failed to understand his deepest needs. In *Our Country, Its Possible Future and Its Present Crisis,* published by the American Home Missionary Society in 1885, Josiah Strong, a Congregational minister, raised the haunting specter of revolution unless the churches took upon themselves the burdens of the less privileged. Strong's best seller summarized the views of those calling for a new Christian commitment to the reform of American society.

In this context the Social Gospel movement gained strength. Built on the premise that social justice and Christianity were synonymous, its advocates emphasized the humanity of Christ, especially His concern for the poor and the destitute. Insisting that individual salvation was not enough, Social Gospel advocates called for major social reforms to achieve a more equitable, a more Christian society. Charles Sheldon's enormously popular Social Gospel novel, *In His Steps,* posed the question "What Would Jesus Do?" One character, a manufacturer, resolved to operate his business solely for the welfare of his employees. Rich philanthropists bought up slum property and rebuilt it for the benefit of its residents.[6]

Few things so drastic as this occurred in real life, but this new activist-reformist bent did have practical effects in some churches. Clergymen determined to reestablish ties with the underprivileged and to purge some of the self-righteous smugness of those remaining in the church, spearheaded the creation of charity and evangelism missions in slums. Institutional churches sprang up in needy areas offering club-rooms, gymnasia, brotherhood societies, and missions.

More important, settlement houses, secular in nature but usually staffed by religious young men and women, were established in major cities. The founding of the Henry Street Settlement in New York City in 1886 and Hull House in Chicago in 1888 began a process that re-sulted in more than a hundred settlements by 1900 and four hundred by 1910. Determined to help ameliorate slum conditions and reconstruct neighborhood ties, settlement workers taught English, sponsored cultural events, and opened child-care facilities. "The Settlement movement," wrote Jane Addams, founder of Hull House, "is only one manifestation of that wider humanitarian movement which throughout Christendom . . . is endeavoring to embody itself, not in a sect, but in society itself." "It is an attempt to relieve, at the same time, the overaccumula-tion at one end of society and the destitution at the other."[7]

Experience with the poor led these activists inevitably to advocate more sweeping social changes. The need for cleaner streets, more play-grounds, and better schools was obvious to settlement workers and others who worked in the slums. Many demanded new child labor laws, factory inspection, regulation of working hours, taxation of inheritance, and strict regulation, or even confiscation, of natural monopolies like public utilities.[8]

Intensifying in influence and strength during the harsh depression years of the 1890s, the Social Gospel movement "was started by 1895 on all the paths it was to follow in later years." The growing ranks of Social Gospel advocates insisted that to be a Christian was to be involved in dynamic change. "The church," wrote Walter Rauschenbush in 1893, "is both a partial realization of the new society, in which God's will is done, and also the appointed instrument for the further realization of that new society in the world about it."[9]

Social Gospel proponents were convinced that society must be and could be changed by men who sought justice. Through Jane Addams, mayors like Samuel ("Golden Rule") Jones of Toledo and Tom John-son of Cleveland, B. O. Flower, editor of *The Arena,* nationally promi-nent politicians like William Jennings Bryan, Theodore Roosevelt, and Woodrow Wilson, and many others, all of whom had close ties to Social Gospel leaders and principles, this notion was transmitted to the core of the progressive spirit.[10] The Social Gospel was a major source of the righteous indignation that made progressivism in its deepest sense a moral movement.

Henry George (1839–1897), spokesman for the single tax and precursor of progressivism. *Arena,* January 1898.

Richard T. Ely, at age forty-one, the academic as progressive. *Arena,* December 1895.

Jacob Riis, student of urban problems, at age fifty-four. *McClure's Magazine,* February 1903.

Trends in academic circles moved in tandem with changes in religious life, reinforcing these new socially grounded precepts. Like traditional Christianity, economics and sociology had long been captives of the conventional beliefs. The sacred tenet of laissez faire, which held that government must not interfere with the natural course of economic development, dominated both disciplines into the 1880s. Then a new breed of scholar emerged, challenging the established ways and placing the obligations of the educator in a new light. In 1885, for example, a group of young men just back from German universities founded the American Economic Association. At war with laissez faire on moral, religious, and scientific grounds, the Association held "that the conflict of labor and capital has brought into prominence a vast number of social problems, whose solution requires the united efforts, each in its own sphere, of the church, of the state, and of science." The presence of twenty-three ministers, including Washington Gladden, on the list of original members, and the close ties which founding economists like Richard T. Ely, John R. Commons, John Bates Clark, and Edward W. Bemis all had to Christian denominations, illustrated the union of socially conscious churchmen with reform-minded intellectuals which the association represented.[11]

Convinced that science and the ideal of human brotherhood were complementary, these new professors committed themselves to progressive social change. "The widening and deepening range of ethical obligations rests upon a basis of solid facts," asserted Ely, the leader of the new economists. The more man knows, the more he will understand his oneness with and his responsibilities to other men. Like many other progressives, Ely was certain that society was evolving from antagonistic competition toward new forms of harmony and cooperation. It was the task of educated men to speed the process.[12]

Motivated by such commitments, sociologists and economists, studying closely the current problems of American society and prescribing possible solutions, contributed to the developing mood of progressive reform. Leaders of social Christianity drew upon their insights in formulating new approaches to problems churches sought to remedy. The inauguration of courses in social problems and social ethics in seminary curricula in the 1880s and 90s helped produce a new breed of clergy.[13] The participation of Ely, Commons, Bemis, and others in church conferences and on church boards formalized the ties.

As the social sciences grew in importance in college and university curricula, students who became aware of societal defects imbibed the progressive solutions which these scholars prescribed. Harvard graduates remembered a course in "The Ethics of Social Reform." In "drainage, drunkenness and divorce," many gained their first acquaintance with charity work, settlement houses, housing reforms, and other efforts to cope with city problems. Numerous progressives affirmed their indebtedness to college courses that moved them to devote their lives to the amelioration of society's injustices. "My life began at Johns Hopkins University," wrote Frederick Howe, a prominent progressive. "I came alive. I felt a sense of responsibility. I wanted to change things."[14]

The influence of university scholars grew as progressive politicians gained power. Reform-minded officeholders sought their advice and counsel, and they helped write numerous progressive statutes. Professors often dominated regulatory commissions and other new administrative agencies. Progressives firmly believed in the power of experts to prescribe solutions to major societal problems.

At times, however, this heavy reliance on highly trained scholars worked at cross-purposes with the principle of expanding popular participation in government. While some intellectuals showed a deep and abiding faith in the people and worked for popular reforms, others emphasized such elitist ideals as the restoration of efficiency and order in economic and political life.[15] The reunion of intellectuals and politicians gave progressivism great innovative strength. At times, however, it proved to be a mixed blessing.

Not the least of the contributions of university professors was their role in helping bring to light relevant parts of the European experience that would aid Americans in achieving a better society. As America's problems, revolving around urbanization and industrialization, came to resemble those with which Europeans were already dealing, many who had earlier viewed Europe with skepticism now sought to learn from its successes and failures.

Obligations to Europe pervaded the reform movement. Henry George relied heavily on European thinkers and the experiences of European countries. The new scholars, often trained in European universities, bore the indelible imprint of trends in late nineteenth century European intellectual life. Their sense of self-importance, and in some cases their elitism, was fed by the insistence of British intellectuals that neither businessmen nor workers had the ability to make effective public policy. By advocating the state as an instrument of constructive change, German intellectuals laid to rest fears of the results of government interference. The settlement idea, the eight-hour day, public ownership of utilities, public housing, unemployment insurance, and old-age pensions all were tried first in Europe, then brought by progressives to America.

The transfer of ideas and programs from Europe to America was by no means direct. Both were changed significantly to suit American predilections and circumstances. But to a greater degree than most Americans recognized, progressives followed Henry Demarest Lloyd's admonition that we "have the wit to make a salad of all the good ideas of Europe and Australasia."[16]

Ideas from many sources fed the evolving definition of progressive change in the late nineteenth century. Before the mid-1890s, however, the ideas had little practical focus. Local, state, and federal governments, with few exceptions, gave little attention to demands for a new order along progressive lines. The confidence of the established order lay in its correct understanding that citizens still responded more readily to specific electoral appeals based on ethnic, religious, social, and economic self-interest than to issue-oriented politicians who spoke of a new tomorrow for everyone.

Other contemporary reform movements offered some support to progressive aspirations by also demanding change, but their concerns differed so significantly that few advanced progressives found them appealing. Distressed by a perpetual decline in farm income, the erosion of their freedom and self-sufficiency as a result of the growth of industrialism, and the apparent lack of governmental concern for their compelling problems, farmers created a series of "alliances" in the 1880s. In 1892 they coalesced into the People's (or "Populist") party seeking to regain the governmental power they required and felt they deserved. In words reminiscent of Henry George, the preamble to the Populist platform declared, "From the same prolific womb of governmental injustice we breed two great classes—paupers and millionaires."

To right the balance Populists called for the democratization of the electoral system to return control of government to the people, and the partial redistribution of economic benefits to restore prosperity to farmers and other wealth-producers. The secret ballot, initiative and referendum procedures, and the direct election of U.S. senators would help achieve the first. A graduated income tax, government ownership of railroad, telegraph, and telephone systems, a sub-treasury system that would allow the government to loan farmers money with crops as collateral, and inflation through the unlimited coinage of silver would bring about the second goal.

In 1892 the Populist presidential candidate won more than one million votes. By 1896 the Populist plea, now dominated by a call for free silver, had become timely enough that the Democrats, after a vigorous fight, embraced free silver as part of their platform and nominated William Jennings Bryan, a Nebraska agrarian with Populist tendencies. Abandoned by conservative Democrats and unable to appeal to urban workers with a program based on inflation and agrarian concerns, Bryan lost to William McKinley. The loss marked the end to farmers' hopes of winning domination of the national government through insurgent politics.[17]

The Populist movement was an important conduit through which many programs which progressives would embrace (and often enact into law) first received national attention. It also stated with a new compelling urgency the nature of the major dilemmas facing American Society. For some who would become progressives, populism was their first crusade.

But for most, populism had little or no appeal. Although valiant attempts were made to win over urban laborers through the endorsement of an eight-hour day, support of labor union organization, and the condemnation of strike-breaking tactics by management, the crusade remained essentially agrarian. Inflation through free silver meant only higher prices for wage earners; other programs seemed irrelevant to their concerns. The Populists had little to say to those who looked to a future America dominated by industrialization and urbanization.[18]

More ambiguous was the Mugwump legacy. These patrician reformers had, since the 1870s, watched the evolution of an industrial society in America with increasing alarm. Appalled by both the crass acquisitiveness of the new industrial barons and the uncouth customs of the industrial working class that crowded into the cities, these men mourned the absence of character, breeding, and ideals that had characterized American society in an earlier era. "Two enemies unknown before, have risen like spirits of darkness on our social and political horizon—an ignorant proletariat and a half-taught plutocracy," wrote Francis Parkman, a historian with Mugwump tendencies.[19]

Especially concerned about the decline of standards in politics, the Mugwumps in the 1870s and 1880s sought to destroy corrupt urban political machines and to rescue government from self-serving politicians. Locally they often embraced nonpartisanship, hopeful that a union of the "intelligent and educated classes," as E. L. Godkin put it, would rescue the cities from the stranglehold of political bossism. At all levels they championed civil service reform, seeking to replace patronage appointees with administrative officials, often Mugwumps themselves, chosen on the basis of their intellectual merits. The passage of the Pendleton Act in 1883, which established the federal civil service, was a major Mugwump accomplishment.[20]

But for the society as a whole, redemption could only come from the reformation of individual Americans. Linked to the pre–Civil War tradition of moral reform, which emphasized the purgation of individual's sins as the key to transforming society, Mugwumps secularized the notion and spoke of building "character" into men. The enforcement of vice laws, temperance and prohibition statutes, even women's suffrage, might help create a climate in which the best in men could be brought out through education and persuasion. But beyond this government could do little. "Whenever we go outside the field of moral suasion, or education, and endeavor to make mankind good by legislative enactments," warned a Mugwump editor, "we check the operation of the best methods of reforming men and induce evils vastly greater than those we attempt to destroy."[21]

Mugwumps shared with progressives an outrage at the excesses and abuses that the processes of industrialization and urbanization wrought. Their determination to restore honesty and efficiency to government presaged a major progressive goal. Futile efforts by Mugwumps to change men's characters in the face of stultifying environmental conditions led many (especially younger) Mugwumps to shift their focus from the individual wrong to the societal injustice. Through this process they became progressives. Frances Willard, leader of the Women's Christian Temperance Union, angered the labor movement in 1887 by urging it to concentrate on the correct use of wages, especially the need to abstain from buying liquor, rather than asking for higher wages. By 1894, Miss Willard had recanted, asserting now that if poverty was first eliminated, then temperance would follow. "It was only our ignorance of the industrial classes that magnified a single propaganda and minimized every other so that Temperance people in earlier days believed that if men and women were temperate all other material good would follow in the train of the great grace!"[22]

For most Mugwumps, however, the "industrial classes" were something to fear and to keep in their places. When Grover Cleveland sent federal troops to support management against striking railway workers in 1894, he expressed the Mugwump penchant to support the top against the bottom. The disorders of the 1890s and the rise of populism led Harvard Professor Charles Eliot Norton to wonder whether our civilization could "maintain itself and make advance against the pressure of ignorant and barbaric multitudes." Appalled by the growing number of proposals for government aid to rescue the impoverished, Godkin labeled them "the most mischievous delusion which has ever taken hold on the popular mind."[23] Fearful of the extension of government and of the power of uneducated masses, Mugwumpery had little in common with efforts to purge privilege and democratize society through the broadening of the powers of government.

The same panic and depression that drove many Mugwumps into reactionary positions proved to be the catalyst that made progressivism a plausible ideal. The economic crisis of the 1890s had a shattering impact on the country, especially in urban areas. As unemployment reached as high as 20 percent over the nation, with higher levels in specific areas, the cities found themselves deluged with hungry, desperate, unemployed people. In New York City at least twenty thousand took refuge in the corridors of the City Hall, and police were sent to guard the railroad station to prevent other indigents from entering the city. When nearly all silver mining in Colorado was shut down, the unemployed inundated Denver. Officials there set up a tented relief camp while they completed plans to ship the unemployed to already hard-pressed Eastern cities.

In the spring of 1894 Washington, D.C., felt the human impact of the depression when a straggling group of the unemployed under the leadership of Jacob Coxey, an eccentric Ohio businessman, arrived to demand that the government undertake a program of federal public works which would give jobs to the able-bodied. The project, they suggested, could be financed by printing $500 million in paper money to pay wages. Only about five hundred in number, Coxey's "Commonweal Army" was quickly dispersed by police who waded into the crowd with clubs, injuring about fifty persons, including some bystanders. Coxey and several other leaders were arrested for trespassing on the Capitol lawn. Nevertheless, those "sandwich-men of poverty, the peripatetic advertisers of social misery," as W. T. Stead called them, pointed out again that things were not going well in the republic. Some sixteen or seventeen other "industrial armies," some larger than Coxey's, set out from as far as California to present petitions "with boots on" and to make the same disturbing point.

The evidence of crisis was abundant elsewhere also. During 1894 there were 1,394 strikes involving over half a million men, the highest number in American history to that date. The conflict at the Pullman Company in Pullman, Illinois, had the largest impact. After many workers were laid off and many others cut in salary, though rent on company-owned housing they lived in and prices in company stores where they shopped remained the same, Pullman employees walked out in May of

1894. A sympathetic boycott of trains carrying Pullman cars by the newly founded American Railway Union shut down rail service in most areas east of Chicago. The strike was ended only when President Cleveland sent federal troops to force strikers back to work. Twelve lives were lost in the violence attending the dispute.[24]

Many wondered at the meaning of this new class conflict in "classless" America. The culmination of an especially violent and disruptive series of labor-management disputes, beginning with widespread rail strikes in 1877 and including the Haymarket Square riot of 1886 and the Homestead strike of 1892, the Pullman affair highlighted anew the social and economic chasms that had developed in the society.

The depression, which peaked in 1894 but lingered fitfully until 1897, was profoundly unsettling. Impressed with the coincidence of economic depression following the 1891 declaration that the American frontier line was no longer discernible, many businessmen stepped up efforts to find new markets abroad. At the same time a comprehensive reexamination of United States foreign policy began. Convinced that America would escape persistent economic disaster and spiritual decline only by expanding its power and influence in the world, imperialists urged the taking of new possessions, the creating of an American empire. Equally confident that such a departure would irreparably damage American values and institutions, the anti-imperialists unsuccessfully combatted pressures for an imperial policy.[25]

At home many governmental officials took steps to protect the republic. President Cleveland urged the repeal of the Sherman Silver Purchase Act of 1890 to guard against dangers which threatened the nation's sound currency. His stand against strikes stemmed from an equally deep fear of social disorders.

Some latter-day progressives shared these attitudes. Especially concerned about the implications of populism, Theodore Roosevelt decried "this free silver, semianarchistic, political revolutionary movement" and only half facetiously suggested "taking ten or a dozen of [the Populist] leaders out, standing . . . them against the wall and shooting them dead." The memory of the social disorder of the 1890s would haunt Roosevelt and on occasion impel him to support reforms to head off a recurrence of this nightmare. Many others shared his horror. "This is the hour of partisanship degenerated into faction, of opinions unsettled, of vagaries abounding, of lawlessness infecting the very air we breathe," lamented Albert Beveridge, later a prominent progressive senator from Indiana, in 1895.[26]

But for many the depression experience was revealing in another way. Young Ray Stannard Baker was sent to cover Coxey's crusade. Disdainful at first, Baker soon wrote his editor: "I am beginning to feel that the movement has some meaning, that it is a manifestation of the prevailing unrest and dissatisfaction among the laboring classes. When such an ugly and grotesque fungus can grow out so prominently on the body politic there must be something wrong. The national blood is out of order." Lawrence Veiller went with a relief crew to the East Side of New York City during the depths of the depression in 1893–94 and concluded that "the improvement of the homes of the people was the starting point of everything." The dilemma of how to help the enormous flood of unemployed men and women trapped in Chicago led Jane Addams into "perhaps the most serious economic reading [she] had ever done."[27]

Baker, Veiller, and Addams became leading progressives. Many others who never gained prominence shared their sense of shock through personal experiences during this period—and grew more receptive to progressive causes. They helped form a base of progressive support. The countless people who were moved by the suffering of the unemployed to help in relief activities found reason to review the prevailing assumption that poverty resulted from personal vice. Although most insisted that aid be given only to those who were willing to work when jobs were available, the breadth of the problem made it impossible to distinguish clearly between those who deserved help and those who did not. A new conviction that all who needed it merited help was one important result of the relief work experience for many.

Many who viewed first hand the suffering of those who lost wages because of strikes during the depression and others who were simply frightened by the violence attending these labor-management conflicts supported federal arbitration of labor disputes and a law insuring an eight-hour day for all workers. They hoped such disastrous confrontations could be avoided and that a limitation of hours would distribute more evenly available work among all able-bodied men.

Most striking was the degree to which the depression experience intensified popular hostility toward the trusts. In this time of widespread suffering, privilege became far more obvious, and was more deeply resented. Many blamed the panic and depression on the manipulations of large corporate barons. Crass displays of ostentatious wealth on the part of the rich even as many verged on starvation aggravated this hostility. It was customary in New York City, for example, during the late nineteenth century, for the rich in their stone and marble palaces on Fifth Avenue to leave their curtains undrawn on New Year's Day so that passersby could see the splendor of their clothes and furnishings.[28] In *The Theory of the Leisure Class* Thorstein Veblen coined the phrase "conspicuous consumption" to describe such shows of wealth in the 1890s. That these same rich seemed to care little about the plight of the poor during the depression gave added cause for censure.

Numerous people wondered about the inordinate power which such men exercised in the society. *Harper's Weekly,* for instance, which spoke disapprovingly of Coxey's army as that "sham crusade," nevertheless pondered the paradox of Coxey's arrest on the Capitol steps. "Up those steps the lobbyists of trusts and corporations have passed unchallenged on their way to committee rooms, to which . . . the representatives of the toiling wealth-producers, have been denied." The trusts, many concluded, preyed on helpless citizens to accumulate profits to line the pockets of the already rich.[29]

The soil had been prepared for the planting of new seeds. The agonizing self-examination which characterized foreign policy debates, centering on questions as basic as the future of American institutions, highlighted the nature of the crisis.[30] A growing number of citizens grasped the enormity of the problem as they lived through the disastrous depression. People viewed the future with fear and alarm.

This "very general popular discontent, the choral accompaniment of the hard times," as Lincoln Steffens called it, opened the way for the promotion of progressive causes. Writers who found fault with America gained access to the public through *The Arena* and other magazines and newspapers in the 1890s. The popular reception given to such stories paved the way for the heyday of muckraking after the turn of the century.[31] The growing sales of such books as *Progress and Poverty,* W. T. Stead's *If Christ Came to Chicago,* Henry Demarest Lloyd's *Wealth Against Commonwealth,* and Sheldon's *In His Steps* indicated a thirst to know the real truth and solve the pressing problems.

This new popular desire for insight into the country's dilemmas was expressed in other ways. When Wisconsin opened new university extension centers around the state, citizens flocked to complex lectures by men like Richard Ely, who analyzed the problems of society and proposed progressive solutions. Campaigning as a reform candidate for Congress, Tom Johnson held tent meetings in all parts of Cleveland and found the reception overwhelming. Lawrence Veiller organized a tenement exhibition in 1900 complete with maps, charts, tables, photographs, diagrams, and cardboard models to illustrate graphically the disease and poverty in slum areas. Ten thousand people attended the exhibit in New York, after which the exhibit was sent about the country.

The success of Veiller's experiment persuaded the Chicago City Homes Association to establish a permanent Municipal Museum in Chicago featuring the same evidence of deprivation.[32] Mass rallies in a number of major cities protesting the arrogance of corporations with franchises to run public transit systems and other utilities reflected the same groundswell.

In this atmosphere of discontent, important gains were made in urban reforms. New concern about tenement housing mushroomed after the publication in 1890 of Jacob Riis' *How the Other Half Lives,* a striking exposé of urban slum conditions complete with the first photographs which many had ever seen of actual living conditions in tenement hovels. The living areas were so dark that only after the perfection of flash photography in 1887 could pictures be taken. Major investigations of tenement conditions in Boston and New York in the early 1890s confirmed Riis' portrait of disease and crime ridden sections of cities that destroyed those forced to live in them, and threatened the public health and social order of entire urban areas.[33]

Chicago's World's Fair of 1893 most graphically illustrated the deplorable conditions. Featured at the Fair was "White City," a massive display depicting the city of the future, beautifully designed, built with the newest architectural techniques, utterly clean, safe, and efficient, with abundant areas set aside for recreational and cultural experiences. Settlement workers, gathered at a conference in Chicago during the Fair, through speeches and exhibits emphasized the sordid contrast between "White City" and the slums of many major American cities.[34]

As the pressure for housing reform mounted, cities acted. Boston prohibited non-fireproof tenements in 1892, Buffalo passed an ordinance setting new housing standards in 1893, the Pennsylvania legislature passed a housing code for Philadelphia in 1895. In the wake of a searing report by the New York Tenement House Commission in 1900 and Veiller's striking exhibit, the New York State Legislature approved a model housing law. The New York Tenement House Law of 1901 established higher standards for new construction, required alterations and improvements in existing structures, and required inspection of all dwellings housing three or more families. The city created a new Tenement House Department to oversee enforcement of the law.[35] Under the masterful leadership of Lawrence Veiller, these early successes gained wide publicity. By 1904, Veiller had created a national housing reform movement.[36]

A spreading awareness of the deplorable working conditions in American industry spurred new efforts to eliminate flagrant abuses.

Most striking was the widespread use of child labor. Beginning in the late 1880s states passed laws prescribing minimum ages and maximum hours for young employees. Especially aware of the effect on children of working all night, Massachusetts and New York placed limits on night work for minors.[37]

In the 1890s these initiatives were expanded. By 1900 twenty-eight states had adopted some legal, though often inadequate, protection for working children. In Illinois Florence Kelley, an early settlement worker at Hull House, became the first factory inspector in the state's history. Through detailed reports she publicized the unhealthy working conditions for children in stockyards, glass factories, and garment industry sweatshops. These reports led to the passage of the Illinois Factory Act of 1893, a model law that included provisions for regular factory inspection and prohibition of the employment of children under the age of fourteen at night, or for longer than eight hours during the day. But the judiciary, a persistent obstacle to reform in this period, intervened. The Illinois Supreme Court in 1895 declared this statute, the most advanced in the country, unconstitutional. Kelley remained at her post until political pressure forced her removal in 1897. She became the leader of the National Consumers' League in 1899. From that post, she spearheaded efforts to prohibit child labor through federal statutes. The organization of the National Child Labor Committee in 1904 gave new strength to the cause that would persist until successful during the New Deal.[38]

Other employment practices also came under closer scrutiny. The New York Consumers' League, organized in 1891 in cooperation with the Working Women's Society, prepared a list of department stores that treated their employees fairly. After five years of agitation using this "white list" it secured a state Mercantile Inspection Law which limited the work week of shop girls to sixty hours and required employers to provide seats for female employees.[39] Such efforts marked the beginning of an array of successful efforts in the next decades to insure a safer, more humane industrial labor environment.

The detailed investigations of conditions in the 90s made a profound impact on conscientious men and women who had entered the field as philanthropists and charity workers. Many who initially had been content to aid unfortunate individuals who, because of their inadequacies, had become the dregs of society, reevaluated the original precepts of their work. Increasingly they concluded that people were poor because of social ills. Social dislocations created poverty rather than the poor creating social dislocations. Dedicated to this new notion, workers for charity societies, settlement houses, supervisors of public welfare institutions, professors and students involved in field studies, who now to an increasing degree called themselves "social workers," sought to identify and eradicate the forces that brought such misery. By 1900 a new view of poverty had become current, and the way was cleared for new efforts at social reform during the progressive era.[40]

The desire to bring about changes in urban, industrial America led not only to efforts to secure new laws but inevitably to efforts to secure better government itself. "I never go into a tenement without longing for a better city government," declared one settlement worker. For those involved in social work in the 1890s, especially settlement workers, filthy streets, the lack of playgrounds and parks, and inadequate schools could be traced to poor government—government by those who cared little about the common citizen. In Chicago, New York, and elsewhere, social workers entered politics in efforts to elect reform slates that would extend the public welfare functions of city government.[41]

The growing disgust of urban dwellers with the utter irresponsibility and arrogance of companies franchised by city governments to provide such vital city services as gas, water, and public transportation was an even more potent source of reform pressure at city level. In city after city in the 1890s this disaffection created a new agenda of grievances which united disparate groups of concerned citizens. Their complaints were essentially the same: unsafe, inefficient, and overpriced public services, the evasion of just taxes by large corporations which resulted in greater burdens to average citizens, and the corrupt alliances between these corporations and city officials. Out of these concerns came experiments with municipal ownership, consumer-owned-and-operated companies, and tighter local and state regulation. These struggles in turn generated a greater interest in breaking up or regulating trusts at the state and national level. In the same way, the growing conviction that the tax problem went beyond selective tax dodging to the issue of the maldistribution of tax burdens themselves led to new proposals for tax reform. The equation of popular and honest government versus the power of corrupt corporations and special interest took on specific meaning in the context of such disputes.

In 1890 Hazen Pingree was elected mayor of Detroit as a reliable, tractable business candidate. Confronted with dishonesty and inefficiency in the city's government, Pingree reacted like many other Mugwumpish advocates of "good government" in the period, and set about restoring honest rule based on good "business" principles. Soon, however, Pingree perceived disquieting outlines of more severe and deep-seated problems that he could not solve by simple morality.

A wide range of groups and individuals used the occasion of a violent strike against the street railways in Detroit in 1891 to protest the disregard by the Detroit City Railway Company of public demands for improved facilities and service. Detroit, like many other cities, issued franchises to private firms to supply vital public services. The ability of the Railway Company to manipulate the city council when necessary emphasized the unhealthy results of the franchise system in the case of natural monopolies. Unfettered by competition and unregulated by a captive city government, the firms were free to supply inferior service and to charge exorbitant rates. Pingree's vetoes of franchise extensions indicated a new concern for the economic and social effects of such an advantage. His actions began a long fight for lower fares and more public control of the transit system.

The mayor soon confronted the massive inequities in the assessment and collection of taxes also. Many large businesses enjoyed special "shelters" from all taxes. The custom of assessing the most valuable real estate at a lower rate than the holdings of average citizens shifted the major burden to those less able to pay. Struck again by the unfair advantages enjoyed by some, Pingree sought to eliminate all such inequities.

The depression of 1893 consolidated the mayor's tendencies toward social reform. Appalled by the human misery about him and angered by the apparent lack of concern by the rich of Detroit for the plight of the poor, Pingree built a political organization designed to bring about a more just social and economic order in the city. Forsaking many business companions, Pingree associated his administration with the needs and desires of the urban working classes. The depression thus completed the vital process of transition from a Mugwump-style good government preoccupation to a broader progressive analysis based on the need to serve "the people" more directly and effectively and to curb privilege.[42]

The dramatic fight against the corrupt nexus between a public transit system run by Charles T. Yerkes and the city government in Chicago in the 90s illustrated even more graphically the new forces in the country during those hard times. William Stead, the crusading editor of the *London Review of Reviews,* visited the Chicago World's Fair in 1893 and also toured the city's slums. In *If Christ Came to Chicago,* published in 1894, Stead argued that Chicago needed a religious and civic revival. On the outside cover of the book was a reproduction of Hofmann's famous painting of Jesus driving the money-changers from the temple. The faces of prominent Chicagoans raking in their ill-gotten gains, however, replaced those of the merchants.

The largest figure was that of Charles T. Yerkes, the callous controller of street railways and public officials.[43] "The secret of success in my business is to buy old junk, fix it up a little, and unload it upon other fellows," confided Yerkes at the end of his career in Chicago. The controller of forty-eight separate transit lines which spanned the city (they were never consolidated in part because passengers could be forced to pay an entirely new fare when they changed from one line to another), Yerkes had a stranglehold on public travel in the city. He refused to run enough cars to keep a regular schedule, used inadequate, poorly maintained equipment—sometimes open cars in the winter—and would not attach required safety devices. On occasion pedestrians injured by Yerkes's cars were rushed to a railway office and forced to sign a liability waiver before they could receive medical attention! Cavalier about the rights of property owners, Yerkes gained permission to extend lines sometimes by forging signatures on permits, and on one occasion, to avoid an injunction from property owners, he constructed an entire line through a neighborhood during the night when no relief could be obtained by residents.[44]

All this Yerkes accomplished because of his ability to purchase control of a majority of the City Council, which compliantly extended his franchises and ignored wholesale violations of the law. The vast majority of Chicago aldermen, fifty-eight of sixty-eight by one estimate, were known to be dishonest.

Responding to growing public indignation, settlement workers, business and professional men, and other concerned citizens founded the Civic Federation. The federation, dedicated to improving Chicago, soon inaugurated campaigns to clean the streets, to eradicate gambling and other vices, and to aid the unemployed. The focal point became the struggle to drive corruptionists out of the City Council and curb the abuses of certain privileged corporations. The major effort began in 1896 when the Civic Federation made common cause with other interested citizens and groups to form the Municipal Voters' League. The league declared its intention to insure the election of honest men, to achieve equitable tax assessment on property, and to reform franchise-granting procedures.

In a three-year battle, punctuated by mass protest meetings attended by thousands of citizens and supported by several of Chicago's major newspapers, the Chicago City Council was purged of a majority of its corrupt members. Unable any longer to manipulate the city government, Yerkes sought permission to extend his franchises from the state government, but reformers beat back those attempts. Defeated, he sold his interests in 1899 and left to build the London subway system. The stage

was now set for more substantial reform achievements in the city after
the turn of the century.[45]

Elsewhere the story was much the same. A broad array of clashes
between determined citizens' groups and corporations operating under
franchises granted by corrupt city governments laid the background to
model statewide progressive reform in Wisconsin under Robert La
Follette beginning in 1900. Reform groups in Milwaukee spearheaded
by the Milwaukee Municipal League challenged the powerful Milwaukee
Railway and Light Company, which monopolized street transit and light
services in the city and wielded enormous political power in the state.
In Superior, Ashland, Wausau, and numerous other smaller cities struggles of a similar character began. Specific grievances like citizens being
killed or injured at unprotected railroad crossings, or the nonpayment
of taxes by corporations which resulted in the closing of schools and the
loss of jobs, expanded into broader considerations. Pressures for change
led to municipal ownership of some utilities, the rapid growth of cooper-
atives, and a strong desire for state regulation. Agitation for a more
equitable tax system made that a major issue on La Follette's reform
agenda.[46]

Even in Massachusetts, a state never noted for its progressivism, disaffection with corporate abuses at the local level was apparent in the
1890s. In Boston the Public Franchise League, the Massachusetts Reform Club, the Municipal League, and the Associated Board of Trade
stood against a syndicate led by Henry M. Whitney, which sought to
extend its control over all street transit in the city under generous franchise terms which would insure no public interference with profits.
These new demands vividly raised the specter of "conspiracy," "monopoly," and "corporate arrogance." In 1899, when the Boston Elevated
Railway Company, Whitney's syndicate, sought to gain control over the
city-owned subway, the voters responded to a reform campaign by de-
feating the authorizing referendum by a two to one margin. An ensuing
three-year struggle over the terms under which the company might lease
the city subway system resulted in 1902 in a much more restrictive lease
than was previously given.[47]

In these struggles can be found the clear origins of a new reform
mood. The 1890s, in retrospect, must be judged a decade in transition.
For many who had followed programs like populism, the decade ended
in despair. After 1896 many late nineteenth-century crusades faded in
strength and importance. Even many progressives, riding the tide of a
discontent which was soon to flower into national prominence, remembered the 1890s as indecisive. Walter Rauschenbusch, one of the two

major figures in the development of the Social Gospel, recalled the period as "a time of lonesomeness. We were few, and we shouted in the wilderness. It was always a happy surprise when we found a new man who had seen the light." Jane Addams characterized that decade in Chicago as "a period of propaganda as over against constructive social effort, the moment for marching and carrying banners, for stating general principles and making demonstration, rather than the time for uncovering the situation and for providing the legal measures and the civic organization through which new social hopes might make themselves felt." Ray Stannard Baker remembered the 90s as the end of an era in which the country "had been swept by the agitation of soap-box orators, prophets crying in the wilderness, and political campaigns based upon charges of corruption and privilege which everyone believed or suspected had some basis of truth, but which were largely unsubstantiated."[48]

Still, by the end of the decade the outlines of a new reform philosophy, buttressed by growing popular support, had become distinct. The National Social and Political Conference held in Buffalo in 1899 articulated this progressive consensus. Mayors Pingree and Jones, Florence Kelley, Samuel Gompers, head of the American Federation of Labor, Henry Demarest Lloyd, Eugene Debs, Socialist head of the American Railway Union, and others ratified a program that sought "direct legislation and proportional representation by which the people shall be able to truly govern themselves," and "direct taxation, in order that all values which society creates may equally benefit all men in common, and give special privileges to no man or class." The conference called for "public ownership of public utilities or of monopolies growing out of natural resources and the existence of society," to achieve "equality of all men in the gifts of God to the common life; equality of economic opportunity and political power; equality in access to all the material and social resources needful for the living of free, righteous, happy, and complete lives."[49]

These three categories—more direct democratic control over government, new forms of taxation to eliminate privilege and assure a more equitable distribution of society's benefits, and the strict control (if not public ownership) of monopolies—formed the very heart of progressivism.

After the turn of the century progressivism gained new national prominence. As it grew, however, it became more and more of a split-level affair. Building on early successes, mayors like Tom Johnson and Samuel Jones achieved an array of urban reforms unimaginable a few years earlier. Others, frustrated by their inability to get results at the local level, looked to the higher rungs of government where success might be more readily achieved. The first major progressive victory at the state level was the election of Robert M. La Follette as governor of Wisconsin in 1900. In the first decade of the twentieth century state progressivism reached its apex as scarcely a state escaped some progressive influence. Although the elevation of Theodore Roosevelt to the presidency after the assassination of William McKinley in 1901 brought an ostensibly progressive figure to the White House, only after about 1906 were there sufficient progressives in Congress to champion a program and lead a national crusade.

As progressivism flowered in the years after 1900 it did so in a different context from its origins. Born in days of conflict, hardship, and despair, it reached its peak of strength in times of considerable prosperity. Although fear of a recurrence of the conflict-ridden 1890s was a leitmotif in the lives of many progressives, reform was easier to achieve, and easier for opponents to accept, in those more prosperous times. The kinds of reforms achieved, however, never were as clearly insurgent as those which early proponents had imagined. The sense of urgency weakened as prosperity returned and social conflict diminished. And as progressivism reached national prominence, its cutting edge was dulled. Reform coalitions that supported nonpartisanship as a means of isolating city government from the vagaries of partisan politics found such informal organization impractical in larger political arenas. They normally were forced to choose between the two major parties. To embrace either meant to enter an arena of compromise, to relinquish parochial local demands that had little broader appeal, and often to embrace candidates whose credentials as progressive reformers were either extremely scanty or hastily assembled.

Hence in 1897 Wisconsin reformers flocked to the side of Robert M. La Follette, a politician at war with those in power primarily because of his enormous ambition. Although his devotion to principle deepened as his political career developed, La Follette in his early public years often determined his political stance by using a popular yardstick. If the people wanted it, he was for it. In his conversion to progressivism, therefore, the initiative was clearly on the side of citizens who sought a leader. Voters chose a maverick to be their champion.[50]

At the national level, Theodore Roosevelt's conversion was similar. During most of Roosevelt's public career prior to his elevation to president his reform concerns had been confined to upgrading public morality and other Mugwump preoccupations. While he recognized the systematic abuses of certain big businessmen, he emphasized the shortcomings and defects of the common man. Like La Follette, however, Roosevelt possessed an uncommon ability to perceive and trim to the popular wind, and in turn to lead others in the same direction. Reading the signs of danger and perceiving the need for change if the society were to remain stable, Roosevelt embraced progressive attitudes. He was, declared Herbert Croly, "the first to realize that an American statesman could no longer really represent the national interest without becoming a reformer."[51]

Under the leadership of such deft politicians progressivism became more a part of a process of give-and-take, with other concerns and interests weighing more heavily in the balance. Other trends of the day militated in the same direction. As industrialization and urbanization unraveled the traditional ties which had bound men into communities, individuals organized along lines of mutual interest and purpose to discuss common concerns and achieve common goals. Businessmen spearheaded this drive by their organization of trade associations, chambers of commerce, and other such groups. Following the tendency toward nationalization such organizations soon combined into national groups whose interests could encompass the dimensions of growing national power and influence. Hence businessmen organized the National Association of Manufacturers and dominated the National Civic Federation.[52]

Reformers participated wholeheartedly in the organizational trend. Dismayed by "the inestimable waste to humanity of vital and uplifting energy through a lack of concerted action," B. O. Flower in 1893 had called for a massive reform organization which he named the "Union For Practical Progress."[53] Some reformers gathered tentatively under the Populist banner, but the closest the country came to Flower's ideal before the Progressive party experiment in 1912 was the Buffalo Convention in 1899.

Although a useful point of reference, the Buffalo gathering led to no long-standing organization. Instead many reformers created groups more representative of their specific preoccupations. The National Consumers' League, the National Child Labor Committee, the National Housing Association, the American Association for Labor Legislation, the Committee of One Hundred on National Health, and dozens of other groups brought their concerns to the attention of the entire nation. They were joined sometimes by groups like the General Federation of Women's Clubs which increasingly after 1900 embraced social reform causes. "When dissenter met dissenter early in the twentieth century, they founded a reform organization."[54]

Although vocal and dedicated, these reform groups, always in a minority, especially in national politics, found it virtually impossible to achieve major goals unless other groups seeking self-interested ends found reason to join them. Sometimes, when the primary ends were the same, such coalitions achieved major progressive aims. Hence tighter railroad regulation came about primarily through the efforts of trade associations and chambers of commerce. The support of small merchants for pure food laws and would-be exporters for federal meat inspection proved crucial in achieving these ends.

At times, however, "progressivism" was merely a term used to conceal other objectives. Many corporations supported the work of new or strengthened regulatory commissions because these agencies helped rationalize their industries, dampen competition, and even forestall further reform.[55] In cities some businessmen sought changes in their form of governance in order to make their cities more efficient and, not incidentally, to insulate government more effectively from the pressures of lower classes. At the national level, the same "cult of efficiency" attracted many to campaigns for change. These self-styled reformers cared little about the ideals which had originally motivated progressivism.[56]

The fate of progressivism was ironic. Spokesmen for its ideals were so successful that all who desired change sought to enlist themselves under the progressive banner. To an increasing degree, *progressive* become a catchall, a cliché that described little because it was used to characterize too much. The people's faith in American institutions had been restored by the growth of new popular leadership, the evolution of new devices for democratic expression, and the writing of new laws to curb corporate abuses. The changes, however, often seemed more profound than they really were. Devices like the initiative, referendum, and recall were little used. The direct primary was an important democratic innovation, but it was subject to far more manipulation than progressives had predicted. Although attempts to control corporations enjoyed some success, big business grew in size and power, affected little by efforts of progressive reformers. The progressives gave the people a new sense of involvement in the affairs of the nation. They could not, however, achieve the new society envisioned in the years when progressivism took root.

2

DIRECTIONS OF THOUGHT
IN PROGRESSIVE AMERICA

R. LAURENCE MOORE

Henry Adams looked forward to the twentieth century with grave misgivings. There were other Americans in 1900, many of them older, who sensed that the United States had lost her sense of unique moral mission and would henceforth be just another nation in the world. Adams, however, the disappointed descendant of two presidents, had special reasons to despair. Private family loss, his peculiar reading of new scientific knowledge, and the defeat of personal ambition all combined to confirm Adams in his belief that mankind had recently turned the corner into a new and chaotic future.

Evolution, Adams said in private, was not a record of human progress but the story of man's increasing unfitness to live comfortably in the world. Reason, which since the Enlightenment had formed the basis for a humanistic confidence in man, had, according to Adams, separated human beings from vital, instinctual sources of behavior. They alone among the creatures of the earth stood mired in miserable self-doubt. Moreover, the centrifugal energies of recent technology had whirled people away from the unifying values that had given purpose and direction to human society in the Middle Ages or in eighteenth-century Boston. Adams found a symbol for his historical era in the dynamo, the machine that had most impressed him at the Great Exposition in Paris in 1900. The complexity of the forces it could unleash made the past obsolete and the future unmanageable. Education was useless. Adams read the future in the Second Law of Thermodynamics: man's creative energy, like all physical energy, could not be destroyed, but it would lose the capacity to perform useful work.[1]

To a lesser degree the fears that beset Adams touched all Americans at the turn of the century. Many of their small-town communities

35

had crumbled in the late nineteenth century, and they faced the impersonal world of industrial, urban society. Ugly labor conflicts, the strange voices of a new wave of immigrants and the rhetoric of "un-American" radicalisms intruded into a homogeneous society and produced a sense of crisis in the culture.

Neurotic self-doubt has always been a submerged motif in individual American consciousnesses, and it plagued many writers and thinkers in the years before World War I. Nonetheless, a bleak outlook on the future never became the dominant public mood. The Progressive Era was characterized perhaps more than by any other thing by the ease with which intellectuals uncovered social theories that overcame their deep concerns about the rapidly changing environment. Men and women of the period asked troubling questions about their society and uncovered problems that had not before been widely recognized. However, they generally found comfortable answers to their questions and never doubted that problems had solutions.

William James, far better than Henry Adams, expressed a faith that conformed to American thinking in the late nineteenth and early twentieth century. James and Adams had a few things in common. Both belonged to a famous American family and both had gone through severe spiritual crises. At one point in his early life, in the same period that Adams had discovered the corruption of post–Civil War America, James's melancholy had led him close to suicide. By the turn of the century James, who had long before given up faith in absolute moral values, saw the future stretching out in indefinite directions that might or might not lead to a better world. However, seeing a challenge at the point that Adams announced defeat, James remained confident about man's ability to exercise choice with respect to the future. His famous philosophy of pragmatism, which received its most popular expression in a series of lectures printed in 1907, aspired to give Reason a new lease on life by modifying its pretensions and expanding the range of legitimate empirical inquiry to include subjective experience. The philosophy assured man that he had options and gave him a formula to evaluate the effectiveness of his actions. The test of any belief became its workability—that is, its ability to satisfy the expectations that had been placed upon it without upsetting other truths established by a similar test.[2]

Some politicians, of course, who subsequently boasted their "pragmatism," wanted nothing more than a respectable tag to cover an unprincipled opportunism. Others, however, had more serious intent in seizing the label. Reformers justified all the social experiments of the

early twentieth century as pragmatic ventures. If one regulatory commission failed to meet a problem, the government could try another.
Pragmatism did not mean unreflective flexibility. Passive men could be
flexible. Properly interpreted it was a cry for people to take responsible
action in shaping a world that would not stay put.

James's open-ended universe did pose dangers. It invited men to
look into neglected and often troubling corners of experience without
the preconceptions of conventional morality or the security of divinely
sanctioned truth. Most failed to go quite that far. Whatever they protested to the contrary, American thinkers entered the progressive period
with some very strong convictions. Traditional commitments to democracy and the old-fashioned virtues of hard work, self-reliance, and individualism informed almost all kinds of thought in the early twentieth
century. Social experimentation in theory and practice was carried out
under the understood judgment of an enduring morality. Men who
called themselves pragmatists operated within the limits of certain established, frequently Protestant, principles that Americans never thought
to challenge.

William Allen White, the influential writer who edited the *Emporia
Gazette,* believed that nothing in his pragmatic outlook required him
to compromise his ties with the past. In that respect he was a typical
progressive. In the first decade of the twentieth century White opened
his eyes to "swamps, morasses, deserts, and wildernesses" in his country
that he had not noticed before. In 1912 he joined Teddy Roosevelt at
Armageddon to battle for the Lord. Changed circumstances forced him
to shift his political stance from that of the 1890s when he had attacked
populist agrarian demands in a famous editorial "What's the Matter with
Kansas?" But his metamorphosis from a foe of populism to a champion
of progressivism required no fresh set of values, only a slight readjustment of the old and a shuffling of priorities. The business of America
remained business, and its natural leaders were Republican, white, and
middle class. Nothing ever led White to repudiate his early beliefs in "the
triumph of righteousness in human relations," "the ultimate triumph of
reason," and the "indestructibility of truth."[3]

According to James and White, values and truths existed within history and suffered, as all transient things, the eroding effects of time.
White, perhaps unwittingly, clung to a few transcendent absolutes of the
sort James had rejected. But James hedged his relativism and insisted
on a right to believe in certain doctrines that men in the nineteenth century regarded as the special tenets of philosophical idealism.[4] Pragmatism in no way lessened James's interest in the spiritual potential of men.

For James and for Americans belonging to generations on both sides of him, the relativism suggested by pragmatism meant that men could get better. It never meant skepticism. It never meant that people could find no standards to distinguish good and evil. Young writers and reformers in the progressive period explicitly accepted the fluid universe that James described, but, with no sense of contradiction, they kept sight of some fixed stars in the firmament by which to set their course.

In the first few decades of this century a buoyant confidence in progress cushioned the impact of philosophies of relativism. Life was malleable, hence improvable. Reform thinking in the progressive years began with an optimistic interpretation of environmentalism. For example, the settlement house idea, which dated back to the 1880s, rested partly on the premise that it was essential to establish havens for workers and immigrants in an otherwise morally dangerous city environment. The poor might always be with us, and few progressive thinkers ever imagined that they would disappear, but at least society could provide places for them that permitted a healthy unfolding of character. Jane Addams wrote in her account of Hull House in Chicago: "Life in the Settlement discovers above all what has been called 'the extraordinary pliability of human nature,' and it seems impossible to set any bounds to the moral capabilities which might unfold under ideal civic and educational conditions."[5] Herbert Croly, who founded *The New Republic* in 1914 with Walter Lippmann and Walter Weyl, set out in his influential *The Promise of American Life* what progressive reformers understood as the fundamental premise of American government: "Democracy must stand or fall on a platform of possible human perfectibility. If human nature cannot be improved by institutions, democracy is at best a more than usually safe form of political organization."[6]

Croly's statement would have startled the Founding Fathers who had tried to frame a government that paid special attention to the permanent flaws in human nature. In spite of that, environmentalism had always formed an aspect of American reform thought. Even the early Puritans, who believed that a bad inheritance had rendered human beings hopelessly imperfectable, never let the inevitable sins of men excuse them from the full responsibility and duty of regulating and improving their communal life. The extreme environmentalism of the French Enlightenment had its impact on the American Revolution, and Horace Bushnell's *Christian Nurture* predated progressive reform by half a century. Nineteenth-century reform movements, whether in behalf of better prisons, freer education, or shorter work weeks, linked the moral progress of individuals to the quality of their surroundings.

The founder of Hull House, Jane Addams, in 1915, at age fifty-five. *Courtesy of Chicago Historical Society.*

The young Walter Lippmann, at age thirty-six. *Bookman's,* December 1915.

Spokesman for midwestern progressivism, editor William Allan White, age forty-eight. *Independent,* February 7, 1916.

Environmentalism came very close to being an absolute faith among some progressive reformers. Emerging professionals in law and in the social sciences assembled a whole new range of empirical data to buttress their arguments for the reform of social institutions. The city slums became their social laboratories. They discovered poverty and studied it as a cause, apart from physiological factors, of insanity, criminality, and other forms of deviant social behavior. Improving the environment could not in every case rehabilitate delinquent adults, nor did dismal living conditions provide blanket excuses for crime. Individual character remained a key factor for most American thinkers in the early twentieth century. However, since they commonly assumed human nature to be good, reformers adopted the humane position that strong moral character inevitably followed the establishment of healthy social institutions.

Reformers concerned about deteriorating urban landscapes pushed for measures ranging from the improvement of tenement conditions to the restructuring of public schools.[7] They tried to raise money to give young delinquents a chance to get out of the city altogether, at least for brief periods. Rural settings were supposed to be wholesome. Americans had believed for a long time that hard work on a farm in the fresh air of nature encouraged a proper respect for decent human values. Supporting a program first launched by the New York *Tribune* in 1877, progressive social workers sought ways of sending the children of the cities' poor to fresh air camps. They thought it natural as well to build youth reformatories away from the city. According to an enthusiastic supporter of one such institution in Freeville, New York, rehabilitation in the country almost never failed. "With healthy physical and social conditions and with society reduced to its simplest terms, the child of bad inheritance and . . . bad environment tends to right himself and throw off the physical and moral disease."[8] Enterprises seeking to improve the environment of the individual often provided no more than temporary relief. Rural camps and reformatories, looked at in one perspective, represented an effort to avoid far-ranging alterations in social institutions. The individual caught his breath in nature and plunged back into the urban maelstrom, presumably with more energy to cope with his situation and with greater respect for social order and self-discipline. The fresh air camps provided at the same time a program of social betterment and a means of social control.

Social thinkers of the nineteenth century had rarely approached the potential optimism of the argument that the quality of the surroundings alone determined the quality of the man. It was one thing to suggest that people, being products of their immediate culture and environment, could be molded within limits. It was quite another to posit perfectibility as a possible outcome of this situation and to suggest as a corollary view the necessity of government intervention to control the environment.

William Graham Sumner and Oliver Wendell Holmes, Jr., who were both turning sixty at the end of the century, vigorously opposed these latter conclusions. Our folkways and laws, they admitted, do evolve and become outdated. Historicism for them, however, implied only a scientific way to express fatalism. If men are shaped by the past and the natural processes of evolution, they have no way to rise above historical circumstances to institute some visionary utopia. They may shed traditions of ages long past and adjust their situations to a changed historical context. (This was truer for Holmes than for Sumner.) They may in addition rid themselves of silly notions about a higher law. Neither man, however, believed it within human power to undo the work of the past or interfere with natural processes of development. Environmentalism, in their hands, supported economic conservatism.

Even Lester Ward and Richard Ely, two pioneers in the revolt against Social Darwinism who lived into the Progressive Era, had difficulty explaining, in view of their commitment to evolution, how man could be both product and master of his environment. John Dewey, who in the early 1900s modified pragmatism into a more self-conscious theory of collective social reform than James had imagined, attempted to formulate an answer to the problem. According to Dewey, free will, as it applied to social planning, only became an issue if people viewed nature and man as antagonistic. Such a notion grew out of the false dichotomies of dualistic philosophies. Once man was properly identified as part of nature, any planned modifications that he made in his environment became altogether natural.[9] They could be nothing else. Man was a product of nature, but his actions upon it in turn altered the situation in nature and introduced new possibilities in the world that previous patterns had not determined.

Other progressive thinkers interested in social change, although few of them shared Dewey's concern with the technicalities of academic philosophy, arrived at the same conclusion. At least, theoretical limitations on environmentalism as an ally of reform did not dampen their enthusiasm for releasing man's full potential through improvement of his social milieu. If temptation led to sin, eliminating the temptation would yield socially useful benefits. In that sense, Prohibition was as much as the settlement houses and child labor laws a logical outcome of the mentality that guided progressive reform. Even many eugenicists in the

Progressive Era shared in a curious way environmentalist confidence. Eliminating the genetically unfit became one program of improving the social environment. The debate between nature and nurture did not have the same sharp outline in the progressive years as it sometimes did in periods both before and after.[10]

In the first decade and a half of the twentieth century the middle class assault on the ideal of a passive Jeffersonian state succeeded in finishing the demolition of the harsher assumptions of Socal Darwinism and made important inroads into laissez-faire economic theory. Certainly not everyone went as far as Herbert Croly and Walter Lippmann, two of the boldest champions of the positive state. Their views ran far ahead of the actual political achievement of the early twentieth century and far ahead of ideas countenanced by the middle-class men and women that historians generally have in mind when they speak of progressives. Progressive reformers were troubled because the American government had never been the strictly neutral umpire that laissez-faire theorists prescribed. Adam Smith's invisible hand had been thwarted time and again when business interests demanded favors. Most reformers sought little more than a restoration of balance in the operation of a free economy, a rewriting of the rules to guarantee equal opportunity for everyone. The idea was important, but it was not radical. It aimed at preserving free enterprise, and it was not intended, as it did not, to preempt private ventures to improve the human condition. The editorial staff of *The New Republic* did its best to lower American respect for the Jeffersonian idea of a negative state. But their arguments, as the editors admitted, never persuaded the majority of the people.

Changed attitudes toward state intervention and environmentalism reflected themselves more boldly in the thought of the various social science disciplines than they did in the area of the practical politics of the Progressive Era. These disciplines had for some time been in search of separate identities. The American Historical Association established an independent status in 1884. The American Economic Association followed suit a year later. Finally in 1903 came the American Sociological Society and the American Political Science Association. American scholars who had studied in Germany and other European countries in the last two decades of the nineteenth century returned to American universities and organized strong graduate departments of history, political science, sociology, and economics. Johns Hopkins, Columbia, and the University of Chicago made the most impressive initial moves to strengthen education in the social sciences, but in the early twentieth century social science studies spread to Yale, Wisconsin,

Michigan, Harvard, Stanford, and Brown. John W. Burgess, Woodrow Wilson, Charles Beard, Franklin Giddings, Albion Small, Charles Horton Cooley, E. A. Ross, John Bates Clark, and John R. Commons tried in their respective fields to bring American scholarship of age.

Specialization did not yet mean overspecialization, and considerable mobility continued to exist between the various disciplines. American social scientists moved toward a common goal of reducing human social behavior, at least partially, to the same calculable elements as the material investigated by the physical sciences. Scholars tried to achieve greater realism in their work, meaning a closer examination of how people actually behave as distinct from how they ought to behave. American students learned to examine interaction in group behavior as a means of understanding how competing pressures influenced political decisions. Their teachers insisted that they devote more time to the study of the functions of human activity and less to the assessment of subjective motives. Man had to be analyzed not as a squirming bundle of nerves reacting to pleasure and pain, but as an active creature moving daily within a complex frame of wants, constraints, and emotions.

Theoretically all this should have meant a great reduction in the moral content of the social sciences. It certainly moved social science thought well beyond the moral exhortation of the Social Gospel movement and brought it into contact with the realities that Lincoln Steffens had uncovered as a muckraking journalist investigating corruption in American cities. Steffens had discovered that graft was not merely the product of the sinister conspiracies of bad men.[11] A corporate executive such as Shelgrim who appeared in Frank Norris' *The Octopus* disarmed the moralist. Political bosses and the captains of industry were normally impressive men who worked hard, loved their families, and showed fierce loyalty to their enterprises and the people around them. Exposing hypocrisy and dishonesty in high places had no effect on society, for the problem resided elsewhere. People did what their circumstances dictated. America, the realists argued, was in trouble because it allowed the huge machinery of corporate production and finance to run along with no central direction other than what fell within the capacity of a few powerful men who served private interests. Hence the social scientists tried to focus community interest on the establishment of a rational set of rules that could direct decision making in all areas of private and public life.

As subsequent history demonstrated, realism could be pushed in directions not really imagined by the social scientists in the period before World War I. Compared to the empirical work that began in the 1920s at the University of Chicago, not to mention the enormous, statistics-ridden studies that computers and foundation grants have made possible, their work remained moralistic and prescriptive rather than scientific and descriptive. That fact did not escape a few of the men working in those years. Arthur Bentley in *The Process of Government,* a book now regarded as a classic study in political science, attacked his colleagues in the progressive period for their persistence in formalism and legalistic description. He rudely went after reputations. Albion Small, who founded Chicago's Department of Sociology in the 1890s, dealt according to Bentley with "soul-stuff." In describing Small's reasoning, Bentley wrote: "It is all a vicious circle which starts with a rough, untested guess, and comes out in a rough, untested guess, with nothing but metaphysics in between." With a European theorist he was gentler but concluded: "He never learned to posit the simple answerable question: 'How are these masses and groups of men doing these things in these ways?' which is the only scientific question. He always asked: 'What is there hidden in these men and in other men which makes them be doing these things which I, or somebody else, can easily think they ought not to be wanting to do?' "[12]

The published work of political scientists and sociologists offended Bentley because it lacked any systematic methodology for gathering and collecting data and injected ethical issues into what he insisted should be matters of strict scientific description. Charles Cooley wrote in his influential *Human Nature and the Social Order* that "I do not look upon affection, or anger, or any other particular mode of feeling, as in itself good or bad, social or antisocial." But while assuming this neutral posture toward the moral potential of specific human instincts, he added: "It seems to me that the essential good, social, or progressive thing . . . is the organization and discipline of all emotions by the aid of reason, in harmony with a developing general life, which is summed up for us in conscience."[13] Cooley knew the difference between higher and lower human instincts as they emerged in a social context, and his goal was a society that allowed men to live a rational and moral existence.

Except for Bentley, and possibly Thorstein Veblen, social scientists in the early twentieth century felt that nothing in their role as objective scientists forced them to renounce ethical concerns. In their work the spirit of the American Institute of Christian Sociology, which John R. Commons and Richard T. Ely had established in 1893, persisted. So did the explicit theism of Edward Bellamy and Henry George. They did seek to understand the mechanism of social behavior and organization, and derive social thought from a description of human nature as it actually existed. Yet their eyes rested on a society that permitted a fuller realization of human potential, and moral norms always flavored their definitions of human potential. Determined to save man's higher nature through the establishment of community values not unlike the ones they had known in the small towns of their youth, they would not have understood a social science that had no use for the concepts of justice, harmony, and democracy, nor one that was not directed explicitly toward social meliorism.

Old patterns of thought that implied some moral standard of judgment were not easy to break even by those who strove most rigorously after scientific objectivity. Charles Beard, for example, displayed a powerful skepticism toward all received truth. In his influential book *An Economic Interpretation of the Constitution* Beard deleted literary flourishes and presented facts that he thought made a case by themselves. His chapters read like appendices and contained no editorial comment. Beard hoped that the work would serve as a model of scientific history, and it did. It proved, however, that empiricism may carry its own cool brand of ethical comment. Despite his admiration for the intellect of the men who wrote the Constitution, Beard regarded their work as a deliberate decision, arrived at under strong pressure from self-interest, to check the spread of democracy and equality. Beard later rejected scientific history in favor of a frank relativism, but in retrospect the difference between a Beard who wrote *An Economic Interpretation of the Constitution* in 1913 and one who spoke in the 1930s of "Written History as an Act of Faith" seems less dramatic.[14] It was a rare work from Charles Beard in any period that did not reveal him troubled by current practices of American constitutional government. Scientific history pleased him at one point because it supported his democratic values. But it was the values that counted most.

Walter Lippmann was younger than Beard and a very different man. After turning in a dazzling undergraduate performance at Harvard, Lippmann wrote two books of political thought. *A Preface to Politics* appeared in 1913, followed a year later by *Drift and Mastery*. In the first Lippmann argued that concern for moral norms and rationality had directed attention away from an investigation of the hard facts of human nature and thwarted creative uses of government to satisfy human needs. Political moralists were misguided, Lippmann wrote, in clinging "to some arrangement, hoping against experience that a government freed from human nature will automatically produce human benefits."[15] Greatly influenced by the Fabian views of Graham Wallas as well as a reading of Freud, who had visited the United States in 1909, Lippmann

used as his most important example repressive sexual laws. Man's strong
sexual instinct had become a taboo subject in the late nineteenth century. Social legislation pretended that it did not exist. Legislators had
gotten it into their heads that they could preserve the chastity of young
girls and the sanctity of marriage beds by banning prostitution, statues
of naked men, and the dissemination of contraceptive information. Such
unwise and unworkable legislation, according to Lippmann, only increased unhappiness and social unrest.

These were strong statements that required a revolutionary approach
to political decision making. But Lippmann mixed his analysis with arguments that were less bold. In attacking bans on prostitution, Lippmann
was not urging more sexual activity as much as he was the creation of
socially acceptable outlets for sexual libido. The reformer had to substitute "attractive virtues for attractive vices." "Instead of trying to crush
badness," he continued, "we must turn the power behind it to good account. The assumption is that every lust is capable of some civilized
expression."[16]

Lippmann's suggestion of community dance halls to combat prostitution grew from an uncritical faith in what Freud called sublimation.
Lippmann saw the irrational side of man and used psychoanalytic insights to criticize the shallowness of many reform measures. Compared,
however, to what Harold Lasswell would write in the late 1920s, or for
that matter what he himself would later write, he did not pursue the
image of Freudian man very far.[17] Man's unconscious side did not shake
his faith in democracy or lead him to doubt the possibility of rational
patterns of social organization that would complement man's deepest
feelings about goodness and truth. He concluded *A Preface to Politics*
saying that men's "intention is to be free. Their desire is for a full and
expressive life and they do not relish a lop-sided and lamed humanity.
For the age is rich with varied and generous passions."[18] So much for
the darker implications of Darwin, Marx, and Freud, and for Lippmann's
claim before the war to be a tough-minded empiricist and realist.

If social scientists and other progressive reformers refused to regard
their ethical and scientific concerns as conflicting, they also had no difficulty balancing demands for increased democracy with an enthusiastic
sponsorship of efficiency, of rational organization, and of anti-partisan
management. The complex industrial world ushered in by the greatly
expanded technology in the late nineteenth and early twentieth century
demanded engineering specialists, efficiency experts, and city managers.
In industry and government, men concerned themselves less with long
range goals and more with the techniques of managing small problems

on a daily basis. The maintenance of order rested on their collective efforts. Rising professional consciousness affected teachers, social workers, architects, and government employees. One could no longer in the twentieth century practice medicine by hanging out a shingle or argue cases for clients in court after reading a few months in a law office. Professional status required a degree, entry into a professional society, and a license from the state. The modern world, it appeared, had to protect its body of technical knowledge or else submit to chaos.

The drive for efficiency and for expert management had several spectacular champions in the period before World War I. Whatever faith Thorstein Veblen had in the future, and it was not much, grew from his hope that engineers would take over the direction of industrial planning.[19] Frederick Winslow Taylor launched a Society of Scientific Management in 1911, which worked to eliminate collective bargaining in favor of a scientific determination of proper wages, hours, and working conditions. His followers intended the stop watch to become a determinant of progress.[20]

John Broadus Watson's psychology of behaviorism, however, embodied the most perfect amalgamation of the twin faiths in environmentalism and technical expertise. The minds of human beings, Watson thought, were blank slates that technicians could program once they discovered the full range of external stimuli appropriate to produce desired responses. With proper research experts could rear a new generation of people conditioned to conform to any social plan. "Give me the baby and my world to bring it up in," Watson wrote a few years after he had left academic life to enter a career as an advertising executive, "and I'll make it crawl and walk; I'll make it climb and use its hands in constructing buildings of stone or wood; I'll make it a thief, a gunman, or a dope fiend. The possibility of shaping in any direction is almost endless."[21]

Watson was pursuing a general trend in progressive thought, but he carried it to an extreme. His work suggested the use of the data of social science as a form of social control undertaken without consideration of possible innate needs of human sociability. Organizations, not men, were rational, and the value of social sciences, once this view was accepted, became their ability to predict human response within any organizational structure. This idea proved acceptable to some social scientists at a later time. However, it typified progressive thought only insofar as the stress laid upon scientific management in the years before World War I raised doubts about the extent of the area remaining to democratic decision making. Herbert Croly, in *The Promise of American*

Life, had no intention of running over democratic aspirations, yet the almost mystical nationalism that he espoused left unclear how much and what kind of power could be left with the people. His portrait of a Hamiltonian state, designed in benevolent fashion to ensure Jeffersonian ends, never really had anything to say about the fate of the common citizen who refused to "imitate his exceptional fellow-countrymen" and other "acceptable examples of heroism and saintliness."[22]

The issue is a complex one. Political machines, which controlled many American cities in the early part of the century, were democratic in the services they provided and the opportunities they offered. Progressives wanted to replace them with a corps of urban experts who were not elected but chosen by a city manager. Yet they fought the "bosses" with the tools of direct primaries and referendums. The leading social thinkers of the progressive period undeniably believed that some were better equipped to govern than others. Many had rejected the democratic impulse behind the populist movement as anti-intellectual. On the other hand they intended the trained expert, in whom they placed confidence, to act not as the subvertor of popular will but as the people's only protector against impersonal forces that threatened to overwhelm them. Louis Brandeis arose before the Supreme Court to argue the constitutionality of a ten-hour law for women workers (in the case of *Muller* vs. *Oregon*) with cartons of data gathered by experts. The "people's lawyer," like later consumer advocates, was not an elected official. He made himself master of material that the masses could never understand, and, in so doing, became their servant.

Efficiency and professionalism were important goals to many writers in the progressive period because those things seemed able to advance the more general cause of human progress and liberation. They wanted not just technical mastery made possible by new technology and were deeply suspicious of "the discipline of the machine" championed by Veblen.[23] What excited them was the diversity and change that machines promised to bring into their lives. They had not had sufficient experience with the potentially deadening impact of routine and standardization to worry about it. The increased complexity introduced by technological innovation uprooted many Americans from the security and insularity of their rural past. At the same time machines made possible more variety and a whole new range of options. In the beginning of this century automobiles, new communications, and electrical conveniences served to underscore the faith of Americans in inevitable progress.

Professional organizations as well attempted to open up opportunity rather than to stifle diversity and individual taste. However rigid and self-protective they became over time, in the progressive period they symbolized dynamic change. Young doctors concerned about the standards of medical care reorganized the American Medical Association in 1901. The new organization recommended the adoption not only of new medical practices but, for a brief moment in 1917, of compulsory health insurance. Order and efficiency coexisted with change and creativity. Progressive education, which found a champion in John Dewey, became in part a movement for more efficient school administrations, for better testing, and for the shaping of citizens who "fit in" with their society. But, of more importance, it attempted to eliminate the social conformity that rigid and unimaginative school curriculums impressed on the young. Theodore Roosevelt told the nation to go out and have some adventures, in the West, in Africa, on the Harvard playing fields; and an eager nation joined his war, admittedly a limited one, against dullness.

The sense of new possibilities found undiluted expression before World War I in New York's Greenwich Village and other artists' quarters that sprang up in many large American cities. Young artistic rebels moved into the cheap apartments in these areas and, especially between 1912 and 1917, welcomed modernist trends in European art that challenged traditional forms in music, painting, and literature. They were joyous, experimental, and anti-bourgeois, although they still showed a sign or two of the middle-class America that had nurtured them. They read the formal Imagist poetry of Amy Lowell as well as the endlessly formless prose of Gertrude Stein. They had love affairs, went to psychoanalysts, and tried hashish. They also paid their rent, frowned on homosexuality, and quite regularly drifted into marriage.

The burst of creative activity in the arts followed the lull of the first decade of the twentieth century. The "Ash Can School" of painting, led by Robert Henri, John Sloan, William Glackens, George Luks, and George Bellows, to be sure, had made its major impact in the early years of the new century. The critic James Gibbons Huneker and a youthful admirer of his, H. L. Mencken, had tried to keep America abreast of artistic ferment in Europe. Jack London and Upton Sinclair had published novels that had carried on the naturalistic traditions of the 1890s. Still, compared to the 1890s, artistic life in the first decade of the twentieth century was dull. Stephen Crane died in 1900 followed by Frank Norris in 1902. Hamlin Garland, whose *Main Traveled Roads* had depicted the despair pervading much of rural America, turned his attention to the investigation of spirit voices and mediums. Theodore Dreiser, smarting under the publisher's suppression of *Sister Carrie,* remained silent.

Mabel Dodge was pleasantly surprised therefore when she returned to America from Europe late in 1912 and found things humming. Dodge, the daughter of a wealthy Buffalo banker, had left the United States in 1902 after the death of her first husband and came back, reluctantly, to get away from the second. New York proved exciting. "Looking back upon it now," she recalled in her famous memoirs, "it seems as though everywhere, in that year of 1913, barriers went down."[24] The Armory Show, which opened in New York, thrilled Dodge just as it shocked genteel tastemakers who were forced by its exhibits into a losing battle against nonrepresentational painting and sculpture.

From Chicago word reached Dodge of a young generation of Midwestern writers who stood ready to pick up with Dreiser the fight against genteelness that he had lost in 1900. Carl Sandburg, Vachel Lindsay, Maxwell Bodenheim, Floyd Dell, Edgar Lee Masters, and Sherwood Anderson were about to achieve their first literary successes. American publishers began to welcome some of the new work, and what proved too strong for commercial marketing found outlets in the little magazines that appeared in the years immediately preceding America's entry into World War I. Harriet Monroe introduced a number of new writers in *Poetry.* The *Little Review,* which Margaret Anderson edited, part of the time while living in a pitched tent on the shores of Lake Michigan, won lasting fame for its unsuccessful attempt to get sections of *Ulysses* printed and distributed in this country.

Mabel Dodge's famous salon, which she conducted after her return from Europe in her Fifth Avenue apartment near Washington Square, reverberated, according to accounts, with talk of new ideas and movements. The most radical progressives mingled there with artists, socialists, and anarchists. Lincoln Steffens, Walter Lippmann, John Reed, Emma Goldman, and William Haywood were among the guests. They all believed in the fight against "rigidity and dogma wherever it was found," which was the slogan Max Eastman used to describe his socialist publication *The Masses.*

Whether American optimism is a vice largely depends upon one's point of view. Henry Adams, in any case, serves as a reminder that it can be overemphasized. Memoirs of people who grew up before World War I, many of which were written in the 1930s and were looking back on youth, probably exaggerated the brightness of those years. The cultural radicals of Greenwich Village pushed the optimism of progressive politicians and reform-minded thinkers as far as it would go. So did the political socialists who won their greatest American victories in the period before World War I. They had no faith in progressive reform but believed, all the same, that the United States stood on the verge of a cooperative commonwealth. There were other writers, however, who, like Adams, do not get into anthologies of progressive thought because they rejected the assumptions behind both reformist and radical demands for change. The same cultural milieu that produced a Carl Sandburg prompted quite different poetic responses in Robinson Jeffers and Edward Arlington Robinson. The first years of the twentieth century only increased the bitterness of Mark Twain and Ambrose Bierce. Ezra Pound and Gertrude Stein fled America, and Henry James, after a visit in 1904, saw no reason to come back from England. The humanist critics Irving Babbitt and Paul Elmer More decried the decline of taste and civilization. "The Love Song of J. Alfred Prufrock" sat on T. S. Eliot's desk in 1911, and Sherwood Anderson wrote most of his somber tales of *Winesburg, Ohio* before America's entry into World War I.

Lower on the social scale, the evangelist Billy Sunday attracted large audiences to hear his denunciations of modernism and the decay of the moral stability of an older world. The village community had been exchanged for impersonal cities that decayed into slums. Waves of new immigrants aroused fears about race suicide. The family had lost its economic significance, and mothers, encouraged by the suffragists and more radical feminists, threatened to desert the nursery to get jobs. Churches had lost a God who could command respect. The great social changes that foreshadowed to many an exciting new world proved in some crowded urban areas to be more liberating to those who could afford a psychiatrist. The vogue of mind-cure movements in the late nineteenth and early twentieth century, while on the one hand serving to illustrate American belief in the pliability of human nature, indicated that the rapid social change so typical of the whole American past created mental fears, depression, and neurosis.

A sober mood, however, was nowhere evident in the initial reaction of progressive reformers to Woodrow Wilson's great crusade for democracy. Moods and opinions changed rapidly in the few years during which America fought against Germany. In the aftermath of Versailles, it seemed clear that many writers, politicians, academics, even a good number of socialists, had been mad with optimism in their support of the war effort. John Dewey wrote articles defending American involvement as an opportunity to change things.[25] The mobilization and collectivism that war necessitated would finally, according to the editors of the

New Republic, move the United States in the direction of a planned rational society.

Randolph Bourne, one of the most promising young members of New York's intellectual circles and formerly a member of the *New Republic* staff, wrote bitter replies to intellectual defenders of the Wilsonian war effort. He protested the kind of thinking that interpreted the national hysteria he saw developing as a chance to install pragmatic social planning. The coming of the war, Bourne said, testified to the helplessness of men to control their destiny. Welcoming it merely compounded the futility of their situation. According to Bourne the sacrifice of the last shred of principle on the altar of a pragmatism that had suddenly accommodated itself to "nebulous ideas of democracy and liberalism and civilization" had hurled America into a crisis almost beyond saving.[26]

Dewey no longer preached what Bourne understood as pragmatism, or at least Bourne now got the point of Dewey's teachings and rejected them. Dewey's justification of the "poison of war" amounted to nothing but a cheap realism that adjusted itself to whatever happened. "Creative mastery" could not survive among a "host of militaristic values" that did not tolerate a "jealous regard for democratic values."[27] The dangers of mere technique and expertise, if they were not kept subordinate to ideas, to values, and to poetic vision, suddenly became clear to Bourne.

Before the war, Bourne wrote, he and others like him had taken Dewey's philosophy almost as "our American religion." But "it never occurred that values could be subordinated to technique, . . . we had our private utopias so clearly before our minds that the means fell always into its place as contributory." Henceforth it would not be as easy as it had been to achieve an innocent blending of scientific and moral perspectives, of democratic and elitist notions, of efficiency and Christian uplift, of liberation and organization. Bourne did what he could to dig man out of Nature where Dewey had placed him, arguing that beyond the ethic of adjustment lay one of transcendence. In that enterprise he invoked the spirit of William James, "with its gay passion for ideas, and its freedom of speculation," for it was the "creative desire more than the creative intelligence that we shall need if we are ever to fly."[28]

World War I and the Treaty of Versailles were enormous events whose impacts, especially their long-range ones, are very hard to measure. They disillusioned many thinkers, confused others, and brought the conserving sides of the progressive reform impulse to the fore. Major trends in social science analysis and literature continued into the twenties, but intellectuals generally showed less respect for the possibilities of government and the wisdom of the populace. The *efficiency* that progressives had championed quickly proved an interchangeable word with *stabilization* or *regularity,* and business usurped it for the cause of profit. Warren Harding had another word for *efficiency—normalcy.* It was not entirely a perversion of progressivism. Even before World War I industry, as much as any reform group, helped bring into being the regulatory agencies that were supposed to control it, all in the interest of order.[29]

Commonsense more than anything else has blamed World War I for the decline of reform and radical impulses so pronounced in progressive America. In fact spirits were flagging before Wilson asked for a declaration of war against Germany. Many were content with what had been achieved. The winning of a major goal, suffrage for women, for example, or the income tax, frequently slowed further reform momentum. Mabel Dodge and some other intellectuals simply got tired. When John Reed, her lover, left her late in 1914, she said "good-by to . . . the gay, bombastic, and lovable boy with his shining brow, to the Labor Movement, to Revolution, and to anarchy" and turned "to Nature and Art and tried to live in them."[30] Her salon evenings ceased, and several years later she left for Taos, New Mexico. She married a Navaho Indian, who was barely literate, and did not move back.

Historians have been increasingly hard pressed to agree about the beginning and terminal dates of progressivism. Some have even doubted whether it existed.[31] Despite the labels that we place on historical periods, continuity in our cultural patterns is very persistent. Certainly the intellectuals and serious political commentators who wrote books and made speeches in behalf of progressive reform and called for a readjustment of public and private interests did not escape the past. Once more, and this can be more confusing, their ability to imagine future possibilities often put them ahead of their age. Later critics of the progressives have had no trouble levying charges of inconsistency against those who tried in the decades before World War I to chart a new course for America. They have attacked progressive thinkers alternatively for their failure to throw off nineteenth-century morality and for capitulation to the directionless course of twentieth-century scientism. What one sees depends on one's biases. Both elements were present. The progressive outlook tried to encompass beliefs in democracy, environmentalism, technology, efficiency, paternalism, moral goodness, and the force of the human will. While it ended in an impossible mélange of conflicting values, the successors of progressive reformers have had difficulty moving onto new ground. They have not, sad to say, found it easy to locate other views to sustain hopes for a better future.[32]

The new age of electricity in the home; woman with a washing machine. *Arena,* December 1907.

An American family out for a drive in a steam touring car. *Review of Reviews,* January 1907.

3

THE REPUBLICANS UNDER
ROOSEVELT AND TAFT

LEWIS L. GOULD

William McKinley's second term began on March 4, 1901, in what Henry Adams called "a very heavy primeval deluge of rain." The gloomy day did not cloud the happiness of victorious Republicans, now securely entrenched as the nation's majority party. McKinley's triumph in 1896 and 1900, following the decisive congressional election of 1894, had created a coalition of voters that made the GOP the dominant force in American politics until the Great Depression of the 1930s. Cohesive and disciplined, the Republicans seemed purposeful and energetic, "the party that does things, instead of one that opposes them." As the decades of electoral deadlock before 1894 receded in memory, men accepted Republican supremacy as the natural order of things. The party became a "synonym for patriotism, another name for the nation."[1]

Unity and cohesion gave way to rancor and discord during the next decade. The open break between Theodore Roosevelt and William Howard Taft in 1912 climaxed years of increasing factionalism and bitterness. This rupture did more than put Woodrow Wilson in the White House. It left the party permanently scarred, its constructive energies dissipated, its leadership enfeebled, and its conservative tendencies ascendant. Though they retained their hold on American voters for another fifteen years, the Republicans were no longer "the party of energy and change" after 1912.[2] These qualities disappeared in the Progressive Era when the GOP proved unable to adapt its policies to the challenge of an industrial, pluralistic society.

The preeminent position of the Republicans in 1901 owed most to the masterful leadership of William McKinley. Conducting a brilliant campaign against the Democrats in 1896, in office he established fruitful relations with Congress, and asserted presidential power in foreign

and domestic policy. The prosperity that followed passage of the Dingley
Tariff of 1897 and new gold discoveries enabled McKinley and his
party to take credit for the good times at the turn of the century. Most
Americans applauded intervention in Cuba and the acquisition of the
Philippines; they also endorsed the administration's caution and sense of
limits in dealing with new imperial responsibilities. Within the party
McKinley imposed order and routine in the allocation of patronage, encouraged younger Republicans without alienating party veterans, and,
with the help of Mark Hanna, deftly managed the various factions to
retain maximum influence for himself. To the ethnically diverse American public the president radiated a benign tolerance of cultural difference
that did much to overcome the GOP's reputation as the party of evangelical Protestant moralism and rigidity.[3]

The shift in electoral loyalty from Democrats to Republicans in the
mid-1890s, coupled with McKinley's successes, made the party ascendant in most of the states outside the South by 1901. Republican policies
of nationalism, hospitality to a wide range of ethnic groups, and government promotion of economic growth had more appeal to voters than the
parochial, anti-industrial stance of the Democrats. In fact "the more
economically advanced a state was the more heavy were its normal
Republican majorities likely to be." In key states like Massachusetts,
Pennsylvania, Ohio, Michigan, and California, the Democrats offered
only a feeble challenge to Republican hegemony between 1900 and
1910. Confined to its southern base and divided between enemies and
followers of William Jennings Bryan, the Democracy no longer was the
formidable adversary of the Gilded Age.[4]

Republican strength in Congress underscored the party's national
dominance. After the Democratic disaster in 1894, the GOP controlled
the House of Representatives for sixteen years with majorities that
reached a high of 114 votes in 1905. In the Senate the Republican hold
was even more secure. The number of GOP senators ranged from fifty-
three in 1899 to sixty-one ten years later, while the Democratic total
hovered around thirty until 1911. In both houses party discipline was
tight. The power of the speaker enabled Joseph G. Cannon of Illinois
to become the reputed "Czar" of the House of Representatives from
1903 to 1910. A small group of senators, led by Nelson Aldrich of
Rhode Island and known as "The Four," directed party policy in the
upper house. Popular grumbling about the presence of millionaires in the
Senate or the excessive influence of the speaker was not sufficiently
strong in 1901 to disturb the even rhythms of legislative routine under
the Republicans.[5]

The vigorous president, Theodore Roosevelt, age forty-seven, relaxes at Oyster Bay. *Review of Reviews,* October 1905.

he stern face of progressivism, Robert [. La Follette, at age fifty-two. *Arena,* eptember 1907.

President William Howard Taft (1857–1930). Library of Congress.

The tariff, "the sacred temple of the Republican party," had been the ideological underpinning of the triumphs of the 1890s. Protection reflected the party's belief in an active government, social harmony, and the encouragement of business enterprise. Viewing society as a network of interdependent producers, Republicans asserted that the tariff spread its benefits by insuring markets and jobs for all classes. It appealed to labor with the promise of higher wages in a protected home market. To specialized farmers, stock-raisers, and extractive industries like coal-mining and lumbering, it offered insulation against imports from Mexico, Canada, and overseas. American industries that faced competition from cheaper British, German, and French products formed a vocal and powerful segment of the tariff coalition. But the political impact of the tariff went beyond economics. In the hands of McKinley it took on na-tionalistic and patriotic overtones, and became a program of progress and coherent social development.[6]

Internal discipline and a tradition of innovation were other essential ingredients in the GOP's success. "The Republican party is preeminently the party of action," observed Senator Henry Cabot Lodge, "and its march is ever forward." Having saved the Union, preserved the nation's monetary honor, and rescued Americans from Democratic depression, the party asserted that it could meet the challenges of the new century. Unlike the discordant and faction-ridden Democrats, respectable and responsible Republicans could be trusted with the burdens of govern-ment. To this task the GOP brought a "facility of cohesion" and an ability to compose factional differences before an election. As a student of the party noted, "it is a standing boast that no man is essential to its success." Seeing themselves as "the party of patriotism, the party of progress and of industrial improvements and advancement," Republicans entered the twentieth century confident that their supremacy would en-dure.[7]

For all these assets there were elements of potential weakness in the party's position that proved troublesome in the ensuing decade. The tariff was not all political gain for the Republicans by 1901. As the na-tion became more industrial, the proliferation of large corporations caused many citizens to question the wisdom of unregulated economic expansion. The tariff was vulnerable to charges that it fostered the trusts. The process was more complex than that, but the GOP never found a convincing response to the allegation. Since customs duties raised prices, opponents of the tariff also blamed it for the rising cost of living, a de-velopment of increasing political danger after 1905. Republican con-nection with protection further solidified the party's reputation as the agent of "Big Business." In an era of mounting consumer consciousness and public suspicion of corporations, this apparent union was an inviting target to Democrats and party insurgents. Throughout the progressive years Republicans were defensive about the tariff in contrast to their assertiveness and confidence in the preceding decade.[8]

Susceptible to the criticism of opponents, the tariff also sparked intraparty friction. In the agricultural Middle West, farmers and industrialists dependent on the farm sought reduced schedules on manufactured goods to lessen the chances of foreign retaliation through duties on American farm products. Some Republicans, most notably in Iowa, argued that the tariff on trust-made goods should be lowered or removed altogether. This "Iowa Idea" became a focus for the Midwestern low-tariff forces during the first term of Theodore Roosevelt and a source of apprehension for protectionists outside the Mississippi Valley.[9]

In the East, manufacturers wanted easier access to raw materials like sugar, Canadian wheat, hides, and wood pulp, but resisted changes in the schedules for finished products. Since a successful tariff policy relied on the willingness of all interests to subordinate their particular claims in the interest of unified action, these sectional demands, and the infighting that accompanied them, place severe strains on the Republican coalition. Sensing trouble, McKinley hoped that reciprocity treaties with competing nations would reduce the tariff within the protective framework, but Senate coolness to pacts with France and Argentina in 1900–1901 demonstrated the volatile nature of protection as a matter of internal Republican debate.[10]

Beneath the smooth surface of party unity in 1901, there were signs in several states of the internecine quarrels that would characterize the Roosevelt and Taft years. In Wisconsin Governor Robert M. La Follette was building an organization of dissident farmers concerned about railroads and taxation, ethnic groups eager for more recognition, and aspiring young Republicans intent on wresting party control from older leaders. Disputes between La Follette's "Half-Breeds" and the opposing "Stalwarts" would soon turn the state into a Republican battleground. A long-time foe of railroad power in state politics, Albert B. Cummins of Iowa won the GOP gubernatorial nomination in 1901 in a campaign that sought "to diminish the influence of permanent organization in the ranks of the party." Embryonic reform movements also stirred in California, Michigan, Illinois, and Kansas. Elsewhere future progressives like Albert J. Beveridge of Indiana maneuvered against other Republicans in familiar power struggles that would become matters of principle in a few years. With national leadership and public exposure, these disparate insurgent factions had the capacity to form a distinct reform wing within the larger Republican organization.[11]

Finally, Republicans in the Progressive Era operated amid a general atmosphere of growing hostility to political parties. The upheavals of the 1890s had weakened the intensity of partisan commitment with a resultant rise in voter apathy and substantial difficulties in waging campaigns. The moralistic spirit of the age also made Americans receptive to assaults on the professional politician and his pluralistic, tolerant lifestyle. Some of the new mood reflected a concern for more honest government and an outrage against corporate corruption. In other cases reformers resented the way office-holders responded to ethnic groups that did not share middle-class values, and they wished to restrict the size of the electorate to purify politics. As the majority party, the Republicans became the arena for controversies over the direct primary, ballot reform, and the regulation of election financing and corrupt practices. In the long run, these changes had profoundly conservative results, but their immediate impact on the GOP was divisive and crippling. They sharpened internal quarrels, raised questions of procedure to the level of principle, and precluded compromise and mutual bargaining.[12]

The death of McKinley in September 1901 injected a new, and often disturbing, element into Republican calculations in the person of Theodore Roosevelt. Like James G. Blaine in the 1880s and McKinley in the 1890s, Roosevelt became the GOP's dominant figure, around whom factions formed and party fortunes fluctuated. A prominent politician for almost two decades, he had, on the surface, sound Republican credentials earned in New York politics, as a Civil Service Commissioner and Assistant Secretary of the Navy, and as an enthusiastic critic of William Jennings Bryan in 1896. Heroic service in the Spanish-American War led to his election as governor of New York in 1898. Two years later, his popularity with western Republicans, the machinations of Mark Hanna's enemies, and the absence of an alternative, gave Roosevelt the vice-presidential nomination. His public statements in these various roles supplied few hints of future progressivism and rarely deviated in substance from party doctrine.[13]

Yet Roosevelt wore his Republicanism with a difference. He was ambitious, impatient, and unpredictable. Some party members remembered a flirtation with a bolt after Blaine's nomination in 1884; a lack of concern about the protective tariff troubled Republican stalwarts. Others noted an occasional public skepticism of corporate wealth, suspicion of party loyalty as an essential political virtue, or rhetorical bellicosity in foreign affairs. "Roosevelt is always in such a state of mind," concluded

McKinley in 1897, a judgment that had become general among GOP leaders by 1901. But the Republican hierarchy found that Roosevelt possessed a hold on the public mind and a capacity for winning votes that offset the qualms he aroused within the party.[14]

As president Roosevelt was a virtuoso in the art of electoral politics. He relished the process of molding public opinion and devoted an enthusiasm to its details that he rarely displayed in dealing with the internal machinery of the GOP. Schooled in the subtleties of influencing the press, he dominated the headlines with deft trial balloons, a knowledge of the rhythm of deadlines, and a ceaseless wooing of sympathetic reporters. The flow of news from Washington increased as reporters found the president, his activities, and his family an abundant source of copy. The range of presidential visitors broadened; in the process Roosevelt's office seemed more accessible to the average citizen. He intuitively recognized the latent popular interest in the presidency and fed the public hunger for information and a sense of participation.[15] The center of the political spectrum was his natural habitat, and he carefully balanced denunciation and praise in a quest to give the competing forces in American society the appearance of a "Square Deal." The president spoke often of the merits of unalloyed Americanism, but his actions comprehended the impact of ethnic loyalties at the ballot box. Yet the basis of his popularity went beyond these semi-calculated effects. The man exuded a free-wheeling exuberance and ebullience that fascinated the public for a generation. Americans retold "Teddy" anecdotes, responded to his moralism, and agreed with the Englishman who called Roosevelt "an interesting combination of St. Vitus and St. Paul."[16]

Masterful on the campaign trail, Roosevelt appeared to less advantage in dealing with Congress and his party. Eager to strengthen presidential power, he had scant regard for legislative sensibilities, and relations between Capitol Hill and the White House steadily deteriorated after the early years of his first term. Within the GOP he pursued an erratic course that left both progressives and conservatives perplexed about his purposes and suspicious of his tactics. Preaching the need for courage in public life, Roosevelt equivocated on hard issues like the tariff and Negro rights. These mixed results stemmed in part from an excessive faith in his political skill. He was at best mediocre as a manager of men. He tended to rely on those who told him what he wanted to hear; men who differed with Roosevelt soon lost the pleasure of his company. A poor listener and susceptible to flattery, he was capable of petty and vindictive behavior toward those whom he disliked. Leaving the presidency, he wrote that it had been his business "to take hold of the

conservative party" and make it "a party of *progressive* conservatism."
For many honest Republican politicians opportunism and expediency
seemed equally plausible explanations for Roosevelt's record as the leader
of the GOP.[17]

Roosevelt's primary political aim in his first term was the presidential nomination in 1904. To that end, he emphasized the more popular
portion of William McKinley's policies, evaded action on the divisive
tariff issue, and sought to commit the party machinery to his candidacy.
After taking the oath of office, Roosevelt announced his intention to
"continue, absolutely unbroken, the policy of President McKinley."[18] In
large measure that is exactly what he did. The new president's early
years were devoted to implementing and enacting the program of his
predecessor; in terms of achievement it represented a second term for
McKinley. But Roosevelt was selective in his application of existing
policy. He could safely expand and extend GOP action on the trusts; he
was more cautious and timid on the tariff question.

On trusts McKinley had already decided that the Republicans must
act. His letter of acceptance in 1900 said that combinations interfering
with competition "should be made the subject of prohibitory or penal
legislation," and he described publicity as a "helpful influence" in dealing with the evils of corporate consolidation. Roosevelt's first message
to Congress concluded that "Publicity is the only sure remedy which we
can now invoke," and this precept shaped his legislative recommendations through 1904. The Department of Commerce and Labor, created
in 1903, fulfilled a GOP campaign promise in 1900. Its Bureau of
Corporations gave the government the means to obtain and publicize
information about business activities as both McKinley and Roosevelt
had advocated.[19]

Roosevelt diverged from McKinley in the public emphasis that he
gave to the trust question and his vigorous assertions that the federal
government possessed the power to deal with it. Large corporations, he
noted in 1902, "are the creatures of the State, and the State not only
has the right to control them, but it is in duty bound to control them
wherever the need of such control is shown." He balanced constantly
the benefits of bigness against the government's capacity to regulate and
did not go beyond publicity as the necessary first step. Yet, even this
modest program alarmed and irritated some men on Wall Street who
preferred quiet presidents on this issue. But most Americans regarded
the Roosevelt position as judicious and his proposals as sound. Though
his tangible achievements were limited, his willingness to air the trust

issue gave public emotions a chance to vent themselves, and proved a major element in building Roosevelt's popular standing after 1901.[20]

Two episodes offered Roosevelt the opportunity to demonstrate in practice his concern with the power of large corporations. In February 1902 the government filed suit to block the merger of several large railroad companies in the Northwest into the Northern Securities Company. Put together by J. P. Morgan, James J. Hill, E. H. Harriman, and the Rockefeller interests, this company, with its attendant stock issues, threat to competition, and potential dominance of the region it served, had come to symbolize the dangers of "trustification." The Supreme Court sustained the government in 1904. On this case, and the prosecution of the Beef Trust, largely rested Roosevelt's early reputation as a "trust buster." While he did not believe that the breaking-up of big enterprises was the proper solution to their misbehavior, his action convinced the public that the president, and to a lesser extent his party, could retain an independence of corporate influence. It became less easy to contend "that the Republican party always legislates to aid the rich and oppress the poor."[21]

Presidential intervention in the Anthracite Coal Strike of 1902 further solidified the impression that Roosevelt could resolve the tensions of an industrial society and do justice to the nation's opposing forces. Entering the prolonged dispute between coal operators and miners in the autumn, Roosevelt acted as a constructive catalyst. The prestige of his office brought the parties together, and cleared the way for serious negotiation. At the same time the president seconded the efforts of Mark Hanna, Elihu Root, and J. P. Morgan to work out a compromise settlement. Success in October averted a power crisis, eased public anxiety about possible violence, and helped the Republicans limit Democratic gains in the congressional elections of that year.[22]

Despite the animus of some segments of the business community, Roosevelt's antitrust program and his role in the coal strike strengthened his party. In other important ways he widened and deepened the GOP's electoral base. Sensitive to the effect of ethnic loyalties in voting behavior, the president offered public sympathy and tangible encouragement to groups long suspicious of Republican moralism. Adroit appointments in the Philippines and on the Indian Commission buttressed policies that wooed Catholic voters away from the Democrats. On such apparently small but politically volatile matters as the selection of chaplains to the armed forces, the president sought to include representatives from the whole spectrum of denominations. From the Italians and Hungarians in New York to the Germans in Wisconsin, the diverse national and religious groups received constant and perceptive presidential attention. "I have not appealed to any man as Jew, as Protestant, or as Catholic," he wrote in 1904, but each was "to have a square deal, no more and no less, without regard to his creed."[23]

Achievements as an administrator and a diplomat added to his appeal at the polls. Maintenance of the open shop in the Government Printing Office offset the apparent pro-labor action in settling the coal strike. Forceful presidential effort against scandals in the Post Office removed a potential source of embarrassment. In foreign policy, the acquisition of the Panama Canal Zone, the assertion of national pre-eminence in the Caribbean, and the resolution of the Alaska Boundary controversy with Canada completed the agenda of problems left over from the McKinley administration and stamped Roosevelt as a champion of American power and influence in the world.[24]

The president's handling of the tariff issue in his first term contrasted strikingly with his strong performance on other matters. His equivocation contributed to the growing Republican friction on the issue. Roosevelt shied away from protection in part because he never fully grasped its ideological implications or economic complexity. "There is nothing any more intrinsically right or wrong in a 40% tariff than in a 60% tariff," he observed in 1903, in a phrase that would have confirmed the worst fears of dedicated protectionists. Afraid that a full-scale tariff debate would split the party, Roosevelt procrastinated throughout his presidency.[25]

There was one serious campaign for tariff revision in Roosevelt's first term. Upon taking office he found McKinley's reciprocity treaties still waiting in the Senate. These pacts, promising negotiated and controlled changes in selected schedules with individual nations, offered a way around the volatile process of congressional logrolling that threatened always to frustrate tariff legislation. In the early weeks of his presidency Roosevelt indicated that he would support the treaties as McKinley had done in his last speech at Buffalo. Pressure from eastern businessmen, the opposition of Senator Nelson Aldrich and other party leaders, and fear of repeating Grover Cleveland's errors led the President to give only the mildest endorsement of general reciprocity in his message to Congress. Caution was excusable and understandable, but a significant opportunity had been missed.[26]

Events compelled consideration of ancillary portions of the tariff before 1904. The economic needs of Cuba led Congress to approve a reciprocity treaty with that island after prolonged debate in 1902–1903.

In the aftermath of the coal strike, the duty on anthracite coal was removed. Otherwise, the rhythm of congressional sessions and elections allowed the president to postpone action. Avoiding the tariff had persuasive short-term justification, but, while it languished, pressures within the GOP on the issue built up to the danger point.[27]

In his quest for the Republican nomination, Roosevelt faced a complex situation, but one in which he had most of the advantages. With the exception of Mark Hanna, potential rivals like Charles W. Fairbanks of Indiana or Leslie M. Shaw lacked widespread popularity or broadly based party support. More important, if Roosevelt made a creditable record, repudiation at the convention would imperil the party's chances in 1904. As Roosevelt's performance unfolded in 1902, Republican state conventions across the nation endorsed him for president. By the end of the year, only a major blunder could interrupt progress toward an easy victory at the national convention.[28]

At the outset of his presidency Roosevelt took up the tangled question of Republicanism in the South. Though the region delivered no electoral votes, its delegates, often predominantly black, composed one quarter of the national convention and were regarded as loyal only to the highest bidder of patronage or cash. Roosevelt wanted to revitalize the party in the South, a perennial dream of Republican presidents, while insuring regional support for his candidacy. With the aid of black leader Booker T. Washington he named "self-made Negroes or paternalistic Gold Democrats" who would endorse him in 1904. Washington's luncheon at the White House in 1901, the president's defense of Negro appointees in Mississippi and South Carolina, and his condemnation of "Lily White" movements in Alabama and South Carolina reassured the black vote in the North and Negro Republican organizations in the South. In practice, however, the selection of Gold Democrats and the reduction of black appointments encouraged the growing pressure for excluding Negroes from the southern GOP. Mixing expediency and mild principle, Roosevelt's southern strategy fulfilled its essential purposes of delivering votes for his nomination in 1904.[29]

For anti-Roosevelt Republicans, unhappy with the president's vigor, assertiveness and program, Mark Hanna represented the only real alternative. Yet, as the Ohio senator recognized, he had striking weaknesses. He was old, in uncertain health, and closely, if unfairly, connected in the popular mind with big business. More important, he knew that the party's nomination would be worth little if it came after the rejection of Roosevelt. Aware of his liabilities, Hanna had no serious presidential ambitions, but did want to retain influence. He was also reluctant, as chairman of the national committee, to foreclose the chances of any other challengers by openly endorsing the president. Roosevelt, on the other hand, watched Hanna with intense suspicion, listened to those who warned him against the Ohioan, and desperately desired a formal commitment from McKinley's old friend.[30]

The two men maintained an uneasy alliance in 1902 as Roosevelt's national backing within the party grew. The president did not pursue a concerted anti-Hanna strategy in seeking delegations; they came to him as his record evolved and his popularity emerged. Roosevelt had the substance of power; by 1903 he sought also public loyalty from his erstwhile rival. In the spring the machinations of Senator Joseph B. Foraker of Ohio and public insistence from the White House compelled Hanna to support a resolution of endorsement in the state convention. At a June meeting Roosevelt believed, probably erroneously, that Hanna had agreed to come out for him. A brief stock market panic in the summer of 1903, resultant business opposition to the president, and the senator's triumphant success in the fall Ohio elections revived talk of a Hanna candidacy and Roosevelt's fears. Still anxious for an endorsement, the president and his allies moved toward a showdown with Hanna in early 1904. Before these plans matured, Hanna died in mid-February and Roosevelt's path to the nomination was clear.[31]

Even with Hanna out of the way, Roosevelt remained cautious and conservative in his dealings with the party in the rest of 1904. The platform, written with Henry Cabot Lodge, slid around the tariff issue, concentrated on the past Republican record, and gave little clue to future policy. Roosevelt kept his hands off the vice-presidency, and the party named a bland conservative, Charles Warren Fairbanks of Indiana. For the chairman of the national committee the president sought first Cornelius N. Bliss, a New York financier and McKinley ally. When Bliss declined, Roosevelt settled on George B. Cortelyou. A former presidential secretary and currently Secretary of Commerce and Labor, Cortelyou brought to the post the efficiency, order, and flair for smooth organization that made him a prototype of the twentieth-century campaign manager. Finally, Roosevelt insisted that intraparty feuds in states like Wisconsin and Illinois be resolved or adjourned in the interest of national success.[32]

These efforts produced a reasonably united party at the national convention in June 1904, and Roosevelt was unanimously nominated. Party regulars still eyed him with occasional distrust, and the convention displayed less than overwhelming enthusiasm. But most Republicans knew that they had a formidable standard-bearer. To run against Roosevelt the Democrats selected the colorless and conservative Alton B. Parker of New York. Badly divided, certain of defeat, and left with opposition to the president's record as the only issue, the Democracy floundered through a pathetic campaign. Last-minute charges about corporate contributions to GOP coffers only enabled Roosevelt to issue a ringing public statement of denial and to dramatize once again the impact of his personality. Although Roosevelt fretted over his prospects, the result was never in doubt. "I am stunned by the overwhelming victory we have won," he told his son.[33]

In the election of 1904 the Republican party reached the peak of its electoral supremacy in the Progressive Era. Roosevelt gathered 336 electoral votes to 140 for Parker, won 56.4 percent of the total ballots, and piled up a popular majority of more than 2.5 million, the largest to that date. The Democrats won no states outside the South and lost all the western states that Bryan had carried in 1896 and 1900. On the sectional border West Virginia and Missouri joined the GOP column. Industrial centers like Pennsylvania and Ohio went Republican by crushing margins. Among urban residents, Catholic, and ethnic voters, Roosevelt's appeals paid off in widespread defections from the Democrats. Gubernatorial defeats in Massachusetts, Minnesota, and three other states that Roosevelt won, indicated that the president was stronger than his party but did not take the edge off the triumph. The question before the GOP was, as Senator Orville H. Platt remarked, "what are we going to do with our victory?"[34]

Some party members hoped that the Republicans could follow Mark Hanna's maxim and "stand pat" on the victory, but the pressures for positive change in Roosevelt's second term were too intense to ignore. Muckraking journalists attacked political corruption in state and nation, exposed corporate wrongdoing, and warned consumers of the hazards of shoddy products. Diverse elements in the business community— shippers, hinterland bankers, and medium-sized manufacturers—sought national legislation to alter the power balance in their sector of the economy. Middle-class Americans rallied behind reform governors and mayors who challenged political machines, entrenched incumbents, and business influence on state and local affairs. Organized labor directed its emerging political clout toward electing candidates and securing laws to improve the conditions of work and a union's chances of winning strikes. The growing size of the Socialist vote alarmed conservatives who feared that change could lead to revolution and progressives who insisted that only reasoned change could avert social upheaval. Within months of the 1904 election the nation was in political ferment. "There is a craze on

now not at all unlike what preceded the Alliance and Populist movement," warned a troubled Kansas Republican in March 1905.[35]

Proponents of tariff revision saw the decisive triumph of 1904 as an
opportunity to secure changes in the Dingley Law from the solidly Republican Congress after March 1905. Friends like Nicholas Murray
Butler and Elihu Root, Middle Westerners still critical of existing schedules, and Massachusetts leaders interested in lower duties on raw materials all urged Roosevelt to summon a special session in the spring or
fall. Exploring the question in late 1904 the president encountered reso-
lute opposition in the House and Senate to any action on the tariff at all.
By the early months of 1905 the prospect of revision had faded; the
practical effect was to defer any changes until after the 1908 election.
Discussion of the issue persisted over the next three years, especially
with rising prices on consumer goods, but the White House avoided facing the matter. Convinced that "a large part of the scream about the
tariff represents simply an effort to draw a red herring across the trail of
genuine economic reform within our own borders," Roosevelt had few
qualms about leaving to his successor a boring and confusing issue.[36]

Railroad regulation, on the other hand, was a question to which Roosevelt could give interest and attention. Appealing to both specific business
groups and a broad popular animus against rail companies, stricter control of railroads also harmonized with the president's desire for orderly,
expert, and administrative management of economic power. In the annual message of 1904 he urged that the Interstate Commerce Commission should have greater authority over the railroad rate structure. Over
the following eighteen months Roosevelt invoked the manifold powers
of his office to gain railroad legislation. Discussion of the tariff helped
convince GOP leaders in the House that legislation on railroads was
preferable to a debate on protection. Speeches by the president and his
cabinet, as well as timely publicity from the Bureau of Corporations and
the Justice Department about railroad indiscretions, defined the regulatory program and offset industry lobbying on Capitol Hill and with
the public. The annual message of December 1905 renewed the call for
congressional action. "What we need to do," said the president, "is to
develop an orderly system, and such a system can only come through
the gradually increased exercise of the right of efficient government control."[37]

The Hepburn Act of 1906 embodied these presumptions. Passing
the House easily in February, it had a stormy time in the Senate where
Republican conservatives, led by Nelson Aldrich, worked to insure the
judicial review of ICC action, and thus dilute the measure. Complex

parliamentary maneuvers eventually produced a law that gave Roosevelt much of what he had sought: the ICC could establish reasonable rates, and the regulatory agency received other power to oversee railroad operations. From this same Congress also came a pure food and drug law and a meat inspection law, the latter in response to revelations about unsanitary conditions in the nation's stockyards. As Roosevelt noted, these measures, "taken together," marked a "noteworthy advance in the policy of securing Federal supervision and control over corporations."[38]

Republicans used these legislative achievements in the congressional elections of 1906 to counter assaults from organized labor, under the leadership of American Federation of Labor president Samuel Gompers, and resurgent Democrats. Although the GOP lost twenty-eight seats in the House, cutting its majority in half, the party retained control of both houses. "It is very gratifying," Roosevelt wrote, "to have ridden iron-shod over Gompers and the labor agitators, and at the same time to have won the striking victory while the big financiers either stood sullenly aloof or gave furtive aid to the enemy." But there were disturbing portents. The appearance of labor as a political force foreshadowed the shift of the unions toward the Democracy in the next decade. Democratic gains in the Middle West, William Randolph Hearst's strong showing in defeat in New York, and congressional victories in the Northeast indicated an opposition revival from the debacle of 1904. Within the GOP, moreover, there had been organizational and financial apathy about the elections, growing criticism of party leaders like Cannon and Aldrich, and an erosion of the cohesion that had so long characterized Republican campaigns.[39]

These problems reflected the serious factional and philosophical differences that had emerged inside the Republican party by the end of 1906. Theodore Roosevelt's regulatory policy was one source of friction. Involving the use of federal power to make business improve itself and thus forestall more drastic social change, the president's program also included a downgrading of Congress, increased authority for the chief executive and administrative agencies, and private governmental understandings with key industries. In aim and tactics these proposals challenged many parts of the traditional Republican creed. It was one thing to use national power to promote economic growth, quite another to employ it to regulate an industrial society. The question of state's rights, so long the exclusive province of the Democrats, now surfaced in GOP thinking. Even mild social legislation also seemed to some conservative Republicans an assault on property, the cornerstone of the party's entrepreneurial premise, or a threat to their special interests. Others simply found the pace of reform too quick. Times were "changing too damned fast now to suit an old-fashioned Republican," sighed Senator John C. Spooner in 1906.[40]

Progressive Republicans countered that the party was not responding to social problems rapidly enough. Strongest in the agrarian states of the Mississippi Valley, and the Far West, such reformers as La Follette, Cummins, and Beveridge contended that the GOP should employ more federal power to restrain business through lower tariffs, stronger railroad regulation, and social justice legislation. These proposals, couched in moralistic terms, also looked to a sectional adjustment of economic strength away from the East in favor of the Middle West. Similarly, in championing procedural reforms like the direct primary or direct election of senators, the progressives cleared away obstacles to their policy goals, but also undermined, to their own advantage, incumbent party leaders. In the House insurgents chafed under the dictates of Speaker Cannon; Aldrich was a comparable target for the animosities of progressive senators. The reformers were sincere and principled in opposing the standpatters but had as much ambition, opportunism, and guile as any of their rivals. In the process of debate between the two sides, party unity ebbed away.[41]

The presidential style and policies of Theodore Roosevelt in his last two years in office accelerated the polarization of the Republicans. The progressives received encouragement from the president's increasing sympathy for their programs and goals. While he did not share all the views of La Follette, Cummins, and their colleagues, he recognized the popular sentiment for reform and wished to give that impulse orderly, personal direction. In messages and speeches Roosevelt urged the party to take up the income tax, federal incorporation of interstate business, and restrictions on the use of injunctions in labor disputes, and numerous other measures. Republican reformers retained residual suspicion of the president's friendship with some of the regulars and his propensity for compromise, but they welcomed endorsement of their ideas and expected the next president to build on that legacy.[42]

As Roosevelt's second term unfolded, conservatives found more and more to criticize. Standpatters in Congress resented the expansion of executive power in conservation and foreign policy and questioned precipitate presidential action in such episodes as the Brownsville affair of 1906. Some of the rancor stemmed from a basic dislike of reform, some reflected a knowledge that Roosevelt was a virtual lame duck, but qualms about executive supremacy also harked back to the GOP's Whiggish past. Conservatives wanted a president less disposed to initiate

Roosevelt and Joseph L. Bristow repel the evil wolves of graft and corruption.
Judge, December 12, 1903.

change, less critical of courts and lawmakers, and more solicitous of party regularity. By 1908 Roosevelt's relations with Congress had worsened, and mutual recrimination stalled the legislative process. Among the business community, especially after the Panic of 1907, the hostility toward regulatory laws combined with tension and irritation at Roosevelt's unpredictability into a desire to elect a more reliable president in 1908.[43]

On election night in 1904 Roosevelt announced that he would not be a candidate in 1908. With commendable fortitude he adhered to that pledge, and resisted entreaties that he change his mind. But Roosevelt was also determined to have a proper, progressive successor, and devoted much energy to advancing the fortunes of his personal choice, William Howard Taft. The president came to Taft in part because of the absence of suitable alternatives. Elihu Root, the first choice, was too old, in bad health, and a corporation lawyer. Charles Evans Hughes, governor of New York, had reform qualifications, but his aloof manner and political independence rubbed Roosevelt raw. The other hopefuls, Philander Knox, Joseph G. Cannon, and Vice-President Fairbanks, were easily disqualified as conservatives without popular appeal. When Senator Joseph B. Foraker of Ohio, Taft's rival in his home state, assailed in early 1907 Roosevelt's dismissal of black soldiers from the army in the Brownsville affair, the chief executive decided to throw his weight behind Secretary of War Taft. Over the next year the administration used patronage, persuasion, and the reminder that if it were not Taft it would be Roosevelt, to win a first-ballot victory for Taft. With the vital aid of the secretary's own efficient organization, that result came in June 1908.[44]

In endorsing Taft Roosevelt maintained that rarely had "two public men . . . ever been so much at one in all the essentials of their beliefs and practices." On the surface Taft amply suited the president's reform specifications. An able administrator, he had done well as governor general of the Philippines and had been an effective cabinet officer. In the latter capacity he took on some of his leader's progressivism and dynamism. "I agree heartily and earnestly in the policies which have come to be known as the Roosevelt policies," Taft wrote in December 1907. Roosevelt reciprocated with fulsome praise of his own. "Taft as President will rank with any other man who has ever been in the White House."[45]

Unhappily for the Republican party the Roosevelt and Taft friendship, for all its apparent warmth, rested on a forced and insecure foundation. As colleagues the two men had not explored their divergent views on presidential power, the direction of social change, and the methods of pursuing reform. Sympathizing with Roosevelt's aims, Taft hoped to a be less activist president, more concerned with orderly, legal procedures. He was also inclined toward laziness, had a well-developed animus against some influential progressives, and lacked Roosevelt's sure sense of public relations. Taft would have been far happier as a Supreme Court justice, but ambition, pressure from his wife and family, and the importunings of Roosevelt pushed him toward the White House.[46]

The process of gaining the nomination and fighting the election mortgaged Taft's future as president and did little to close the party's wounds. The appointment policies that secured pro-Taft delegates limited the patronage power at the disposal of the new president in March 1909. In response to popular agitation and presidential pleas, the GOP promised to revise the tariff in a special session following the inauguration. Deliberately ambiguous on the direction of revision, the platform plank became a pledge to lower the tariff in Taft's campaign speeches in the fall of 1908. These promises were genuine on the part of the candidate and politically necessary for the party, but they aroused popular expectations that Republicans found troublesome six months later. At the national convention the conservative thrust of the platform, the standpat officers, and the selection of Congressman James S. Sherman of New York as Taft's running mate underscored that the regulars intended to contest progressive demands. As the public heir of Roosevelt Taft would have to seek some accommodation between the increasingly discordant Republican factions.[47]

In the 1908 campaign Taft overcame a variety of obstacles to defeat William Jennings Bryan. The Democratic hopeful made his usual wide-ranging personal canvass, on this occasion with a relatively harmonious party. The Brownsville episode left black voters potentially disaffected, organized labor was unhappy with Taft's record on injunctions and unions, and some Protestants grumbled about both the candidate's Unitarian faith and tolerance toward Catholicism in the Philippines. Quarrels over prohibition hurt the GOP in the Middle West. Mounting criticism of the speaker of the House led Taft to conclude that "the great weight I have to carry in this campaign is Cannonism." Internal disputes and apathy further weakened the Republican effort. In early September George B. Cortelyou warned: "There are too many State fights. . . . We are not at the moment the militant organization we ought to be."[48]

The combined efforts of Taft and Roosevelt turned back Bryan and the Democrats. Through open letters and public statements, the president injected his personality, program, and an element of drama into the race. Presidential denunciation of Senator Foraker's connections with Standard Oil counteracted Democratic complaints about GOP campaign funds. At the same time Taft abandoned a front-porch strategy for an effective series of speaking tours in the last six weeks of the canvass. Republican orators like Hughes and Root hammered away at Bryan, the party had a larger supply of money than the opposition, and the campaign organization, after false starts, regained some of the GOP's heralded efficiency. Meanwhile, Bryan never found a winning theme for his campaign, and apparent Democratic assets melted away. Organized labor did not deliver for Bryan, the black vote stayed Republican, and Taft made inroads among Catholics while combating Democratic efforts to exploit the religious question. By mid-October "Taft stock" was "going up every day."[49]

"We have them beaten to a frazzle," proclaimed Roosevelt on election night, and the results seemed to bear him out. Taft won 321 electoral votes to 162 for Bryan, and polled 7,675,320 popular votes, nearly 50,000 more than Roosevelt in 1904. The Republican candidate did well in the cities and found his majorities in the Northeast "exceedingly gratifying." Close attention to the returns, however, showed more danger signs for the GOP. Taft's margin was less than half of Roosevelt's, Democrats won governorships in Indiana, Ohio, Minnesota, and two other states that went for Taft, and the party had a small loss of seats in the House of Representatives. More ominous still were the divergent analyses of Taft's task as president. The conservatives looked for if not a repudiation of Roosevelt's program at least a slower and more measured pursuit of the goals. Progressives, who believed that Taft owed his nomination to their support, expected a continuation or an acceleration of the pace of reform. "The Roosevelt policies will not go out with the Roosevelt administration," wrote a new progressive senator. "If Taft weakens, he will annihilate himself."[50]

The first two years of Taft's presidency satisfied none of the elements within the party. Regular Republicans disliked the selection of Democrats as secretary of war and secretary of the treasury, lamented the absence of strong politicians in the cabinet, and generally regarded its members, whom Taft selected with little party consultation, as mediocre. The president's approach to his office evoked further discontent. He made decisions slowly and seemed unable to adhere to those he made. Beginning with congressional good will after Roosevelt's last two years, Taft's stubbornness and ineptitude over policy and appointments angered Capitol Hill. The White House staff was weak, the presidential family

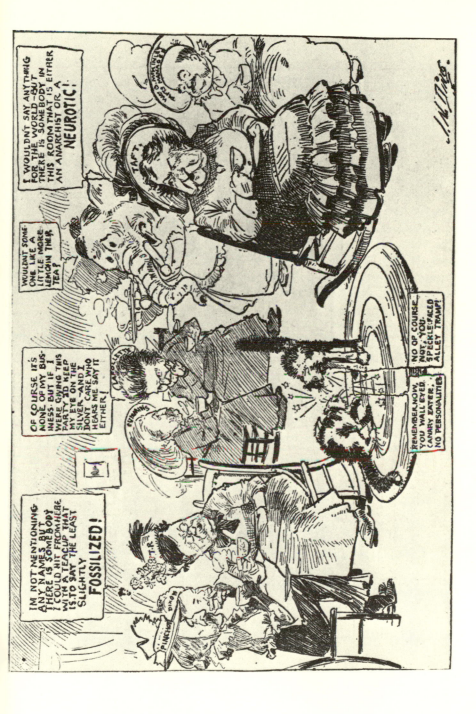

Taft, Roosevelt, and La Follette at a Republican teaparty in 1912. New York Globe and Commercial Advertiser in *Review of Reviews*, May 1912.

indulged in unwise personal vendettas, and Taft allowed grudges and memories to influence his judgment of men and issues. As a journalist later recalled, Taft's "bump of politics" was "a deep hole."[51]

Conservatives in and out of office viewed Taft's policies with wary suspicion. The Payne-Aldrich Tariff of 1909 did not please the more doctrinaire protectionists, and the administration's advocacy of a tariff commission and reciprocity with Canada reinforced these qualms. Taft and his attorney-general believed in enforcement of the Sherman Anti-trust Act. The suits they filed to break up combinations and the legislation they sought to increase governmental power provoked unhappiness in the business community. Erratic handling of the patronage disturbed the network of relationships within the GOP and cooled commitments to presidential goals. With progressives on the offensive, the right wing of the party could not break away, but its loyalty to Taft was measured and negative.[52]

Taft's relations with the progressive faction began badly, deteriorated rapidly, and reached open hostility within a year of his inauguration. His Cabinet, filled with corporation lawyers, was an initial source of reform concern. Shortly after the election, the new president explored the chances of unseating Speaker Cannon. Taft soon backed away from the effort, on the advice of Roosevelt and in the clear absence of sufficient votes. Insurgent Republicans challenged Cannon in March 1909 and looked to the White House for aid. Since the rebels were a minority, the president could not imperil his legislative program at its inception and did not oppose the speaker. This wavering course aroused further doubts that Roosevelt's successor would be a copy of his patron.[53]

The struggle over the Payne-Aldrich Tariff and its aftermath crystallized progressive discontent. Taft did not perform badly in seeing the bill through Congress in the special session that began shortly after he took office. The House passed a measure revising duties downward, but the Senate restored most of the cuts and raised other schedules. By hoarding his influence until the bill went to conference, the president probably secured as many concessions as the balance of forces in Congress would allow. But such a course left Taft open to charges of being the agent of Cannon and Aldrich. Midwestern progressives, with La Follette, Beveridge, and Jonathan P. Dolliver of Iowa in the lead, attacked the bill as injurious to the interests of their section and consumers generally. They assailed the White House for not supporting an income tax and lower tariff rates, and they blamed Taft for the final version of the legislation. Seven Republican votes in the Senate against passage indicated the extent of middle western displeasure. Still, the bill had passed, and popular reaction was initially mild. If the president could woo back the progressives, the party would face the regular session of Congress and the elections of 1910 in a more favorable posture.[54]

With characteristic maladroitness, Taft widened the split. On a public tour in September, he praised Nelson Aldrich, and then, in a hastily prepared speech at Winona, Minnesota, called the Payne-Aldrich "the best tariff bill that the Republican party ever passed." The statement was accurate but indiscreet. It rekindled the anger of the insurgents, and released the long-suppressed tensions over protection inside the GOP. Although the regular session of Congress in 1910 produced useful legislation like the Mann-Elkins railroad act and a postal savings measure, and saw the reduction of Cannon's power, the parliamentary battling further polarized president and progressives. At the same time Taft's bumbling attempts to deny patronage to his enemies and his encouragement of anti-progressive movements in midwestern states hardened the opposition to his policies. By the spring of 1910 a long-time GOP stalwart concluded: "Our Republican party is in about as bad shape as it is possible to be."[55]

For Taft the erosion of his friendship with Roosevelt was more dangerous than the coolness of the regulars or the animosity of the progressives. Numerous minor incidents clouded relations between the two men during the months after the election and in the early stages of Roosevelt's trip to Africa. There was misunderstanding about the composition of the cabinet and unease when Taft asked for the resignation of Henry White, a close friend of Roosevelt's, as ambassador to France. The Taft and Roosevelt families waged a quiet but intense social struggle in the drawing rooms of Washington. To avoid charges of undue influence, Roosevelt did not write his successor while in Africa, and the two men depended on intermediaries for information. Past accord became distance and distrust by August 1909.[56]

The Ballinger-Pinchot affair brought matters into the open. In a long, complex bureaucratic struggle over conservation in late 1909 and early 1910, Taft sided with his secretary of the interior, Richard A. Ballinger, against Roosevelt's confidant and ally, Chief Forester Gifford Pinchot. There were legitimate questions of public policy on both sides, but these faded before the political impact of the imbroglio. Involving the presidential program that Roosevelt valued most, the controversy prompted Taft to review his qualms about the expansive administrative style of his predecessor. Pinchot's ouster, coupled with mounting information about the president's other lapses, strengthened Roosevelt's judgment that Taft had been an adequate subordinate but was a weak leader.[57]

When the former president returned in June 1910, Taft looked for an endorsement of his administration and support for 1912. Adopting a position similar to Hanna's in 1903–1904, Roosevelt avoided a direct commitment on Taft's renomination. At the same time, progressives turned toward Roosevelt for assistance and as a possible candidate for president. It was a trying situation, and neither Taft nor Roosevelt negotiated the months before the congressional elections very well. Again relying on bad advice and amateurish subordinates, the president became further identified with the right wing and seemed, in New York, to encourage opposition to his predecessor. In state after state the forces allied with the White House suffered setbacks that even belated moves toward party harmony could not avert.[58]

Roosevelt spent the summer and fall in a fruitless search for a Republican middle ground. In an extensive speaking tour he proposed the doctrines that became known as the "New Nationalism." At Osawatomie, Kansas, at the end of August, he recommended increased national power to supervise large corporations "in the interest of the public welfare." Calling for laws to regulate child labor, provide workmen's compensation, and safer working conditions, as well as income and inheritance taxes, Roosevelt asserted the claims of presidential leadership and executive action. "This New Nationalism regards the executive power as the steward of the public welfare." Criticisms of legislative impotence and judicial restrictions on the popular will underscored Roosevelt's conviction that progressive Republicanism depended on the exercise of the powers of the presidency. The contrast with Taft was obvious.[59]

A striking absence of political deftness lessened the effectiveness of the Rooseveltian appeal to the party center. He seemed to have lost his touch in Africa. Abandoning a strategy of silence on party quarrels, he was drawn into New York politics to the detriment of his relations with Taft and at the expense of prestige when his handpicked gubernatorial candidate lost. The "New Nationalism" pleased progressives, but speeches for Henry Cabot Lodge and a pro-Taft platform in the New York state convention renewed old doubts about Roosevelt's sincerity. Conservatives brushed off calls for harmony and labeled the Roosevelt program "the world old despotism of one-man power decked out in the rainbow promises of a benevolent socialism."[60]

No longer cohesive or unified, the GOP lurched toward the election of 1910. Rising prices gave the Democrats a potent rallying cry against the high cost of living and the injustices of the Payne-Aldrich Tariff. With Republican disarray, they had an easy task. The Democrats won the House of Representatives for the first time since 1894, cut the GOP majority in the Senate to ten votes, and virtually controlled the upper house with the aid of the insurgent Republicans. Electing governors in New York, New Jersey, Indiana, Massachusetts, and Taft's own state of Ohio, the Democrats anticipated victory in 1912. Among the Republicans, eastern conservatives fell before the opposition tide. In the west progressives survived and looked toward dominance in the party in two years. "The old gang ought to realize," remarked a progressive, "that those of us who were fighting for a decent revision of the tariff had a little sense."[61]

The last two years of Taft's presidency completed the destruction of Republican harmony. After the disaster of 1910 the president performed more creditably, but success still eluded him. Pushing courageously for a tariff reciprocity agreement with Canada, he won congressional approval after a hard fight, only to have the Canadians reject the proposal. In the process Taft further alienated western progressives, who disliked the lower rates on Canadian farm products, as well as eastern farmers and protectionists. Progressive appointments to the cabinet did not win back permanent support from that quarter, and the continued antitrust efforts left business restive. In the spring of 1911 the president quietly began his campaign for renomination, with encouraging progress by the end of the year. Yet Taft recognized, as did Republican professionals, that he might, in the absence of a Roosevelt challenge, gain the party's nomination, but an election victory in 1912 was unlikely.[62]

The progressive wing had ambitions of wresting the prize from Taft, but they lacked an attractive alternative if Roosevelt did not run. Neither Senators Beveridge nor Cummins were ever more than potential dark horses. Senator La Follette, convinced that he was the genuine reformer, spent 1911 in diligent organization and speech-making. He gathered around him Wisconsin friends, some well-heeled campaign contributors, and progressives who would accept him in Roosevelt's absence. A reputation as a radical, sectionally focused policy proposals, and a general lack of broad support left him well behind the president as 1912 began. If the choice came down to La Follette or Taft, it was clear how the party would decide.[63]

Roosevelt was the key to the Republican situation. After suffering badly at the polls and with public opinion in 1910, he recaptured support over the next year as Taft's electoral prospects worsened. If he remained out of the race, his nomination in 1916 was all but assured. This alternative became increasingly unpalatable as 1911 progressed. A post-election rapproachment with Taft did not last, and his public and private criticism of the president, over such matters as international arbitration, intensified. As La Follette's candidacy faltered, progressives urged Roosevelt to seek the nomination. When the administration filed suit against the United States Steel Company in October 1911, the government's case implied that company officers had deceived Roosevelt during the Panic of 1907 to secure presidential approval of the purchase of a crucial steel company. An outraged Roosevelt attacked Taft's trust policy and listened more sympathetically to pleas that he declare his candidacy. Many motives impelled the former president to act. The progressives clamored for leadership that La Follette could not provide. Taft had failed on conservation and antitrust to extend the Roosevelt legacy, and there were the precepts of the New Nationalism to enact. But the dominant impulses were more personal. Bored with private life, Roosevelt wanted the gratifications of office and revenge for Taft's slights. That his candidacy might split the GOP seemed less important than a return to power.[64]

Once Roosevelt allowed friends to rouse popular support on his behalf in December 1911, it was a short step to formal entry. A disastrous speech in early February removed La Follette as a competitor, and paved the way for Roosevelt's announcement late the same month. The situation seemed propitious. The prospect of a winning candidate swayed regular GOP members toward him, key businessmen found his ideas on governmental acceptance of industrial combination congenial, and the party rank and file viewed him enthusiastically. Then Roosevelt blundered. In a speech at Columbus, Ohio, he added an appeal for popular review, or recall, of judicial decisions by state judges. With this assault on the courts, the citadel of the established order, moderate and conservative Republicans quickly fell away. The speech, said Henry Cabot Lodge, "has turned Taft from a man into a principle."[65]

From March to June Roosevelt waged an uphill battle for the nomination. Taft controlled the South and the states where party conventions selected delegates; here the president's early campaign bore fruit. Roosevelt dominated the preferential primaries and challenged the seating of more than two hundred Taft delegates. In a bitter convention at Chicago, the regulars had the machinery of the conclave narrowly, but securely, in their grasp. Neither side would accept a compromise. Rather than agree to the renomination of Taft or a third candidate, or to fight for a more progressive platform within the convention, Roosevelt

decided to bolt the GOP. Some politicians thought he might have won
had he remained, but anger at the tactics of the Taft forces and the conviction that he could defeat both major parties drove Roosevelt to leave.
While Taft was named on the first ballot, his adversary laid plans to
create a third party.[66]

The Progressive party that Roosevelt led embodied the contradictory tenets of the reform wing of the Republicans. Its candidate spoke
for a recognition of the merits of industrial bigness and efficiency, and
government regulation to manage enterprise rather than to dismantle it.
His followers from the Middle West retained a suspicion of eastern
corporations and remained uncomfortable with the business leaders who
bankrolled the party. The social workers and committed reformers in the
movement applauded its endorsement of legislation for unemployment
insurance, child-labor laws, and minimum-wage measures. At the same
time the party wavered on civil rights and offered little to the nation's
black citizens. When the Democrats selected a progressive in Woodrow
Wilson, they effectively countered Roosevelt's appeal and lured away reformers still dubious about his commitment to change. Never more
than the sum of Roosevelt's qualities and political appeal, the third party
lacked the money, organization, and cohesion to persist successfully beyond the inevitable defeat in November.[67]

The Republicans had no chance in the three-cornered race. President
Taft went through the motions. Speakers took to the hustings, reports
flowed in to headquarters, and the candidate even allowed himself occasional bursts of optimism. But there was no real hope. The party was
short of funds, enthusiasm, and, in the end, votes. Many Republicans
cast ballots for Wilson to insure Roosevelt's failure. Taft finished third,
carried only two states, and won eight electoral votes. Both houses of
Congress went Democratic. "It was a crushing defeat," wrote the president's personal secretary. Since the combined Taft and Roosevelt vote
exceeded Wilson's, the GOP retained the electoral resources to regain
supremacy. Wilson's leadership, the lingering effects of 1912, and the
peace issue in 1916 postponed the return to power until Warren G.
Harding in 1920.[68]

All sections of the Republican party bore some responsibility for
the split in 1912. William Howard Taft was an honest, clumsy, conservative whose political blunders overshadowed the general competence of
his policies. Conservatives stubbornly preferred to preserve outmoded
doctrinal purity in defeat than to win and face additional reform and
constant change. The progressives brought fresh programs and goals to
the GOP coalition, but their impatience and occasional unfairness even-

tually weakened the binds of party loyalty. But the primary agent of division was Theodore Roosevelt. His proposals had great merit, but his two key decisions, to oppose Taft and to bolt the party, ultimately turned on personal considerations that reflected more emotion than policy.

Yet the Republicans could ill afford to lose the Roosevelt of 1912. With all his faults he represented the best parts of the GOP's future. He spoke for an inclusive party, receptive to new groups of voters, young men with creative ideas, and a measured program of innovation. Roosevelt understood that the problems of an industrial society could not be ignored, or resolved through a reliance on older precepts of social harmony or an indiscriminate promotion of economic expansion. In the absence of Roosevelt, and the progressives who accompanied him or defected to the Democrats, the GOP stagnated. It allowed the opposition to become the party of the cities, of labor, and of blacks and newer ethnic groups. By 1932 it had no answer to the political genius of another Roosevelt. In 1912 the Republicans decided that they could live without Theodore Roosevelt and what he stood for. The next half century revealed the political dimensions of that error.

THE DEMOCRATS FROM
BRYAN TO WILSON

JOHN J. BROESAMLE

The Democratic party passed through the eras of William Jennings Bryan and Woodrow Wilson in an exhausting search for a national coalition and for its own identity. A legatee of dual constituencies, sharply rural and sharply urban, the party sought leaders who could unite these two cultures and a host of factions. The initial choice of the Democrats, Bryan represented only an agrarian–small-town America whose influence was fading. During the campaign of 1912, Wilson bridged the gulf between city and country primarily through ambiguity in his own rhetoric. But eventually both wings of the Democracy joined to help compel him to reshape party ideology. In response, Wilson haltingly led the nation in the general direction of the welfare state. For a time he managed to hold the Democracy together; yet the Wilson era proved a mere interregnum. In the 1920s, with Wilson's coalition shattered, the party returned to the debilitating cultural conflict and political impotence that had characterized it during the Bryan years.

Until the mid-1890s, when the Bryan era began, Gilded Age politics had been based on relative equilibrium in party strength and hence, stalemate. But a severe depression in 1893 caught the Democrats with one of their own in the presidency. To the party's already conservative image was added the unpopularity of the Cleveland administration and a label as the party of depression that stuck for a generation. The upshot came quickly: the 1894 congressional election brought violent shifts in voting behavior, with the Democracy suffering rural erosion and a spectacular urban collapse. One of the great political realignments of American history had begun; the GOP emerged from the election as the nation's majority party. Meanwhile, between 1894 and 1896, a division that had begun along economic lines turned into a heated version of the old agrarian-industrial split, a revolt of many farmers against urban domination.

In 1896 the Democracy, together with the Populists, nominated William Jennings Bryan for president. It was a sectional victory of the rural West and South against the urban Northeast. Bryan's platform was skewed to the left, and his narrow emphasis on silver, a rural panacea, made it hard for the party to appeal to a variegated electorate. The Bryan triumph horrified Democratic conservatives. Many chose to back a splinter gold ticket; others opted for the GOP.

To cover these losses, the Democracy had to go beyond the rural-sectional convention triumph by enlisting other elements. Bryan tried to forge a coalition of the disadvantaged by joining farmers, plus urban workers and middle-class small businessmen, together as an incongruous bloc, with silver the common denominator. He went on to wage a distinctly middle-class campaign, and the class approach to political realignment soured: having rejected Cleveland's Democracy, the labor rank and file proceeded overwhelmingly to reject Bryan's Democracy as well.

Just as Bryan lost labor, he lost the cities where most workers lived. In the first presidential contest to center on the social traumas industrialization had produced, the Democratic convention practically ignored urban America. The GOP won the industrial Northeast and all of the nation's ten largest cities; several that had previously been Democratic remained Republican long after the turn of the century. In these cities every class, together with immigrants, swung toward the GOP. How much of this reflected economics and how much represented a reaction against Bryan's agrarian, old stock, Protestant parochialism can be debated. Most of the support left to him was rural, though a unified farm vote did not develop. The Democracy managed partially to offset Republican gains in the East by making lasting advances in the rural, small-town, and mining regions of the Midwest and Far West.[1]

The greatest importance of Bryan's decisive defeat—46.8 percent of the total popular vote against William McKinley's 50.9 percent—lay in its long-term implications. The politics of the nineties transformed a stalemated party system with a Republican edge into a remarkably stable alignment dominated by the GOP. The 1896 system involved the least party competition since the early nineteenth century. According to one estimate, during the period 1896–1930 eighteen states were competitive, thirty noncompetitive. The 1896 system also constituted one of the sharpest and most enduringly sectional political alignments in the nation's history. In broad areas of the North, the Democratic party collapsed; in parts of the South, where the greatest drop in competition occurred, the

GOP practically disappeared. In most of the border states competition survived the holocaust of 1896, and it continued to be significant in such states as New York, New Jersey, Indiana, and Ohio. But most of the nation split into "the big Republican monopoly in the North and the little Democratic monopoly in the South."[2]

The important point is that the big monopoly belonged to the GOP. The Republican grip on it was not as firm as that of the Democrats on the South; yet until 1912, the GOP held every state but one that had gone to McKinley in 1896, including all fourteen in the Northeast. Northern Democratic governors and senators became a comparatively rare species. The Republicans controlled the most populous, urbanized, and industrialized regions of the nation. Between 1896 and 1928 (excluding only the election of 1912), Democratic presidential candidates mustered 84.5 percent of their total electoral vote in the South and the border states, heavily agricultural regions that bore a quasi-colonial economic relationship to the urban Northeast. Democratic deterioration manifested itself in other ways. There was a hemorrhage of big business and newspaper support. Contributions nationally and in eastern and midwestern state and local elections declined to the point that wealthy individual candidates could simply purchase some state Democratic organizations. And the nature of the political system changed even further.[3]

In 1896, levels of political participation had reached a new high, with extremely lopsided results. After the turn of the century, a staggering drop in voter turnout occurred compared to nineteenth-century norms. As a general rule, sectionalism inhibits party organization and vigor; certain progressive reforms had a similar effect. The image of party itself had been tarnished, and the functions parties had performed diminished. The lower classes—including southern blacks, who faced systematic disfranchisement—showed the greatest constriction in voting; this suggests that many among the disinherited simply disfranchised themselves. Degeneration of parties and voting turnout went farthest in the Democratic South: in 1904–16 mean turnout of qualified voters for presidential elections in the eleven southern states plunged to 29.8 percent, less than half the mean of 1884–96. At a time when the Democracy needed new blood at the polls, the party system itself was deteriorating.[4]

Democrats entered what would be the urban-industrial twentieth century with their party discredited and utterly crippled by the politics of the nineties. Bryan had given the Democracy's appeal a severe pruning. For years the party would largely orient itself toward and be led by representatives of rural America, from which most of the votes were expected to come. The GOP would speak for and appeal to the great middle strata, urban and rural alike, leaving the Democracy with the political remains. These included a fringe of "unrespectable" and anti-pathetic extremes: outspoken agrarians of the Jeffersonian or Populist stamp, particularly in the South, and urban enclaves marshaled by powerful and notorious political machines. The Democracy was a crazy quilt amalgam of interests and decentralized, autonomous bastions of strength, locked into an unfavorable sectional alignment. Ordinary shifts in voting behavior were quite unlikely to have any serious impact on this alignment or free the party from it. For decades, the Democracy had borne the reputation of being slightly disreputable, the party of rum, Romanism, and rebellion. Now it had become the party of depression. It had also become the party of Bryanism.

Bryan found himself portrayed as a "slobbering demagogue."[5] Yet he was never deeply alienated, and if he could be considered radical at all, it was strictly in economic matters. His political programs reflected the Protestant, evangelical, middle-border morality with which he viewed all issues. Courageous, idealistic, but often simplistic, he reacted to situations intuitively and emotionally. He had the most loyal following of any leader of his time, but the loyalty went to his character, not his intellect.

A provincial sectionalist symbolizing a party too multifaceted for such an image, Bryan never functioned as the head of a genuine national coalition. His contemporaries dubbed him the Great Commoner. But he really mirrored only the southern and western agrarian and small-town Populist-progressive middle class. Bryan might be called the Peerless Leader in Nebraska, but New York labeled him the Peerless Loser. He never built a program around which the entire party could join. Suspicious of urbanism and city types, he did not really view the Democracy as an integrative institution but preferred to win his crusades without tainted urban-northeastern help. Urbanization, industrialization, the new immigration—these were things to which he never adjusted. As a candidate and responsible critic, he served as an important link between populism and progressivism; and he successfully controlled the Democracy year after year and shaped the rural wing, at least, around his principles. But while the Commoner lived a quarter of the way through the twentieth century, his mind never fully left the nineteenth.[6]

Democratic survival in the Bryan era depended heavily on the party's ability to hold onto isolated outposts of power. The old Confederacy and northern machines served as oases of patronage and votes. After the 1890s the GOP became in some degree the party of society-oriented cosmopolitans, while the Democracy turned more localistic and community-oriented. All of this proved costly. Localism heightened the party's pluralism and persistent divisiveness. Always affected by national differences more deeply than the GOP, the Democracy became a stage for acting out the ethnic struggles of the early twentieth century. Meanwhile, by harping on the principle of silver "democracy" versus "Clevelandism," Bryan, more than anyone else, kept Democrats divided and distrusted. Saddled with leadership that could not unify a coalition of warring groups and divergent sections, the party pulled itself apart in the first years of the new century.[7]

In the cities of the Northeast and Middle West, the Democracy's strength flowed from its longstanding alliance with immigrant ethnic minorities, institutionalized in the political machine. The most important group in this equation was the Irish, whose urban political ascendancy accelerated with the disappearance of old-stock Bourbon respectables in 1896 and after. Machines lent an element of cohesion to a socially fragmented urban environment. The function of the Democratic boss in these years typically involved centralizing and smoothly operating vestiges of power that the American constitutional system had purposely dispersed, in order to meet the needs of subgroups whose desires did not fall under the aegis of conventional institutions. The machines assisted the needy in a humane and personal way, and they furnished avenues of social mobility for the poor. In return, their beneficiaries supplied them with votes. Machines also served as intersections between legitimate and illegitimate business, which, through collusion with the organizations, found the connections with government they needed in order to maximize stability and profits. Most city bosses were closely tied to business, which, in exchange for favors, fueled the machines with money.[8]

The many reform movements of the Progressive Era that aimed at overturning machines often stalled because reformers who won office failed either to provide substitute structures that could duplicate the functions of the organizations or to eliminate the need for these services altogether. Middle-class municipal reformers might complain that politicos with names like "Bathhouse John" Coughlin and "Honey Fitz" Fitzgerald could never run a city efficiently or well, but machine politicians had a high rate of survival. The organizations thrived by dealing with the poor, and particularly with immigrants. Boss Richard Croker of Tammany Hall probably came close to the truth when he remarked that "there is not a mugwump in the city who would shake hands with them." The suspicion was mutual; men who waged war on corruption often found themselves involved in ethnic battles as well. When municipal reformers spoke of "turning the rascals out," they usually meant ousting from power social and ethnic groups a cut or two below them. This meant, for example, trading a mayor without an Irish surname for a mayor with one. To the immigrant, ward politics met life's practicalities better than rarified notions of honest and aloof government. No wonder urban reform movements faltered; in the words of Tammany ward boss George Washington Plunkitt, "they were mornin' glories—looked lovely in the mornin' and withered up in a short time, while the regular machines went on flourishin' forever, like fine old oaks." When municipal reformers went beyond providing honesty to furnishing public services for the working class, it generally meant that their ranks had been infiltrated by representatives of this class.[9]

The cities served the Democracy as outposts of power in the North, but the party's only safe sectional bastion lay in the South. In 1900, the South was recovering from the Populist insurgency, whose attempt to forge a coalition between poor blacks and poor whites had aroused the specter of Negro domination and ended in the triumph of white supremacy, black disfranchisement, and a temporary reprieve for Bourbonism. Reform went into eclipse for a time; Populists returned to the Democratic fold, ideology and all, or else dispersed. With the South safety Solid, and with reform cleansed of its connotative threat to white unity, the time had arrived for progressivism.

Largely indigenous, middle class, and urban, southern progressivism embraced movements for social justice, good government, the regulation of business—and continuing agrarian radicalism. The movement had at its core the demand of the urban and rural middle classes for property ownership and development. Where large corporations had stacked the odds against the bourgeoisie, progressives argued that the state had a responsibility to intervene in the interest of individualism. Despite a lingering regional atmosphere of conservative traditionalism, the drive for positive, interventionist government became a hallmark of the progressive movement in the old Confederacy.[10]

Across the section, Democratic progressives challenged conservatives for control of the party. Apologists for what was denounced as northern plutocratic colonization of the South, who frequently ran the party through state machines and bosses, found themselves under attack by vehement anti-monopoly, anti-corporate, anti-railroad reformers. Enormously popular in the region, but anathema to the entrenched leadership, Bryan proved a high card for southern progressivism. The drive for reform was complicated, however, by the section's political demagogues: Benjamin Tillman, James Vardaman, Cole Blease, Theodore Bilbo, and

the rest. These men had made of themselves a peculiar southern institution with special appeal to the poor whites. They were often trimmers,
or overblown, or ideologically irrelevant, and virtually always racist. But,
at the expense of much race and class baiting, they produced a number
of meaningful reforms.

Because the South had a way of weighing issues and candidates in
terms of their racial implications, the race issue poisoned Democratic
ideology and served as an impediment to the party's revival during the
early Progressive Era. Southern Negrophobia fused with paranoia on the
subject of threats from Washington. This led the party to summon its Jeffersonian, states' rights ideology in support of its racial predilections. Yet
Jeffersonianism had more to do with the politics of the early nineteenth
century than with the early twentieth. To an extent, racism diverted the
attention of politicians from the Democracy's national functions and
from the development of positive programs. But it also drew the sectional
elements of the party closer together by providing one subject, at least,
on which the membership could agree. Not only did racism, together
with ruralism, reinforce the Democracy's notorious parochialism and
undermine other causes that even the South had an interest in; it also
spilled over into immigration policy, Democrats working to slash entries
from southern and eastern Europe at a time when immigration actually
offered potential party recovery in New England.[11]

With the Democracy foundering on these issues of race, national
origin, class, and section, Bryan tried to keep a grip on the tiller. He
filled the titular leadership longer than any Democrat largely because no
national figure remained to challenge him. His first serious test as an
opposition spokesman came with the Spanish-American War, and his
behavior was erratic. Like the overwhelming majority of congressional
Democrats, Bryan declared for U.S. intervention in the conflict, but then,
like most of them, he soured on the imperial consequences of the war.
The treaty drawn up to end the contest provided for U.S. annexation of
the Philippines and Puerto Rico. Bryan had the power to block ratifica-
tion, but instead, he advised Senate Democrats to vote for the treaty. He
wanted a national referendum on imperialism, as 1896 had been a
referendum on silver; and for this, he reasoned, the treaty must pass,
as it did. But in 1900 imperialism had to coexist and coalesce with other
issues: free silver, a boon to the Republicans which Bryan insisted on
despite its economic and political obsolescence; and antitrust, which
proved to be politically premature. The public greeted all three questions
with apathy. The GOP made prosperity the key issue, and to many
Bryan still threatened that. McKinley did better than he had four years

before, countering slight losses in the South and urban Northeast with gains in the Middle and trans-Mississippi West and the rural East. The Commoner's shaky coalition of Bryan Democrats, Gold Democrats, Populists, Silver Republicans, and anti-imperialists recovered much of the Democratic vote in cities and industrial regions, including the ballots of immigrants and workers. After being stretched out of shape by the unique strains of 1896, the fabric of Democratic politics had predictably reassumed a bit of its old appearance. But Bryan polled only 45.5 percent of the total popular vote against McKinley's 51.7.[12]

Following the 1900 debacle, a number of Democratic conservatives opened a campaign to liberate the party from Bryanism and overcome public satisfaction with the Roosevelt administration by a march to the right. Their "reorganization" drive failed to come to terms with progressivism; it was essentially a nostalgic restoration movement, maladjusted to the new century.[13]

While the reorganizers wandered across the desert of party leadership hunting for a candidate, an interloper moved in: publisher William Randolph Hearst. The very presence in the race of this master of the sensational and the bizarre shocked Republican and Democratic politicians alike. Hearst was a millionaire who viewed himself as a champion of the toiling masses against the rich. A moderate imperialist, as a domestic reformer, he tended to parallel Bryan but had more of a socialist bent. Besides this class appeal and radicalism, other factors helped spawn the love-or-hate reaction Hearst inspired in the party. For one thing, he coveted power. For another, he had feuded with much of the the party leadership. Finally, there was Hearst's personal life—rumor had it that he was an "unrivalled voluptuary."[14]

But Hearst also held political assets. Since 1903 he had represented a working class Tammany district in the House, where he had become a pariah; he controlled the three-million member National Association of Democratic Clubs; and he was famous. Populist and labor leaders backed the maverick publisher, who called for nationalizing the railroads and the eight-hour day. With primarily western delegate support, he emerged as one of the two leading preconvention candidates. Though he did not develop enough strength to be nominated, the party had not seen the last of him. Reelected to Congress in 1904, he remained a power in New York politics, stepping out of and back into the regular Democratic party. He lost races for mayor and governor in the following two years, and after 1906 the serious possibility of Hearst candidacies faded; so did his demagogic but remarkably effective appeal to working-class voters. But Hearst had proved that masses of these voters would defect from Tammany Hall for a candidate with his kind of appeal, personally magnetic and programmatically promising.[15]

The ultimate beneficiary of all the conservatives' preconvention maneuvering in 1904 was New York Judge Alton B. Parker, whose anonymity provided his chief asset at the convention—a remarkable comment on the state of the party. Bryan and Hearst could not get together in opposition, and the Commoner prepared for 1908 as he backhandedly campaigned for Parker. A good judge but a lackluster person of questionable breadth, Parker found himself in an impossible situation. Nominated by a convention that wanted to skirt the money question, still the party's hottest issue despite the rise of Roosevelt and progressivism, Parker insistently took a strong stand on gold. Anonymity, a convention asset, turned into his greatest liability. A man with less political experience than any presidential candidate in a generation, he tried at first to wage a dignified, cautious front porch campaign when he should have been on the stump. He never found an issue adequate to win on, and, as the progressive crescendo rose, he ironically tried to outflank Roosevelt on the right. The aim was to lure eastern business into the party; yet the GOP could still outdraw the Democrats in business support and money.[16]

The Bourbons had arrived at their political oasis only to find it dry. In a dull election, Roosevelt handed the Democrats one of the worst popular defeats in their history, taking 56.4 percent of the total popular vote to Parker's 37.6. The combined Republican majority in both houses of Congress was the largest since the Civil War. Parker won a million fewer votes than Bryan had in 1896 and 1900, losing every state outside the South and the border states and suffering defections to socialism and populism even there. The GOP regained the Pacific Coast and western mining states where Bryan had been strong eight years before, enlisted progressive support, held onto labor, and polled massive margins in the big cities. Though the total presidential vote fell in 1904 by nearly a quarter million, the Socialist presidential tally quadrupled; many Democrats either opted for Roosevelt or Eugene V. Debs or did not vote at all.[17]

If Clevelandism took a drubbing in 1904, so did the South. Its union with the West in 1896 and 1900 had proved barren. Hating Roosevelt, the South had subsequently forged a renewed alliance with the Northeast and much of the Midwest. Because of the erosion of Democratic leadership in 1904, the old Confederacy enjoyed its biggest role in the party since before the Civil War; but the November disaster to the New York–Atlanta axis left the South to stew once again in its own isolation from federal power.

Significantly, where Democratic progressives had been nominated in 1904, some state and local tickets ran ahead of Parker. With the decline of the money question after 1904, the extreme party split of the nineties had substantially ended by the following year and the two wings rejoined. The Democracy's new focus involved a heightened concern with reforming state and local government. This offered a key to party identity and to the Democracy's belated emergence into the twentieth century. Reformers who were neither Clevelandites nor Bryanites had begun to appear in the cities; these men eventually united those who remained among the two older groups and took control. In 1906, long-term Democratic revival—measured by success in seating members of Congress—began. It was concentrated in a belt of six states: New York, New Jersey, Pennsylvania, Illinois, Indiana, and Ohio, particularly the latter two. Just why things occurred in this pattern remains uncertain. Surely the new degree of unity and emphasis on reform did not hurt; another factor may have been the rising prohibition issue.[18]

But at the presidential level the Democracy still groped in the twilight of 1896. After the 1904 disaster Bryan quickly moved back into the role of party spokesman. Meanwhile, however, the charismatic Roosevelt had siphoned off much of the Commoner's reform program and appeal, and many radicals and Populists had gone Socialist.

Bryan needed some issue which might make his warmed-over candidacy more palatable. He became increasingly interested in nationalization, and here he stumbled badly. In the summer of 1906 he came out for federal ownership of trunkline railroads and state operation of feeders. In the party-splitting uproar over "socialism" that followed, Bryan backed off; he also dropped silver, the other most divisive segment of his program. Then he attacked the GOP for government centralization.[19]

Bryan won the nomination handily. But despite his enduring popularity in the party and a comparatively high degree of loyalty from the Clevelandites, and despite his increased respectability even after the railroad fracas, Bryan's magic had faded. The Boy Orator of 1896 had grown middle-aged and slack-bellied by 1908. The campaign dragged despite Bryan's tireless efforts, and he simply could not crack the Republican coalition with issues. He came out with a formula for curbing the trusts, called for lower tariffs and the government guarantee of bank deposits, and took a strong position on campaign contributions. But he

Master of "the sensational and the bizarre," publisher and politician William Randolph Hearst, at age forty-two. *Review of Reviews,* December 1905.

The "Peerless Leader" of the Democracy, William Jennings Bryan, at age fifty-two. *Review of Reviews,* June 1912.

Secretary of the Treasury William G. McAdoo, at age fifty-two. *World's Work,* December 1915.

Champ Clark, a leader of the Democrats in the House, at age sixty-six. *World's Work,* January 1916.

seemed to be trimming in order to pick up the East, and differences between Democratic and Republican positions blurred. Bryan did tie the party together more closely than it had been since 1893, and he did not polarize voters as he had in the past; but he lost the election nonetheless.

He lost for many reasons, among them continuing, crucial defects in the party he had led so long: its isolation from the leverage of national power, its small campaign chest, its lingering vestiges of disunity, and its usual shortcomings in leadership and organization. Of greatest importance, the third Bryan crusade could not breech the political barriers erected against the first Bryan crusade. On the surface, things looked bleak: Bryan won the smallest percentage of the total vote of any Democrat but Parker in nearly fifty years, 43.1 percent to 51.6 for William Howard Taft. Bryan took almost as thorough a beating in the electoral college as Parker had, losing one of Maryland's votes and regaining three western states. Taft won only half the plurality over Bryan that Roosevelt had amassed over Parker, but this suggested that Bryan had simply recovered votes Parker had lost to Roosevelt and Debs.[20]

Yet reason for hope remained; the Democratic revival went on despite Bryan's candidacy. Turnout had jumped 10 percent over 1904, practically all the gain going to Bryan. Taft had run ahead of Republicans in nearly every state, and the Democracy made advances in Congress and in almost all the state legislatures.[21]

One other aspect of 1908 contained potential significance for the future: in an unprecedented move, the American Federation of Labor officially endorsed Bryan for president. Hearst fielded his own National Independence Party that year, but his ties with labor leadership had frayed. From 1906 on, organized labor leaned toward the Democracy more than toward the GOP. This developing relationship was symbiotic: the party's weakness in the urban-industrial East and the Middle West led it to respond to union demands. The AFL claimed it backed principles not party in 1908—the Democrats had taken a comparatively pro-labor position and had included a guarded anti-injunction plank in their platform. Gompers failed to deliver the votes and there is little reason to believe any great shift took place; but the AFL's need for a Democratic revival continued, simply for the sake of its own political leverage.[22]

Two years later, the Democratic party won a congressional landslide. Everywhere but the Pacific Coast, districts changed hands. For the first time since the election of 1892, the House went Democratic as the party picked up fifty-nine seats; significantly, most of the new majority came from outside the South. Though the GOP held onto its edge in the

Senate, the Democrats caught up sufficiently that they could control it together with Republican insurgents. Several Republican states chose Democratic governors. Still divided and drifting, the Democracy had at least gained new morale and a fresh crop of potential leaders, most of them from the East.[23]

The Democratic record in Congress since the turn of the century had been uneven. At first Democrats on the Hill had been split and outnumbered. With no steersman in the White House, constructive planning and simple unity over issues proved difficult, and the Democratic congressional delegation found itself dragged along in the wake of Republican numbers and Roosevelt leadership. In the Senate, what little party coordination existed was shared rather than vested in a single figure. In 1903 House Democrats chose John Sharp Williams as minority leader. A Jeffersonian traditionalist from Mississippi, Williams spent the next five years trying with some success to subordinate Democratic parochialisms to a sense of cohesion.

Beginning in 1909, the Democrats' campaign for unity received unexpected aid from the Republicans. Within a very short time after he took office, William Howard Taft had proved himself a political bungler and the GOP lapsed into the agonies of divisiveness that had characterized the Democracy for so long. Taft's flirtation with the South, begun in the 1908 election, cooled. In both the House and the Senate, Democrats and Republican insurgents managed to join successfully, if fitfully, against the administration. Between 1910 and 1913, a number of social reforms passed into law, most with the backing of Taft yet guided through a Democratic House and a Democratic-insurgent Senate over the opposition of conservative Republicans. The Democrats could take credit for these and other positive measures—including an unprecedented amount of legislation backed by labor—and yet at the same time embarrass the president by rejecting his appointments and passing tariff bills they knew Taft would veto. On one issue dear to the president, a tariff reciprocity treaty with Canada, Taft worked with congressional Democrats (which earned him the onus of Republicans), only to have Canada turn down the proposal. Meanwhile, the Democrats conducted hearings and investigations designed to reinforce their positions on national policy, and joined with Republican insurgents in pruning the powers of the speaker of the House.[24]

The 62nd Congress (1911–13) proved a failure for the administration for some of the same reasons it helped the Democracy, particularly in the House. Democratic leadership had already become adept at the parry and thrust of minority party politics when, in 1911, the initiative was given to skillful Majority Leader Oscar Underwood. Underwood made great progress toward forging a unified, able majority, particularly through use of his trademark, the binding caucus. Order had at last been imposed among Democrats on one end of Capitol Hill, for the first time in a generation and despite lingering progressive-conservative differences. Even the erratic Senate Democrats had begun to head in the same direction.

By 1912, the Democratic party had reached a crossroads. The names of the men at the helm over the past sixteen years—Parker on the right, Hearst on the left, Bryan a three-time loser—suggested the state it was in. Yet the party had done well in 1910, and might again. The key (as Bryan himself realized) lay in finding a new leader who could break away from the irrelevancies of the past and capitalize on the party's southern and urban strength, its growing unity, emphasis on reform, and relationship with labor, and its emerging role in local and congressional politics.

The new leader was Woodrow Wilson. A beginner in national affairs, Wilson had been elected governor of New Jersey in 1910. By birth and identification, he represented the South. Like Bryan a Presbyterian elder and a moralist, Wilson had similar illusions about the voice of the people being the voice of God. He was easy to respect, but deep affection came less readily.

Wilson had first been adopted by conservatives and party bosses, who pushed him for governor and president. But he had a way of being politically cold-blooded, and he demonstrated that he could use these people and then discard them. Such was the case during his governorship; substantially the same thing occurred again when the first Wilson presidential boom, spearheaded by editor George Harvey and a phalanx of anti-Bryan Democrats, collapsed in disillusionment and recriminations. Bosses and conservatives had tried to use Wilson against Bryanism and progressivism in the party. But they had not counted on Wilson becoming a progressive in the process. Wilson followed his break from Harvey with a rapprochement with Bryan and the acquisition of a new coterie of boosters. The most important of these men were transplanted southerners living in New York.

As the 1912 primaries proceeded, Wilson split the South, much rural and conservative support going to Oscar Underwood. But Wilson's most formidable rival turned out to be Champ Clark—progressive, speaker of the House, and the pride of Pike County, Missouri. The contrast between the capabilities of Wilson and those of Clark, whom the party came within a hairbreadth of nominating (and who would probably have gone on to win) could not have been more striking. Clark's intelligence and temperament were questionable, and his provincialism equalled his progressivism. But the primaries made it clear that he had the support of many ordinary politicos and organizations, and had inherited most of the western and midwestern Bryan following. He had also inherited Hearst.

The Wilson forces entered the Baltimore convention with fewer than a third of the pledged delegates; Clark had pulled in sight of a majority. But Wilson's managers quietly and successfully dealt with bosses and others to swing the convention to him. Meanwhile the Wilsonites and Bryan, with some feckless aid from Clark, obscured Clark's personal progressivism. In the eyes of many delegates the convention turned into what it really was not, an internecine party struggle between progressives on one hand and conservatives on the other. The illusion of a head-on ideological confrontation went far toward undermining Clark's candidacy, and Clark grew so furious at Bryan that according to one account the Missourian arrived in Baltimore carrying a gun and had to be talked out of shooting him. On the forty-sixth ballot, Wilson won the nomination. The Bryanesque platform that he ran on was the fifth the Commoner had written.[25]

During the campaign, exploiting possibilities that Hearst had demonstrated, the party aimed special appeals at urban voters: Catholics, Jews, immigrants, and workers. The goal was a genuinely national coalition. The Wilsonites went out of their way to prove that the Democrats had become capable of governing—something that still demanded proof. Wilson patterned his campaign after efficient business models. The party called for subscriptions from the public alone and refused money from corporations. Wilson also took care to maintain a properly awkward relationship with the party's New York financial wing and with Tammany Hall, the epitome of city bossism so important in middle-class progressive demonology.[26]

The 1912 election produced a classic confrontation not just of men but of ideologies, the most important among them Roosevelt's New Nationalism and Wilson's New Freedom.[27] Wilson believed that the national character and democracy itself stemmed directly from the liberty of petty capitalists to "release their energies" and expand the economy. The emergence of huge trusts seemed to imperil all this by closing whole industries to newcomers. In Wilson's view, certain big businesses and largely unidentified political "bosses" had formed an oligarchic alliance; the government as well as the economy had been concentrated in the grip of a handful of men, and freedom had begun to slip away.[28]

President Woodrow Wilson (1856–1924). Library of Congress.

Louis D. Brandeis, foe of monopoly and bigness, at age sixty. *World's Work,* March 1916.

As a result, in his speeches Wilson conducted a determined, though restrained, assault on what he labeled the "system"[29]—the power and decision-making processes of the country's social and economic leadership. Amoral, or immoral, corporate values, he realized, would dominate the society if current trends continued; the organization man would reign supreme. Individualism and the national character would die along with small enterprise if this happened, and the ultimate victim would be democracy.

Despite its obvious crudities, Wilson produced a remarkably broad diagnosis of the nation's economic and social ills in 1912, but—and this is the most crucial point about the New Freedom—he negated much of his critique by offering equally narrow prescriptions for curing them. If certain big businesses involved in unfair practices could be restrained and the petty capitalist could be set free again, Wilson argued, all would be right once more; he clearly underestimated the tenacity of the system he intended to defeat. Fully as important, he remained uncertain about how much of a defeat he wished to inflict; he was ambivalent toward accepting large industry as a permanent fact of American economic life, trapped between Roosevelt's belief, which Wilson shared, that big business had become inevitable, and a longing for the creative individualism of the nineteenth century. Progressive lawyer Louis D. Brandeis, who largely shaped Wilson's antitrust program, erased some of Wilson's confusion, but the basic issue remained the same: how could opportunity be restored and broadened in the United States and accommodated to the new corporate order?

Just as he denounced unfair competition and trustification, Wilson attacked paternalistic, "big-brother government"[30] in 1912 and seemed to oppose special privilege of any kind. He intended to democratize America by bringing each class into common counsel rather than consulting only one—and without formally recognizing or specifically supporting any. He wished to unite all interests in a joint sense of mutual reconciliation. But Wilson spoke primarily for the middle class and its mores; and in doing so he predictably tried to avoid the subject of labor and social welfare legislation. On the other hand, he left the back door open to such measures through vague phraseology. While no class legislation or special privilege of any sort could be tolerated, he argued, no such thing as a working class existed—nearly everyone, after all, was a worker. This suggested that since labor did not comprise a class, labor legislation was unnecessary. But it also suggested that since everyone toiled, no labor measures could be construed as class legislation;

hence such bills seemed entirely legitimate. Wilson drew *both* conclusions, leaving himself perfectly flexible on the subject.

If any one answer appealed to him as a cure for America's social and economic difficulties, however, it was not welfare statism but the prospect of stimulating prosperity through the cultivation of foreign markets. This called for lower tariffs, increased exports, and expansion of banking facilities and the national merchant marine. Wilson also intended to overhaul the antitrust laws and the domestic banking and currency system.

Each of these goals would require the enlistment of experts on the side of the government, yet in 1912 Wilson denounced reliance on expertise because such dependence would short-circuit public debate. It would also amount to a tacit admission that, as Roosevelt claimed, government experts could control business without any risk of falling under the sway of the industries they were supposed to regulate. In addition, the very necessity for a permanent bureaucracy of experts amounted to another admission that Wilson was not ready to make, an acknowledgment that huge corporations would have to be regulated permanently.

The New Freedom did not add up to a coherent philosophy, any more than the Democratic party had a coherent philosophy in 1912. Wilson had not arrived at a final, comprehensive series of programs to end the larger difficulties he identified—alienation, class conflict, dehumanization, and the distribution of power. He did not fully understand the insufficiency of strictly economic solutions to these problems. He remained substantially noncommittal on government centralization and intervention in the economy. He was unwilling to risk class strife by calling explicitly for class legislation. And he tried to ignore a permanent working class whose existence would make the welfare state a necessity. Wilson's solutions fell far short of meeting the imperatives implicit in his own analysis or of giving the party a sense of identity and direction. Yet this eloquent but tangled philosophical jungle of ambiguity, irrelevance, and superficiality concealed at least one crucial quality: flexibility.

Wilson garnered fewer popular votes in 1912 than Bryan had ever polled, slipping into office with 41.8 percent to 27.4 for Roosevelt and 23.2 for Taft. Percentage turnout dropped from 1908, and apparently Wilson lost some Democrats to both Roosevelt and Debs. The AFL leadership supported Wilson, but less energetically than it had Bryan. Wilson's principal strength lay in the South and the border states; his second strongest region stretched from Iowa to Nevada. The old Confederacy gave him a popular majority in every state, but outside the

South only Kentucky and Arizona did so. Wilson swept the electoral college so thoroughly that he could have won without the South, but the results did not point the way to the party's permanent resurgence. Nonetheless, whether Wilson won simply because the GOP split in 1912, as has commonly been assumed, is questionable. The Democrats considerably widened their 1910 House majority and took control of the Senate. Success in the West and the northern cities brought men into Congress who would eventually have to be weighed on the party's ideological scales.[31]

During his academic years, Wilson had become the first systematic American proponent of responsible party government. Nothing could have tested his expertise more severely than the Democracy of 1913, the mosaic of urban progressives, Bryanites, Bourbons, and bosses that so far only he had been able to cement together. Wilson himself was so uncertain the party could accomplish what he wanted that before the inauguration he contemplated an overhaul intended to isolate conservatives and align with the party progressives of all stripes, in keeping with New Freedom ideology. Soon he dropped the idea. Perhaps a strong party could have stood such an overhaul; but the weakness of the Democracy, particularly in the Senate, left him with little choice. Wilson could not afford to alienate the conservative wing if he wanted to pass a reform program; so he learned to play the role of party, not factional, leader and took the Democracy largely as he inherited it from the congressional level on down. Without altering the grass roots, where he had never served and which he may not have understood, the president superimposed a layer of leadership at the top. Rather than allocating patronage specifically to the emerging, struggling Democratic progressives, the Wilsonites generally distributed it to factions already in power from state to state regardless of ideology, reinforcing conservatives here and progressives there. In practice the policy stunted southern progressivism most. But it paid handsome dividends by recruiting the support of state and city organizations and their congressional delegations.[32]

Of the cabinet choices, two proved especially important. Wilson made Bryan Secretary of State, absorbing his personal power base into the cabinet out of sheer political necessity. "The trouble with Mr. Bryan," Wilson grumbled, "is that he cannot think."[33] Easily the president's most impressive appointment, however, was maverick New York businessman William Gibbs McAdoo, Secretary of the Treasury and a wizard in domestic policy.

The choice of McAdoo, a southerner turned New Yorker, symbolized things to come. In the past, the South had been politically hobbled by its stubborn loyalty to a single party—a party that consistently lost and which could count on the section without taking its wishes seriously. Now Wilson's impact supplanted Bryan's in the South; but at the same time, the old Confederacy finally got a grip on the levers of power and policy. Five of the president's ten cabinet members had been born in the South; Edward M. House, his closest adviser, came from Texas; nearly all of the critical Senate committees, and fifteen of the seventeen most important House committees, had Southern chairmen; in the lower chamber, more than two-fifths of the Democratic majority was southern, in the Senate more than half, and southerners predominated in both caucuses. Under Wilson the South received its biggest slice of patronage since the Civil War. Southern Democrats had reversed the politics of 1904 and achieved a revolution in the allocation of power; now they dominated both the Democracy and the government.[34]

During his initial years in office, Wilson established a degree of personal control over his party rare in American presidential history, and this quickly became apparent in the 63rd Congress. The large Democratic majority in the House was laced with newcomers whom Wilson could easily master. Older Democratic leaders in both chambers, accustomed to fighting in opposition and unready to battle the president for command over legislation, proved cooperative for the sake of party, ideology, and the necessity of offsetting the charge of Democratic incompetence. Oscar Underwood still marshaled Democrats in the House. His counterpart in the Senate, the very effective Majority Leader John Kern, had been chosen by party progressives in a sweep of most of the leadership posts. The pivot in legislative strategy was the caucus and the binding caucus. When the Democrats proved incapable of developing a majority among themselves, they found it difficult to engage in coalition politics with either the conservative or progressive Republicans whom they had systematically isolated. But at the time Wilson took office, his party had been primed for unification under forceful executive leadership; and with the battle over the Underwood Tariff behind him in October 1913, his hold was secure.[35]

Wilson's reinforcement and rearrangement of the powers of the presidency may have been his most enduring contribution to American politics. He proceeded as if he had a strong party and a genuine mandate, which he did not. Wilson established such a firm grip on the party that he could shape and alter its policies without its prior consent. Viewing himself as the Democrats' one leader, he played a direct role in the process of organizing his forces behind a complete legislative program sent to the Hill package by package. He personally delivered messages to both houses, employed careful timing and constant pressure, haunted the president's room in the Capitol, working continuously with members and advisers, wielded the patronage and the influence of powerful figures like Bryan, threatened vetoes, and, when the time came and other resources had failed, appealed to the public over the heads of Congress. Ambivalent toward compromise, intolerant of dissent, Wilson's strategy carefully blended flexibility with inflexibility.[36]

When Underwood left the House in 1915, Wilson took over direct legislative leadership rather than working any longer through the majority leader. Meanwhile, dissension erupted. Unity had not been total even during the amicable 63rd Congress; and Underwood's successor, Claude Kitchin, could be cantankerous, particularly on matters of war and peace. With a less tractable majority leader, the binding caucus died as a means of mobilizing Democratic majorities.

An upwelling of political fundamentalism in the South produced still more complications. By the time Wilson left office, the southern and western wings of the party were developing "a complex of political, social, and moral attitudes" comprised "of nativism, fundamentalism, prohibitionism, and a conviction that the American character resided in the farm and hinterland town." This intrusion of religious and regional reactionism into politics, exaggerating familiar themes of the Bryan era, undermined reform in the South and posed a potential threat to the administration.[37]

It also forced Wilson to walk a political tightrope. The president initially met the rising prohibition issue with studied equivocation. But he had less latitude on the ethnic question. Wilson did haltingly resist the anti-Catholic, anti-Semitic bigotry that typified particularly the rural South; the appointment of Brandeis, the first Jew ever to sit on the Supreme Court, symbolized this. Yet the ethnic issue continued to rankle. Immigration restriction attracted the support of both bigoted and unbigoted, but it was the xenophobia of the agrarians—locked into the same party with urban ethnic machines—that had always made the question politically dangerous. In 1915 Wilson delivered a hedging veto of a literacy test for immigrants; two years later, he had a second veto overridden.

If Wilson trimmed a bit on immigration restriction, he proved utterly regressive on race. In 1912 the Wilsonites had cultivated the black vote, practically an unprecedented strategy for the Democracy. W. E. B. DuBois and a number of other black leaders supported Wilson despite their misgivings; how many Negroes followed their example remains uncertain. As president, Wilson came under intense pressure from southerners to segregate and expel blacks from office, and he succumbed. Making it clear that "I will never appoint any colored man to office in the South because that would be a social blunder of the worst kind," he apparently allowed his cabinet members a free hand in racial matters; a wave of segregation, discrimination, and dismissals ensued, with the Great Commoner joining in. Wilson's decision was political. No rabid race baiter, he nevertheless agreed with the general white consensus on the relative superiority and inferiority of races. Under pressure from his most important constituency, it was only a small step to active discrimination. The long-term political future—an incipient black Democratic movement and all its moral and social implications—had been sacrificed to the prejudices and legislative demands of the present.[38]

Discrimination formed only part of a cohesive southern approach to government to which any Democratic president would have found himself vulnerable. In Congress, southern Democrats split roughly into two groups: an administration faction typified by Underwood, generally conservative but loyal to the party and the president; and a larger number composed of men like Kitchin, agrarians who, despite lingering states' rights sentiment, plumped for federal intervention in the name of weak interest groups. Frequently well to the left of the administration, this latter faction's leverage increased as a result of the 1914 election. Although the southern agrarians comprised the party's most active proponents of class legislation, they had an agenda planned almost entirely for farmers. Meanwhile, other forces pushed Wilson toward a more comprehensive social welfare program.[39]

The urban working class may have had little use for farm legislation or prohibition, but it did have a direct interest in the welfare-state approach to reform. Nowhere did this become clearer than in New York. The biggest year for progressivism in the Empire State was 1913. Tammany controlled the governorship and the legislature and proved it could produce labor and social welfare legislation without cutting its close ties to business. Among other things, this movement symbolized the rise of machine reformers who would play a crucial role in the party's future, men like Al Smith and Robert F. Wagner. But for city machines, abstract theories of good government—which early Wilsonian ideology and so many progressives held dear—seemed almost meaningless.[40]

McAdoo, House, Franklin Roosevelt, and a number of others in Washington took a keen interest in "cleansing" New York politics and rendering state and city government more "efficient." In 1913, the year Empire State progressivism reached its zenith, McAdoo and House, with the collaboration of the president, opened an offensive against the New York Democratic organization. It was a typical, middle-class, anti-machine reform campaign, and it quickly turned into a "mess." The only political glue that could hold together the incredibly splintered but aptly named Independent Democrats was patronage, and at the same time McAdoo fed jobs to the Independents, the postmaster general succored the regulars. A fusion ticket won the New York mayoralty in 1913, practically shutting off Tammany's lifeline of patronage and weakening the organization so severely that many regulars wondered if it would die. If it did, however, the powerful Tammany delegation in Congress might try to take the president's cherished legislative program down with it. In the face of this Wilson scuttled party reform in New York in return for Tammany support. The Independent movement stumbled on a little farther before collapsing in a chorus of bitter recriminations.[41]

In 1912 Wilson had argued that American democracy had begun to give way to a cynical alliance between businessmen and bosses. Before the convention, the city machines had been among his most powerful opponents. Yet throughout the gamut of New Freedom ideology, nothing died more quickly in practice than anti-bossism. The realities of passing legislation forced the president to choose between attacking local machines or passing bills which he thought would destroy oligarchy, or at least mitigate it, at the national level. It was a distinction Wilson undoubtedly did not want to make, but from the immediate standpoint of his legislative program he chose correctly. The era of fitful patronage policies had largely ended by the fall of 1914, and the administration had reached understandings with virtually all of the Democratic machines.[42]

Meanwhile the president gradually began to move a bit farther down a road he had already set out on, the road toward the welfare state. By 1913 Wilson had advanced further ideologically than historians have given him credit for. Mounting pressure from the party's urban and agrarian constituencies followed him into the presidency. Wilson did not have the political alternative of sticking out his chest like Cleveland and standing still against the reform tide. He had argued for several years that the Democratic party must become progressive in order to survive; the nature of progressivism changed, and from 1913 to 1917 his response had to as well. He was probably concerned with other factors too, among them social justice, business desires and requirements, heading off strikes, and mobilization for war. In order to ameliorate and minimize class conflict—which he lived in dread of—government and the presidency had to be enlarged sufficiently to deal with its causes. This did not compel Wilson to "surrender to the New Nationalism,"[43] but it did force him to exercise his options under the New Freedom.

As early as 1913, Wilson's suspicion of large power clusters had ironically led him to begin expanding the federal government, ostensibly to liberate the small businessman. Then he held back for a time, because of his own lingering inhibitions, because of an economic recession that led to cries for an end to reform from a business community that already feared administration "radicalism" and a Clevelandesque "Wilson panic," and perhaps for other reasons as well. But the Democratic trek toward the welfare state had already begun—particularly in the policies of Secretary of the Treasury William G. McAdoo, who contributed one of the most remarkable cabinet performances in American history.

The New Freedom, whose ideological flexibility McAdoo constantly exploited, envisioned a promotional role for government. McAdoo was a promoter. He worked toward a massive expansion in the number of services performed by Washington, but without a drastic hike in expenditures. These two seemingly contradictory ends proved compatible because during the New Freedom years the Wilsonians enlarged the administrative structure of government and its role as a referee and provider of services for the private sector without trying to usher in a full welfare state. Year after year McAdoo utilized treasury funds to manipulate the money market in new, creative ways, in order to support important interests, particularly farmers. An empire builder, if he had one supreme goal it was to bring the money market and the new federal reserve system completely under treasury management so that these operations could continue and expand.[44]

McAdoo did not always give farm interests everything they wanted, but he gave them a great deal. He tinkered with the national economy to keep it from stalling, worked to drive down "usurious" interest rates, attempted to shore up the cotton market under the strain of world war, and from 1913 on risked antagonizing bankers, not just in Wall Street but frequently in the South and West as well, in order to apply treasury leverage behind an easier credit flow for agriculture. McAdoo insisted on keeping his distance from a hostile Wall Street during these years at the same time that he mobilized the treasury in back of other capitalists, particularly farmers and entrepreneurs, who often shared his suspicion of big finance and could claim him as their champion against the banks. All of this was important ideologically as well as politically: three years before Wilson is commonly supposed to have capitulated to class legislation, McAdoo, and thus the administration, had already started furnishing aid to farmers—primarily those in the Democratic South, where most of the demand for intervention arose—at the expense of other interests.[45]

As this continued, in an adroit feat of political juggling the president began to allocate balanced legislative concessions to farmers as well as to a number of other interest groups. Less carefully programmed than early Wilsonian measures, the president's later bills were arranged around no great schematic blueprint; but throughout, he dealt with some of the most important questions and the best organized groups capable of applying political pressure.

By the end of Wilson's first term, the administration had extended federal aid to agricultural and vocational education and interstate highway construction (a major rural demand). Wilson also approved legislation, most importantly the Federal Farm Loan Act of 1916, setting up machinery for long-term rural credit. In all of this, added to the treasury policies and warehousing, tariff, and banking and currency reform, the administration went a long way toward meeting southern agrarian pressure and rural desires that had been pending for years.

But from the standpoint of the party, the most arresting gains went to workers. Wilson had originally shared and proceeded from the common middle-class progressive suspicion of organized labor. Neither he nor Bryan had ever sponsored an outright program of labor legislation. But party leadership meant responding to change. Having shelved anti-bossism, his first response to the cities, Wilson reoriented the Democracy toward a positive urban program. He backed a model workmen's compensation system for federal employees, went along with the extension of protection to maritime labor, established a standard eight-hour day for interstate railroad workers, and took a major (and, the Supreme Court declared, unconstitutional) step toward ending child labor. Wilson's degree of cooperative involvement with the labor movement—and the results—were unprecedented and portentous. Gradually accepting organization on the AFL model as a good thing, he appeared increasingly in the company of the union's relatively conservative leadership. And while he never overstepped balance and compromise in the allocation of benefits to labor in conjunction with other interests, he soon had William Howard Taft grumbling that the administration was "surrendering everything to Gompers." Leading the Democracy toward urban, social welfare progressivism turned out to be Wilson's foremost maneuver as party leader.[46]

If workers and farmers got concessions from the administration, so did business. From the start, the realities of power forced adjustments in the New Freedom outlook toward private enterprise. This became clear in two of the most important measures of 1913–14, the Federal Reserve and Federal Trade Commission Acts. Both made major commitments to centralization and expertise through the establishment of powerful, independent regulatory commissions. In the case of banking legislation, these commitments emerged in part from the necessity of placating Bryan and the agrarian wing in Congress by meeting at least the shadow of their demand for government control and short-term agricultural credit. Wilson had ambivalently supported the trade commission idea during the 1912 campaign. But through the FTC Act, together with the Clayton Antitrust Act, the president simply wrote much of his old ambivalence concerning business-government relations into law. Wilson amply demonstrated that he had no intention of destroying large industry. The courts were given broad power to review FTC decisions, which fell into rough accord with Wilson's 1912 demands for "the certainty of law" in government-business affairs.[47]

Later the president showed a striking unwillingness to meet New Freedom imperatives by staffing some of the new regulatory agencies with business-oriented conservatives and bunglers. These men proved that his earlier concerns about the leverage big business could wield over government experts had been well-founded. But from the party's perspective the most important point was that Wilson had cut through the Democracy's old ambivalence toward federal power by personally opting for centralization and then pushing his legislation through Congress.

The New Freedom aimed at liberating the energy of industrial and agrarian capitalism but at the same time directing much of that energy abroad for what Wilson termed a "conquest of the markets of the world." Economic expansion overseas was the key New Freedom plan for guaranteeing national prosperity. The president's view of the vital relationship between foreign commerce and full employment at home provided a crucial backdrop to an emerging consensus over trade policy between the administration and large elements of the business community. In 1912 Wilson had spoken of a redistribution of opportunity rather than of income among different groups, but if American commerce and investment expanded abroad all interests would benefit. With business influence in the administration rising—and in the face of the European war and a desire to protect American industry from it—the president made a number of policy changes. Among other things, he went beyond the foreign trade aspects of his earlier legislation by accepting a larger degree of tariff protectionism, establishing a tariff commission, backing anti-dumping legislation, and sponsoring a measure (passed in 1918) that allowed manufacturers to combine in the export trade. Wilson aimed to reconcile increased economic nationalism with increased sales abroad. He had not abandoned his 1912 argument that a distinction must be drawn between business on one hand, and government and the public interest on the other; but the distinction had certainly blurred, and his tolerance for business-government cordiality had grown. Because cultivating foreign markets required levels of collaboration between bankers, big corporations, and government that Wilson had not fully foreseen in 1912, the administration opted for commerce at the expense of competition.[48] The main target was Latin America. With Europe at war, the U.S. economy bloomed and the Latin American markets opened.

New Freedom trade philosophy, southern orientation, ideological flexibility, and promotionalism all fused in a drawn-out fight over shipping legislation that began in 1914. McAdoo produced a bill to create government lines designed above all to benefit the rural exporters of the West and especially the South.[49] It was a dose of nationalism aimed at spurring capitalism and helping to goad businessmen into expanding overseas at a faster pace than many of them wanted. When the bill finally passed in 1916, after triggering one of the longest and most bitter legislative battles of the era, it went through in watered-down form as a preparedness measure.

Meanwhile, preparedness itself had divided the Democratic party and created a crisis in the progressive movement. Bryan, who had worked hard and effectively for Wilson's domestic program, resigned in the summer of 1915 over the president's handling of the *Lusitania* affair. The Commoner went off on a crusade to rally the rural South and West against the East. The departure did little political harm to the administration; bitterly condemned, Bryan saw his influence in the party wane. But he was not the only rebel. The antipreparedness battle centered in Congress; the main insurgents were between thirty and fifty Democrats, most of them southerners and westerners, under the leadership of Claude Kitchin. Progressives and labor and farm organizations generally wanted peace and opposed Wilson's preparedness program. If Bryan, Kitchin, and their allies captured Congress, they could win.[50]

The president defeated resolutions threatening his control of foreign policy, and his antagonists failed to block plans for a big navy. But they did emasculate the administration's military program. Southern agrarians and their western partners also seized control of revenue policy in 1916, overturned the administration's regressive taxation proposals, and jammed through legislation aimed at making the East pay for preparedness. The new income and inheritance taxes met growing labor demands and provided the clearest triumph of the agrarian left—all of this in the face of an upcoming presidential election.

The Democrats had done so badly in the 1914 Congressional and state races that their House majority slipped from 73 to 25. Only the Senate, where the Democracy gained several seats, remained stable. This had occurred despite political confusion caused by the eruption of war in Europe and a momentary erosion of partisanship, despite a lackluster GOP campaign, and despite the continuing struggle of the Progressive party to eat into the Republican vote. In midterm elections the president's party generally loses seats in the House, but the significance of 1914 went beyond this. Many of Roosevelt's followers had rejoined the GOP and the normal Republican majority had already begun to re-emerge. The GOP had doubled its congressional representation in the East and had made considerable gains in the Middle West.[51]

Confronted by the implications of 1914, in 1916 Wilson would have to succeed at constructing the coalition Bryan had failed to unite twenty years before. The 1916 Democratic platform squarely committed the party to internationalism for the first time, and it went farther than any previous Democratic platform in backing direct government intervention to guarantee social and economic progress. The convention's keynote was intended to be "Americanism," but the delegates demonstrated wildly for peace. With preparedness no longer a major party question, and in the face of Roosevelt's bellicose militarism, Wilson wound up running on the effective slogan "he kept us out of war" with both Germany and Mexico—though he was never really sure how long he could avoid belligerency in the future. The Democratic campaign became a peace crusade, with Bryan leading it in the Midwest and Far West and attempting to turn the election into a referendum against war just as he had tried to make 1900 a referendum against imperialism. In the end, the peace issue may have been more important to Wilson's victory than any other.

Like Bryan in 1896, Wilson needed labor in 1916. The passage of the Adamson eight-hour act in the face of a threatened railroad strike, and the business anger that followed, led GOP candidate Charles Evans Hughes to label the measure "labor's gold brick." But it turned out to be a hot brick for the GOP. Years before, Hearst had called on the Democracy to associate itself with organized labor; he had also shown what the results could be. Wilson's method of intruding federal power into labor relations had been unprecedented, and he responded to Hughes by backing benefits for workers. Capping its emerging relationship with the Democracy, the AFL gave Wilson complete support. Although still not firmly marshaled, the labor vote largely went to the president. This may have signaled a turning point in American political history, the beginning of the significant integration of labor into the Democratic coalition. If Wilson did activate a proto-New Deal coalition so far as labor was concerned, he did so at varying places in different degrees. Ultimately the labor vote made an important contribution to the Democratic victory in at least six states: Idaho, New Mexico, Washington, California, New Hampshire, and Ohio—the latter three never carried before by the Democracy in a two-party election. Workers' ballots appear to have been decisive in Washington, Idaho, and New Mexico.[52]

Clearly, the president's urbanization of Democratic politics had begun paying dividends. Since 1901, the Socialist vote had mounted steadily. But between 1912 and 1916 it slid from 901,873 to 585,113, apparently as a result of Wilsonian reform and the extreme antiwar position of the Socialist party. Most of the lost ballots seem to have been cast for Wilson. Socialist trade unions, impressed by the legislative record, switched en masse from Debs to Wilson in those four years.[53]

Other elements besides organized labor joined in the 1916 Democratic coalition. With Hughes and his party equivocating on social reform and Wilson not, plus the fusion of the peace cause with prosperity and progressivism in the Democratic campaign, a well-developed division on domestic questions ensued between progressives and conservatives. In 1916 presidential turnout rose above the total of 1912 by a remarkable 23.2 percent, with Wilson's vote 45 percent over the level of four years before and Hughes just 12 percent above the Taft-Roosevelt tally. Wilson made gains in every section and every state. He garnered perhaps 20 percent of the ex-Bull Moosers; independent progressives, together with independent newspapers and periodicals, advocates of social justice; pacifists and isolationists; radicals; many farmers and farm spokesmen, more businessmen, perhaps, than usually voted Democratic; and most enfranchised women, who opted for peace. Urban America weighed heavily in this coalition; yet Democratic strategy involved concentrating on the states west of Pennsylvania and virtually writing off the Northeast as hopeless. In the end, the Wilson coalition was electorally strongest in the rural South and West. Though he ran ahead of Bryan's 1908 vote in the industrial states, of these Wilson won only California, Ohio, Washington, and New Hampshire. He picked up most of the West; but with the exception of a handful of states—most important among them

Ohio, California, and Kentucky—the Democratic electoral vote had been virtually pruned back to the Bryan states of 1896.[54]

All things considered, Wilson may have done well to win as many ballots in the cities as he did. As in 1900 and 1908, the percentage of the urban presidential vote that went Democratic rose; but the party's urban congressional representation, which had gone up sharply in 1910, then dropped in 1914, continued downward. In New York, Boston, Chicago and other cities, the Democratic machines, suffering from an unprecedented diminution of their power in the party despite the president's trimming on bossism, knifed Wilson or else campaigned sluggishly. But ethnic participation jumped in 1916. Some elements of the Catholic hierarchy were hostile to the administration, but a deviant Roman Catholic alignment largely failed to materialize. More Irish voted for Wilson than for any previous Democratic candidate. Many Scandinavians opted for the Democratic column on the peace issue, and so, it appears, did some Irish, Germans, and Austrians. Wilson's seeming partiality toward Britain was one thing, but he was "right" on the literacy test and labor legislation, and to many Germans Hughes seemed a mixed blessing or no blessing at all. Thus the Democrats succeeded in making major inroads into the German vote. Understandably, Negroes went for Hughes.[55]

Wilson defeated Hughes by 49.3 percent of the total popular vote to 46.1 percent. But the president had run well ahead of the rest of his party. Hundreds of thousands more votes went to Republican than to Democratic congressional candidates, and while the Democrats held onto the Senate by a comfortable margin, they would be able to control the House only with the aid of progressives and independents.[56]

Two things seem especially impressive about the Democratic party in the years between the turn of the century and the 1916 campaign. The first is how much it had changed; the second, how little. Unlike Bryan, Wilson had combined moralism with political realism and in the process led the party away from states' rights and laissez-faire. He had fashioned a remarkable if fragile coalition; yet it won him only the narrowest of victories against an inept and divided opposition. Partly because of Wilson's failure to create a fresh base for a permanent party realignment, the coalition proved transitory. Wilson had offered Democrats power, a measure of unity, purpose, and respectability, a national outlook, and a chance to minimize their factional squabbles. But even under his leadership the party suffered lingering maladies: an inferior sectional base, organization that had been improved but little, financial problems, and the continuing and in some ways worsening urban-rural schism. The decline of the New York branch of the party in 1916 actually delighted many Democratic progressives, among them William Jennings Bryan, who hailed the election as a triumph of "the West and South without the aid or consent of the East."[57]

The politics of the twenties proved that 1916 had been a deviating election. Democrats fell back into the perennial quarreling of the 1890s and lost elections by landslides. Even in the Wilson era the party had been chided as incompetent to govern, and this criticism cannot be dismissed lightly. Because of his ability as well as his success, Wilson proved an aberration in the course of Democratic politics between Grover Cleveland and Franklin D. Roosevelt. Eventually the party would be decisively urbanized; key precedents for this had been set during Woodrow Wilson's brief years as an urban reformer and coalition leader. Yet half a century after the end of the Wilson era, the Democratic party would still suffer from multiple identities and crumbling alliances.

"One Good Term Deserves Another," Wilson is reelected in 1916. Sioux City Daily Tribune, *Review of Reviews,* December 1916.

5

THE PROGRESSIVES
AND THE ENVIRONMENT

Three Themes from the First Conservation Movement

JAMES PENICK, JR.

In 1900 Americans lived in an urban industrial nation, and they lived with rapid change. Few could predict where it would all end—perhaps in some final awesome consolidation of the mass such as Edward Bellamy foresaw in his best-selling novel, *Looking Backward*. But Bellamy's imaginative leap to a greater generalization, first conceived as a dream, could easily become a nightmare. The past was something else again. There the scene was dominated by stereotypes: stately mansions, quiet villages, restful farms, country churches, pastoral vistas to calm the spirit and soothe jangled nerves. What any of this had to do with the reality of another past that included human slavery, stifling conformity, loneliness, backbreaking labor, religious intolerance, and other violations of the human spirit was quite beside the point. Men read the past for meaning, and a meaningful past for a generation doomed to live with turbulence was orderly above all.

Few Americans wanted to turn back the clock, tear down the factories and the cities, and restore the Jeffersonian republic of farmers and artisans. The "growth of the city," Theodore Roosevelt occasionally found it necessary to remind himself and his countrymen, "in itself is a good thing and not a bad thing for the country," just as the growth of material, technological America was a cause for pride and congratulation.[1] Yet Roosevelt was uneasy in the face of this accomplishment, mirroring, as he did so often, the anxieties of the era.

The worm in the apple was a series of unresolved paradoxes. The number of farmers had declined drastically, farm tenancy was on the increase, and cities waxed while the countryside decayed; yet "from the beginning of time it has been the man raised in the country . . . who

115

has been most apt to render the services which every nation most needs."[2] The city corrupted everything it touched and left to itself would drown in its own filth; yet it was the "center of thought and therefore of influence in National affairs."[3] It depended on transfusions from the country of "fresh blood, clean bodies and clear brains"; yet it took the best breeding stock, and the heart of the nation, its countryside, seemed threatened with depopulation and decay.[4] As Liberty Hyde Bailey put it: "the fundamental weakness in our civilization is the fact that the city and the country represent antagonistic forces."[5] The theme of confrontation was very pronounced. At least one irate observer demanded that "urban aggression and power" be placed under "salutary restraints."[6] Few people had anything good to say about the city as a place to live, which may explain in part why so many American cities were allowed to become unlivable as the century advanced.

While many urban Americans of this generation were born on farms or in villages, and nostalgia doubtless colored their recollection, very often those who sentimentalized the "yeoman," and saw him as the only sound breeding stock, were men whose experience with rural life went no deeper than a reading of *The Adventures of Tom Sawyer*. "The most valuable citizen of this or any other country," in the opinion of Gifford Pinchot, whose own country home was modelled after a French chateau and whose income came from inherited investments, "is the man who owns the land from which he makes his living."[7] The men who shaped national policy in the Progressive Era were saturated in this arcadian ideology. Theodore Roosevelt repeatedly threatened dire consequences if the migration to the city of the better part of the brains and energy of the country was permitted to continue unchecked. His commission, appointed in 1908 to study country life and recommend measures to reverse the drift toward "national degeneracy," viewed the problem as urban imperialism and a confrontation of cultures. The city "exploits the country; the country does not exploit the city," it reported.[8] To resolve this conflict the commission prescribed the era's most popular remedy, science.

Liberty Hyde Bailey, who wrote these words, was himself a scientist, but even he did not mean to limit the word *science* to its narrowest sense, viz., science was what scientists did. Science meant being effective—indeed, the phrase "scientific method" was used interchangeably with "sound business management," and *efficiency* summed up both in a word. Thus a hard-headed word like *science* was enrolled in the service of naive ends. For many, the crisis presented by the nation's urbanization was no more sophisticated than any of the endless variations on the theme of how to remain vigorous and virtuous among the fleshpots of the city. But a significant number, especially among public officials and opinion-leaders, focused on the issue of national efficiency. Like Governor George Pardee of California they could predict only doom for a nation whose rural population did not "greatly outnumber its city dwellers."[9] Pardee himself became an irrigation enthusiast. He hoped to prevent the impairment of the "efficiency" and "effectiveness" of the United States by calling upon the scientist and the engineer to make the desert bloom and open up new frontiers for rural expansion.[10]

A kind of back-to-the-land movement threatened to flourish. In 1900, 500 million acres still remained open to settlement under the general land laws, not counting Alaska. Annual rainfall was too scanty to sustain agriculture on most of this land, but great things were expected of irrigation. "The lands awaiting irrigation will easily sustain a number of inhabitants greater than the present population of the whole country," was the guess of one enthusiast.[11] Estimates that as much as 100 million acres could be brought under cultivation by irrigation were by no means rare.[12]

George Maxwell, a California lawyer, became the leader of a movement to use this garden to relieve social tensions. Back-to-the-land became a veneer of broad appeal to cover the specialized concerns of the farmers, speculators, and regional boosters who gathered annually in the National Irrigation Congress—a powerful lobby financed by the largest landowners in the arid region, the railroads. In 1896 Maxwell converted this congress into an instrument supporting federal aid to irrigation. Through his own organization, the National Irrigation Association, and a monthly periodical, *Maxwell's Talisman,* he argued that irrigating the arid West would serve as a safety outlet for surplus urban populations and minimize the social violence, class warfare, and radicalism breeding in the cities.[13]

These efforts bore fruit in the passage of an act, guided through the United States Congress by Francis G. Newlands of Nevada in 1902, which began a federal program to irrigate lands in the arid region. Administration of the Newlands Act was entrusted to engineers in the United States Geological Survey, who split off to form a separate agency, the Reclamation Service, in 1907. Men like Maxwell and Pardee saw federal irrigation as a way of utilizing science to promote reform. In the progressive engineer they found a kindred spirit with a pronounced point of view all his own, reinforced by his professional self-image and by his training, that the methods at his command to control nature could be used to control human affairs.[14]

President Taft protects Secretary Ballinger as Roosevelt lurks behind Pinchot.
St. Louis *Post Dispatch,* September 1, 1909, Richard A. Ballinger Papers,
University of Washington Library.

By 1921 the Reclamation Service had built reservoirs with a total capacity of 9,610,423 feet of water, constructed 11,258 miles of canals, and brought 32,385 farms into being.[15] The accomplishment was considerable. If it seemed paltry when measured against the extravagant expectations of two decades earlier, it should be remembered that the emotional problem of the era was how to accept the twentieth century and the new urban industrial America. The arcadian misperception led frequently to grandoise, even feverish plans. It also left a legacy of solid achievement in homes and watered fields. The back-to-the-land movement had failed to materialize; indeed, the census of 1920 announced that the nation had turned its back, perhaps irrevocably, on its rural past. It is true that a thin trickle of young people in flight from middle-class materialism flocked to rural communes five decades later, but it may be doubted that Governor Pardee would have seen them as a bulwark against national degeneracy. As for the engineers, although they had pioneered in high dam construction, they broke no ground in the management and control of human affairs. That remained the domain of politics.

No single individual was more representative of the link between progressivism and concern for the environment than Gifford Pinchot. For one thing he was a patrician, a class which provided significant leadership of the national effort to control the impersonal forces remaking American life. The progressive wing of this class fought their reactionary counterparts, squabbled with one another over tactics and strategy, and appealed for mass support in the rhetoric of democracy. In the early years of the century they took the lead in formulating a foreign policy, sought in about equal parts to regulate economic power and end destructive competition, founded the social welfare profession, and worked for urban reform. The progressive conservation movement was the most ambitious and comprehensive program to evolve from this multidimensional attempt to make a bureaucratic response to industrialism, and its chief architect, Gifford Pinchot, was one of the most creative and innovative leaders of his generation.[16]

Trained abroad in French and German forestry practices, and imbued by family background with a sense of responsibility to make some return to society for the privileges he had inherited, he began in the 1890s to preach the gospel of regulated forest management. His great achievement was to raise his infant profession to a fortress from which he could dominate a terrain encompassing far more than the narrow mission of forestry. Yet an abundance of nervous energy and a reckless attraction for the show-down in a tight corner eventually led to a widely held judgment of instability that clouded his accomplishment.[17]

From the time he took command of the tiny Division of Forestry in the Department of Agriculture in 1898 until he secured the transfer of the extensive western forest reserves from the Department of the Interior in 1905, Pinchot demonstrated enormous political acumen. Preaching a doctrine of maximum economic utilization as a contrast to the conservative forest policy of the Department of the Interior, he won the support of important economic groups, such as the lumber and grazing industries, and their trade associations. He openly championed the Newlands Act, and the several columns of the irrigation movement increased his ranks. The committee of arrangements of an American Forestry Congress, organized by Pinchot as a final push to drive the transfer through Congress, included the presence of two important railroads, the presidents of the National Lumber Manufacturers Association, the National Livestock Association, the National Irrigation Association, ranking bureau chiefs, senators, congressmen, editors of trade journals, educators, and miners. A more impressive coalition could not be found in the annals of bureaucratic politics.

Pinchot's political skill was equally as evident in his dealings with Congress. Even before he acquired the forests he had nursed the appropriation for his bureau from a paltry $28,520 in 1899 to $439,873 in 1905. After the transfer the appropriation jumped to $1,195,218. By 1908 it had risen to well over three million dollars. Renamed the Forest Service, provided with a broad mission—management of the national forests (194,505,325 acres by 1909)—armored by powerful interest groups and their allies in Congress, the bureau quickly became a power to reckon with. Pinchot devised a decentralized organization capable of a flexible response to local conditions and manned it with an elite force of specialists fiercely loyal to himself.

The legal staff broke the trail for a dynamic new approach to executive power. Reasoning that the president was a steward with full powers to protect the interests of the people, the bureau first formulated the concept of broad executive discretion that came to be known as the supervisory power of the executive. Existing legislation did not specifically open the forest reserves to full commercial use, but neither did it exclude the possibility. Building on this sweeping interpretation the legal officers of the Forest Service worked out a program requiring fees for grazing and permits for hydroelectric power development within the forests which left power in the government to specify the terms of use.

Even more than timber cutting, grazing became the predominant commercial activity on the reserves. Significantly, most of this program could not have won approval in Congress, although it was later upheld in the courts. The bureau brought rational management and regulation to a theater formerly marked by confusion and jurisdictional conflict. Range wars and bitter conflict between independents and giant corporations, a common feature of western life, were brought under control in the national forests. Thus the Forest Service, working from its narrow forestry mission, pioneered in the formulation of innovative bureaucratic procedures to deal with problems central to the Progressive Era: the control of economic power, the resolution of conflict in the community, and the coordination, centralization, and extension of governmental authority.

The administration of Theodore Roosevelt provided a fertile setting for such innovation. The president was in any case already committed to the idea that rational management could reduce social tensions. The government, he believed, should be "as well planned, economical, and efficient as the best machinery of the great business corporations."[18] Eventually he came to look on conservation as his most important domestic policy because it offered an opportunity for independent action by the executive that could not be duplicated elsewhere. His solution to the trust problem, for instance, to license corporations engaged in interstate commerce, had little chance for adoption in Congress. But as the Forest Service program demonstrated, corporations and individuals using public resources could be licensed and regulated, with priorities on the use of resources set by the government, without additional legislation. Pinchot became a close and trusted presidential advisor, with influence unparalleled in a bureau chief—a conductor cutting across departmental lines, linking up the working agencies with the highest level of political power and investing them with extraordinary energy and direction.

As the movement broadened, presidential commissions studied a variety of special problems, such as the organization of government scientific work, administrative efficiency, and public lands policy. The Geological Survey began to inventory and classify coal and mineral resources. An administration bill for the leasing of range lands on the public domain as well as proposals for the leasing of coal and mineral lands were inspired by the belief that power to regulate the use of such resources should be retained in the government. The culmination of these years of activity was the creative work of the Inland Waterways Commission (IWC) which recommended that the waterways of the nation be treated nationally, and that regional river systems be developed as units for the multiple-purpose use of water resources. Out of the rich and varied activity of the era the movement had finally produced a comprehensive and unified concept of development in the report of the IWC.

Meanwhile, as the program broadened congressional resistance hardened. In 1907 Congress revoked the authority of the president to create additional forest reserves in six western states, and a year later the administration program, from grazing to waterways, was hopelessly stalled. The frantic activity of 1908—the National Conservation Commission, the first Governor's Conference, and the Country Life Commission—was designed to capture public attention and rally popular support behind the administration. A great deal of support was generated, but at considerable cost to clear and accurate thinking. A movement to adjust the resource disposal policies of an agrarian past to the realities of modern industrial enterprise became overnight a great national crusade to save the nation's material wealth from the grasping clutches of monopolistic capital. The crusade did not, however, advance the administration's program in Congress. Resistance there was rooted in genuine interests in the West which the policies formulated in Washington had increasingly disturbed.

That the conservation policies had produced resistance nearly equal to their own force became abundantly clear once Roosevelt had retired from office. His hand-picked successor, William Howard Taft, quickly found himself divided between his loyalty to his former chief and his own grave doubts about the legality of parts of the conservation program. As the secretary of war he had reluctantly implemented those resource policies which had impinged on his jurisdiction, but he had taken a dim view of the influence Pinchot wielded in War Department affairs. His department had been the weakest link in the conservation program, if only because it was the home of the U.S. Army Corps of Engineers, which had refused to support the recommendations of the Inland Waterways Commission. Taft did not include Pinchot in his inner circle of advisers, which seriously undermined the forester's influence. But a graver challenge arose from the new secretary of the interior, Richard Achilles Ballinger, who had already, as a bureau chief under Roosevelt, demonstrated his willingness to enter the lists against Pinchot as a champion of the growing western opposition to conservation.

There is little doubt that Ballinger threatened everything Pinchot had built. For instance, in the closing months of the Roosevelt years the policy of regulating hydroelectric power, developed by Pinchot in the forests, was extended to all of the public lands by Ballinger's predecessor, James R. Garfield; this and other plans for expanding the conservation program were shelved. Even the program of the Forest Service was endangered. Although management of the reserves had been transferred to the Department of Agriculture in 1905, enforcement of the law within their confines was left to the jurisdiction of the Department of the Interior. The inevitable confusion and jurisdictional conflict was avoided by informal agreements between the departments—an attempt at coordination characteristic of the Roosevelt years—which enabled the Forest Service to enforce its program. Those agreements, and hence the entire forest service program, were in danger from the moment Ballinger assumed command of his department.

While conflict between the men was unquestionably rooted in honest differences over policy, it would have been naive in the extreme to expect a man of Pinchot's passionate nature to watch placidly as his life's work was dismantled. He struck back with whatever weapons became available. When a disgruntled agent of the General Land Office approached him with charges of dishonesty against the commissioner of the land office, Pinchot and imaginative lawyers in the Forest Service had little difficulty convincing themselves that the accusations should be shifted up to focus on Ballinger. They placed formal charges before the president. When Taft rejected the charges as unfounded Pinchot forced his own dismissal from the government, and submitted his case before the court of public opinion in a congressional investigation that ensued in the spring of 1910. A brilliant battery of lawyers wreaked a bloody vengeance in the corridors of the Taft administration. Louis Brandeis, in particular, adroitly conveyed an impression of lurking skullduggery to be unearthed if only digging were allowed. Besides the personal character of Ballinger, the prime issue was the fidelity of the president to the policies of his predecessor. The controversy contributed to the estrangement of Roosevelt and Taft and the breakup of the Republican party in 1912.[19]

In one sense, this complicated struggle for supremacy ended as a clear victory for the conservationists, with Ballinger broken in spirit and influence, his good name permanently damaged. But since Pinchot himself was forced to leave the government, the victory was Pyrrhic. Of more lasting significance, in any case, were the forces each man represented in the clash.

Pinchot was the heir to a legacy of which he, if one is to judge by his autobiography, was but dimly aware. The conservation mentality originated among the scientists who manned the great public land surveys in the last four decades of the nineteenth century. Between Josiah Whit-

ney and John Wesley Powell an understanding of the relationship between the power to gather data and the power to regulate worked its
roots into the interstices of the federal bureaucracy and nourished the
main stem of utilitarian conservation. It reached Pinchot through sources
such as the Great Basin Lunch Mess, a genial group of bureau chiefs
and division heads who had worked with Powell, to which the forester
gained access when he joined the government.[20] They had long been the
enemies of unregulated entrepreneurial capitalism, and they passed on to
Pinchot a point of view that remained with him, essentially unchanged,
until his death in the 1940s. But they could not teach what they did not
themselves recognize, and they never understood that to many residents
of the West, whom they sometimes patronizingly called "locals," they
were the instruments of eastern influence and extensions of eastern
capital. One historian has recently identified what he called the "central
dilemma" of the history of conservation: "If efficiency and waste are
the guiding lights, then how does one avoid an alliance between a knowledgeable elite and the highly organized upper class?"[21] This was not a
question that Pinchot would have recognized as valid, and he never
grappled with it.

Nevertheless, the question was asked many times by opponents of
the Forest Service and later by enemies of the expanding conservation
movement. One man who certainly believed in the existence of such an
alliance was Richard Ballinger. As a pioneer citizen of Seattle he had
watched the local dream of empire on the Pacific shrivel. The decisions
that governed the growth of the city were made by James J. Hill and
others who resided east of the Mississippi and controlled the capital
needed for development.[22] Ballinger's law firm served a large number of
clients—independent, often affluent, men of affairs—rather than a few
giant corporations paying large fees. Like Ballinger himself they were
men on the make, thwarted by large pools of established capital, owned
by men who lived elsewhere.

Although Pinchot damned Ballinger as an agent of the "special
interests," Ballinger's own supporters had a somewhat different view.
They saw him as the champion of the "small man." In their view eastern
capital had first cornered and expoited western resources and then supported conservation policies designed to eliminate competition, policies
formulated and implemented by men whose social standing and associations clearly identified them with the oppressive "masters of capital."
As more than one western newspaper editorial insisted, Ballinger had
behind him "the ever hopeful prospector" and the "small rancher," and

against him "the monopoly and aristocracy of wealth."[23] Not the least accomplishment of the political machine which Pinchot had made of his bureau was its success in branding Ballinger as the agent of big capital and in consigning to oblivion his charge that the Forest Service was founded on a conspiracy of bureaucracy and economic power.

Pinchot spoke for conservation with a strong utilitarian voice. The purpose of forestry was "to make the forest produce the largest amount of whatever crop or service will be most useful, and keep on producing it for generation after generation of men and trees."[24] For the Forest Service "the greatest good for the greatest number" became a watchword and a war cry. But another point of view emerged simultaneously and did not lack spokesmen. Emphasizing preservation, especially the preservation of natural beauty, but also of game and wild-life, they deplored the despoliation of the environment for crass economic reasons, and strongly resisted Pinchot's efforts to open the forest reserves to greater commercial development.

The prophet of the nature lovers was John Muir, a Scot raised in rural Wisconsin, who had consciously donned the mantle of Ralph Waldo Emerson. Until his death in 1914 he was the nation's best-known and best-loved naturalist—a mystic who walked the woods and returned periodically to preach the gospel of Nature as his covenanter ancestors once had preached salvation from the Holy Writ. He and Pinchot became friends. But in 1897 Muir broke permanently with Pinchot when the latter came out in favor of grazing sheep in the forest reserves. Such organizations as the American Civic Association and the Sierra Club, on which Muir could count for support, also remained shy of Pinchot's coalition—although, admittedly, he made little effort to woo them.[25]

In 1905 an issue arose that drove the final wedge between the two factions. The city of San Francisco petitioned the federal government for permission to use the Hetch Hetchy Valley, which was a part of Yosemite National Park, as a reservoir. The dozen national parks that had come into existence since the creation of Yellowstone National Park in 1872 had no strong citadel of defense within the government such as the forest reserves acquired in 1905 after their transfer to the Forest Service. Four were patrolled by the United States army, the remainder received minimal custodial care from the Department of the Interior, and nothing approaching a national park policy existed. Pinchot's solution was to recommend their transfer to the control of the Forest Service, and twice, in 1906 and 1907, friends of the parks had to fight off bills introduced to accomplish this. It should have surprised no one, therefore, that Pinchot supported the petition of the city of San Francisco to have a portion of Yosemite National Park placed at their disposal for use as a city water supply.

With other Sierra Club members John Muir founded the Society for the Preservation of National Parks, and launched the last great campaign of his life, to save the beautiful Hetch Hetchy Valley. In the bitter controversy that ensued, conservationists hesitated to oppose Muir, whom many regarded as a saint, a latter-day Francis of Assisi. Yet many did, even many friends of the national parks, on whose support Muir had always been able to count. Included in their number were the California progressives, who concluded reluctantly that Muir and his followers were being used by the state's powerful private utility, the Pacific Gas and Electric Company. Also, prominent among Muir's supporters was the bugbear of progressives in the state, the Southern Pacific Railroad.[26]

Yet this kind of support was the key to a potential power base for the parks. Muir rejected any commercial use of the parks. Nevertheless, for years he had urged his countrymen to break with the confinements of civilization and restore their sagging spirits in the wilderness. His audience, the readers of the mass-circulation periodical press, were to be found in the burgeoning cities. In the larger cities in the 1890s a great many organizations existed to campaign for city parks, recreation areas, and city "beautification." In 1900 they joined to form the American League for Civic Improvement, and following another reorganization in 1905, emerged as the American Civic Association, under the leadership of J. Horace McFarland, a civic leader and newspaper editor from Harrisburg, Pennsylvania. This new organization broadened its scope and campaigned for state parks and national parks.[27] Thus Gifford Pinchot was stating the simple truth when he noted that the "center of distribution" of preservationist sentiment was "in the towns or cities." Rather less shrewdly he thought it was "concerned with purely sentimental considerations."[28] But the growing demand for recreation from an expanding urban middle class was a demand that resources be made available for its use. Any resource that large numbers of people wanted to use had a commercial dimension, quite unsentimental in character. Indeed, recreation became a utilitarian Trojan Horse to breach the preservationist defenses.

Muir did not live to see the act in 1916 bringing the National Park Service into existence, but he had helped to coalesce the forces making it possible. Significantly, however, the park service bill was sponsored by Congressman William Kent of California, a long-time friend of the national parks, who had broken with Muir over Hetch Hetchy.[29] With the controversy laid to rest, the divided forces of the preservationist wing were reunited with greater strength than ever. The final push for a park service brought together a coalition that included the nature lovers of the Sierra Club, as well as the commercially minded travel agencies, railroads, highway associations, automobile clubs, and others interested in the western tourist trade. The first director of the bureau was a glad-handing borax salesman and manufacturer who set out to "sell" the parks as America's "great national playgrounds."[30]

Whatever else it meant, creation of the bureau did not mean that beleaguered esthetes had taken the offensive finally against the crass materialists in the Forest Service. Even the confrontation of Pinchot and Muir had not been quite so simple. Pinchot loved the outdoors. Life held few pleasures for him comparable to a trek in the woods armed only with a compass, a pocketful of hardtack, and a sporting chance of contracting pneumonia. The two bureaus were rivals from the beginning, but a common utilitarian ethic united them as brothers under the skin. To the Park Service "natural beauty" became a commodity, different only from those sold by the other park concessioners in the techniques of salesmanship employed. Rivalry between the two was less a matter of differing philosophies than of different constituencies. A bureau that regulated and serviced producers of raw materials, such as wool, lumber, and hydroelectric power, and their carriers, competed for space, influence, and money with a bureau that regulated and serviced the recreation needs of an expanding urban middle class and its supporting industries.

The death of Muir before the passage of the National Park Service Act may have been merciful, under the circumstances. It is doubtful that the old naturalist would have viewed the new bureau with unmixed pleasure. Despite the fact that his role as a publicist of nature helped to create the public demand that turned natural beauty into a marketable commodity, Muir represented a romantic, discriminating sensibility that could not have remained comfortable for long with Park Service policy. He had broken with Pinchot over the introduction of those "hoofed locusts," sheep, onto the national forests; one can only wonder what his name would have been for the tourists who descended on the parks in the 1920s. But he would probably have agreed with Madison Grant, another naturalist and wilderness lover, who ended by deploring the "general exploitation of National Parks" by the "Peepul" and the disregard of the Park Service for "the preservation intact of our heritage in nature and wild life."[31]

The scientific conservationist, Gifford Pinchot, at forty-five. *World's Work,* February 1910.

John Muir, at age seventy-two, naturalist, preservationist, and defender of Hetch Hetchy. *World's Work,* February 1910.

The themes discussed in this essay do not exhaust the subjects of the progressives and the environment. A study equally as long might have dealt with any one of a variety of topics—the drive for city parks, beautification, the anti-billboard campaign, concern for air and water pollution—many of which would problably strike the modern reader as more topical than the irrigation movement. Yet this, and the other two themes of this essay, was each in its own way characteristic of the era. Each also represented an attempt to formulate national policy. The creation of policy—rational (above all, predictable) programs to deal equitably with problems shared by a broad spectrum of the community —is never as simple as the historians and political scientists make it sound. The land has always been too large and sprawling, the interest groups too diverse, the opportunities for conflict too numerous. When a national policy does emerge it usually has been the product of a fortunate, or at least fortuitous, convergence of circumstances.

For historians of conservation it has become customary to chide Pinchot for allowing complex resource matters to degenerate into questions of right and wrong and personal honesty and for allowing a program which should have remained in the competent hands of experts concerned with applied science to become a popular crusade to keep corporate greed from despoiling the nation's natural resources. Pinchot, with his flair for the melodramatic, has always aroused considerable impatience among scholars. His pervasive presence seemed to reduce politics to personality and to inhibit sound analysis.[32] Unfortunately, this has always been the wrong way to state the problem.

It is true, but only in a sense, that the political implications of conservation derived from the implications of applied science (and the new sophisticated technology of industrialism, sometimes mistakenly called science) rather than growing out of the controversy over the distribution of wealth. In another sense the reverse might be said to be the case, and such popular issues as monopoly were very much to the point. The conservation movement was the product of a convergence of the concerns of scientists and the anxieties and concerns of the general community. In a given era science will accord prestige to certain kinds of activity at the expense of others. Thus in the years after World War II physics attracted money, energy, and talent and dominated the scientific scene. More recently the same could be said for biology. In the latter part of the nineteenth century the nation's scientific imagination was invested in natural history. In such fields as geology and vertebrate paleontology Americans did basic work and excelled. Many of the scientists who had done so much of this work in manning the great public land surveys of the late Victorian era were still salted among the bureaus of the Interior and Agriculture departments in the first two decades of this century. Long accustomed to thinking of natural resources in social as well as technical terms, profoundly critical of unregulated development in the old free-wheeling entrepreneurial way, they possessed an ideology that centered on the dual concepts of control and efficiency. Meanwhile, Americans of every kind and persuasion faced the emotional problem of how to deal with the twentieth century and the new urban-industrial age that had already dawned. The focus of this anxiety was the dominating image of monopoly. The convergence of activity of great appeal to scientists with a related set of concerns to the general community provided the fertile context for creative activity on the national level. Great promoters like Pinchot, or the engineers of the United States Geological Survey, or the wilderness and park advocates, seized the opportunity provided by convergence, opened new avenues, and forged new systems.

From whatever angle it is viewed, however, the great weakness of the conservation movement, and still its soft underbelly of ambiguity, was its failure to deal with the problem of elitism. This was the fundamental issue of the Ballinger episode, which somehow never received a hearing. It continued to lurk beneath the surface. Engineers with a utopian vision of their social role found there was more to getting widespread acceptance of that vision than simply invoking their expertise. Gifford Pinchot, like Josiah Whitney and John Wesley Powell before him, had to make way against strong popular currents and anticolonial resistance. As for the Park Service, it has always divided the human race into locals and tourists, and any ranger knows instinctively that the locals are worse nuisances than the bears. The three themes discussed in this essay each cast a broad net for popular support. The irrigation movement invoked the arcadian myth; Pinchot conjured up the people versus the vested interests; and Muir tried to throw the money changers out of the temple of Nature. Yet for each of the three the most significant support came from organized groups and powerful economic lobbies rather than from the collective weight of the "democracy."

The implications of this alliance still accounts for the peculiarly soft character of conservation ideology. What might be called the Muir syndrome—an overriding concern for design in nature—has predominated and informed every idea. For ecological folk caught up in this syndrome the collective "people" rank somewhere with those noxious quadrupeds, sheep, so long ago branded as "hoofed locusts" by the patron saint. There is not much ideology in the Muir syndrome, but what there is is profoundly reactionary. Because of the longstanding alliance between conservation and "good" capitalists, unaccompanied by any very widespread popular support, the examination of roots and causes has usually been fuzzy, lacking in focus, and generalized. There is a dreary sameness to the ideological landscape. The theory of evil is very Calvinist. Evil is Human Greed. The Enemy is the Exploiter. External vigilance over the Special Interests, eternal exposure of their Machinations, eternal readiness to spring to the defense of Nature, the inability of the Common People to understand complex resource problems—these have long been familiar stocks-in-trade of conservation rhetoric.[33] The need to distinguish constantly between greedy and altruistic capitalists has produced a curious failure to look closely at the political and economic dynamics of capitalism itself in its relation to natural resources. Meanwhile, for most of the history of the conservation movement, evil continued to reside where Calvin said it belonged, in the human heart, and there, presumably, it would remain entrenched until the millennium.

6

URBAN REFORM IN
THE PROGRESSIVE ERA

MELVIN G. HOLLI

The traditional dates assigned to delineate the Progressive Era, 1900–15, do not provide the best possible fit for describing reform in the American city. The years 1893–1920 offer better limits for describing the municipal reform impulse. Historians of the national scene have viewed 1900 as roughly the breaking point between populism and progressivism and have stressed, with few exceptions, the discontinuity of reform. They have tended to see two separate and discrete reform movements, one rural and backward looking and the other more urban, and perhaps urbane, and forward looking. This was not the case with reform in the city.

Although urban reform was also evolving and unfolding into different political and social configurations during this period, there was nothing comparable to the sharp demarcation that has separated populism from progressivism. Within municipal reform the approximation to a great divide or watershed is the depression of 1893. The shock of that event reverberated throughout the land, but it shook the cities with a special ferocity. Nevertheless, the changes occurring after 1893 in municipal reform were basically refinements of older concepts. Even before 1893 in anti-Tweed reform groups in New York City were elements that were developed and refurbished during the high noon of progressivism—for example, the old Mugwump solutions of a strong executive, nonpartisanship, and the separation of administrative from political matters. On the other hand, the city was not immune to the main currents of change in the nation's economic and social sphere. Much of the advanced modernization of business would be expressed first in the city's governmental forms, and some important aspects of this modernization proceeded continuously from 1894 through and beyond the end of the

133

progressive period. In that larger sense the mainstream of urban reform was organic and continuous. The shift of the locus of reform from large cities to small cities or to medium-sized cities signaled no sharp break in ideology comparable to that which presumably took place in the populist-progressive shift of locale and programs. The divergence that occurred in urban affairs was between two important concepts of reform.

The first important benchmark in modern urban reform was the publication by British writer and American observer, James Bryce, of *The American Commonwealth* in 1888. This massive two-volume study was initially intended to set forth the "salient social and intellectual phenomena of contemporary America" along with descriptions of "scenery" and aspects of nature and human nature. Instead, the study focused most appropriately and almost exclusively upon American behavior as expressed in politics and modes of governance. Bryce was a perceptive student of American political and social mores and this was reflected in several important chapters on the city. "An American View of Municipal Government," written by Brooklyn mayor and municipal theorist, Seth Low, was clearly one of the more knowledgeable efforts on that subject. "The Tweed Ring" by Frank J. Goodnow, who was to become the single most important theorist of municipal administration at the turn of the century, covered maladministration in New York City. Both chapters, along with Bryce's considerable contribution, comprised the single best summary of their respective topics up to that time. Bryce set a high standard for discourse about the ills of the city. He brought the urban malaise to the attention of the nation as no other writer of his time had.

Bryce made the first systematic effort to seek out the underlying causes of the urban crisis. His contention that "the government of cities is the one conspicuous failure of the United States" rested on several premises. The city's chief faults, were incompetent and unfaithful officials who "wasted, embezzled, and misapplied" revenue on needless public works and thereby increased municipal taxes to an unbearable level; the introduction of partisan politics into municipal affairs by spoils-oriented politicians who catered to "ignorant" newcomers and the "vicious elements" and thereby discouraged the "thrifty classes from engaging in the 'low business' of politics"; and the intervention by state legislatures into urban affairs, which undermined the principle of local control. On the third point, Bryce acknowledged that the subversion of municipal government had brought its own punishment with it. "Good citizens in the supposed interest of reform and good government" had first sought legislative intervention to control the city; their "fitful and clumsy" efforts had, however, proved disastrous. This good-government "ripperism" had backfired, for urban politicos learned the technique and outmatched the "goo goos" in using state intervention to enlarge and protect their interests in the city.

Bryce's catalog of urban ills was not simply the indictment of a well-bred Englishman but the account of a keen analyst who reflected some of the best-informed views of students of the American urban scene. In addition to the three fundamental causes of municipal misgovernment, Bryce added a fourth, which he described as the "mechanical defects in the structure of municipal government."[1] In so doing, Bryce unveiled a diagnosis of misgovernment that the business culture and patrician class would later find attractive and which became the structural reform tradition. Bryce's four points had presciently canvassed the main outlines that structural reform would follow for the next quarter century.

Bryce's assessment found increasing corroboration in the early 1890s. In 1891 Andrew Dickson White, a prominent educator and college president, called American cities "the most corrupt in Christendom."[2] Yet remarkably enough very little change occurred in American cities through 1893. In the third edition of his book in 1894 Bryce asserted with confidence that during the intervening six years since first publication nothing had happened that would require him to alter substantially anything he had said in 1888. Thus, although the groundwork for municipal reform had been prepared, no single event had touched off in the cities the kind of moral and political conflagration then sweeping the Populist prairies.

The depression of 1893 sparked urban reform. The business cycle had clearly played a role in stimulating nineteenth-century reform: the 1873 slump had triggered an ephemeral movement that flashed briefly through the night of economic despair but fizzled with recovery. The reform effort that followed the 1893 depression was different in character and of much greater magnitude. The economic crash struck all segments of urban society. Some of course were hurt and damaged more than others but all felt the economic decline. An immediate effect was the rapid proliferation of citizens' associations and taxpayers' groups bent on eliminating waste, cutting costs, and lowering taxes. Many of the early groups gave the promotion of "honest, efficient, economical" government a high priority.[3]

What saved the reform effort that began in 1894 from the fate of its short-lived predecessor was that public leaders and others had devoted serious thought and effort to the urban malady, had cultivated a following, and were prepared to lead urbanites toward a more sophisticated analysis of city problems that went beyond simple tax cutting. The effort of the 1890s was also diverted from control of the economizers because a highly visible and publicly significant group of mayors and their supporters, who were inclined toward social reform, directed their administrations toward meeting the social and welfare needs of the urban masses. These social reform mayors identified their administrations with measures that diverged from the direction of associational reform. Another reason that the *ad hoc* tax cutters' associations did not dominate and define exclusively the municipal reform of the 1890s was that early in the crisis nationwide organizations formed and quickly became the captive organs for professional students of the city.[4]

The First National Conference for Good City Government and the National Municipal League were set up in early 1894, and both gave to the municipal reform impulse a life that reached out of the depths of the depression onto the high plain of McKinley prosperity and beyond. The league and its annual conferences not only imparted to reform an elan and sense of national purpose but also provided an institutional framework for municipal reform that assured continuity.

In the wake of economic catastrophe reform groups and reform concerns mushroomed almost overnight. When the National Municipal League was organized in 1894 its secretary reported the existence of forty-five municipal reform organizations. By the end of that year the number had skyrocketed to 180. Within sixteen months after the organization of the First National Conference for Good City Government, four national conferences had been held, municipal correspondents had been appointed in cities in thirty-one states, and every large city had one or more reform organizations. Some like Chicago and New York had several.

Other indices also underscored the unprecedented concern with city problems. During the decade ending in 1902, for example, twice as many articles were published about the city as during the the entire nineteenth century. In 1897 the first magazine devoted exclusively to municipal affairs was established. Just three years earlier the University of Pennsylvania created the first lectureship in municipal government. Before the end of the century several national organizations were founded. The League of American Municipalities in 1897 aimed at providing a meeting ground for municipal officials; the American Society for Municipal Improvements had a limited technical mission and enrolled city engineers; and the American League for Civic Improvement sought to involve unaffiliated laymen for interacting with their city governments.[5] They joined the principal associational vehicle, the National Municipal League, in carrying forward the reform effort through the nation's great urban crisis.

From 1894 through 1897 municipal reform entered its vital descriptive stage. The descriptive phase was never as neat as the National Municipal League hoped, for it always possessed elements of diagnosis and even prescription mixed with a great deal of moral indignation and rage and occasionally some foolish-sounding boosterism. Yet for all of its amorphous character this was the vital information-gathering time, as league officials who looked retrospectively at the period recognized. Even some of those caught in the midst of the municipal commotion perceived what was underway: a Boston *Herald* writer at the first National Conference told the conferees: "We are not unlike patients assembled in a hospital, examining together and describing to each other our sore places."[6]

A plethora of municipal ailments were discussed in a variety of public forums but nowhere perhaps more systematically than at the annual conferences for Good City Government of the National Municipal League. Many of the delegates during the first three national conferences were painfully distressed by the alien franchise and deplored over and again, as did a New Orleans spokesman, the "thousands of immigrants from the slums and prisons of Italy and Southern Europe" who added to the "corruptible vote of the city." Others such as a Chicago delegate related how the newcomers from the "bogs of Ireland, the mines of Poland, the brigand-caves of Italy, and from the slave camps of the South but one remove from the jungles of Africa" made poor grist for milling civic patriots. Some speakers, like the chairman of the Baltimore Reform Clubs, complained that the "saloons and gambling houses and brothels are here nurseries for [urban] statesmen." One conferee argued vigorously that the "vice regions should have no representation. Such sections are to be governed and not to govern."[7]

Others saw the advent of businessmen and business systems as the salvation of the city. The secretary of a San Francisco reform association called the entry of businessmen in municipal affairs the "most encouraging omen in the dark annals of municipal history." The inferior moral fiber of foreign-born and lower-class electorates and their representatives and the dereliction of upper classes was one of the most pervasive themes in the early Conferences for Good City Government. The editor of *Municipal Affairs* concluded in 1897 that in the municipal "Book of Lamentations" no two subjects occurred more frequently than the "degeneracy of councils and boards of aldermen" on the one hand and the "lack of interest among businessmen and the so-called better classes"[8] on the other.

The critics developed another important theme, the inadequacy of most governmental systems in cities. Municipal structures were full of mechanical defects such as the absence of home rule, practices that permitted ward representation, and political interference in administrative matters. Cities had been misled by false attempts to use the federal model to shape municipal organization. This vein of exploration received widespread support. By 1897 two main lines of diagnosis emerged: the affliction was moral, but it was also structural and mechanical—a matter of both men and measures. These two lines of diagnosis informed the drafters of the National Municipal League's model "program" in 1898 and influenced the design of reform charters.[9] The moral-failure line of analysis underwent an important transformation early in the new century that would act as a bellwether for the coming of the "efficiency movement."

The 1897 Louisville Conference for Good City Government opened what officials would fondly refer to as a "new era" for the league. Up to that time there had been no generally accepted theory of municipal government. This realization prompted the league to appoint a committee to report on the feasibility of a program that incorporated the best principles of municipal government and to formulate not only a plan but a program for putting such principles into practice. The committee, after two years of deliberation, presented a final report to the league in November 1899 that won acceptance.

This model municipal program prescribed several important structural changes. It brought together in one package the mélange of charter reforms, revisions, and nostrums that had been discussed and experimented with during the previous twenty years. The program called for a strong mayor plan with a unicameral city council elected at-large for six-year terms and advised that councils should be no smaller than nine or larger than fifty members. The number of elective officers should decrease for only the mayor and council were to be elected on a short ballot. The document specified that appointive offices ought to increase and that administrative positions should come under civil service and be divorced from political matters. Partisanship was banished along with ward and district representation. Municipal elections were separated from state and national elections, and state legislative interference in city affairs was limited. The model advised that cities should receive a large measure of home rule, including the power to adopt and amend their own charters. Bonding and tax powers of municipalities should be enhanced.[10]

Thus the structural and mechanical elements of charter revisionism had crystallized themselves in the new municipal program of 1899. The switch from a descriptive to prescriptive style was a permanent and enduring feature that would characterize structural reform for most of the twentieth century. The institutional base and the framework for effecting far-reaching changes had been established before the new century opened.

Simultaneously a divergent municipal reform tradition was developing outside the institutional framework of the National Municipal League. A more radical group of reformers saw differently the causes of the municipal malaise and proposed alternative solutions that have been called social reform. Social reform had no firm institutional base and was more an *ad hoc* movement that embraced like-minded persons and public officials with similar views of the urban condition. Their ties to the main body of associational reformers were weak and never well established. When three of the most important social-reform mayors— Hazen Pingree, Tom L. Johnson, and Samuel Jones—spoke at Conferences for Good City Government, the evidence suggests that they received a very cool reception. And for good reason. None of the three considered the National Municipal League a significant force for social reform. For the most part they remained skeptical about the league's preoccupation with municipal administration and opposed aspects of its model charter such as those that attempted to depoliticize cities by depriving neighborhoods and natural areas of a voice in urban government by abolishing ward representation. Social reform also departed from the older tradition of nineteenth-century Mugwump reform, and it would be at odds with the city-commission and city-manager movement that rose during the twilight of the Progressive Era.

Social reform was blessed with a uniquely accomplished group of political leaders. Detroit Mayor Hazen S. Pingree (1890–97), Toledo Mayors Samuel "Golden Rule" Jones (1897–1903) and Brand Whitlock (1906–13), and Cleveland Mayor Tom L. Johnson (1901–1909) exemplified the central tendencies of social reform. This reform persuasion was in sharp contrast to the older "throw the rascals out" approach of the nineteenth century. Unlike their good government predecessors, social reformers were not as concerned with paring away inefficiency and bringing the wrath of their administrations to bear upon small time "boodlers." Although such measures were often necessary, they were not the solutions for the major problems that bedeviled the city. These men were also concerned that the drive for austere and clean government might exclude more fundamental reforms, as the history of nineteenth-century reform movements showed.[11]

The social reformers approached the city with a set of assumptions different in diagnosis and tone. The whole thrust of the social-reform effort was humanistic and empirical. The movement did not prescribe standards of personal morality nor did it draft social blueprints or city charters that sought the imposition of middle-class morality and the values of corporate business upon the masses. Unlike the structural reformers who tended to view the problems of the city in terms of the immigrant and the lower classes, the social reformers were convinced that the urban utilities and large businesses that benefited from favors in franchises, taxes, and public services were the major causes of corrupt city government. They rejected the structural view that businessmen and experts were best fitted to rule the city and should dominate municipal government. If anything they accepted a traditional, democratic faith in the ability of the masses to participate in the process of ruling themselves. Tom Johnson, like his aide Frederic Howe, believed that what the city needed was not systems to mute the demands of mass electorates but methods to increase popular control. Detroit's Hazen Pingree was a stormy and volatile proponent of enhancing popular power and amplifying the force of public opinion.

Detroit's reform mayor, Hazen Pingree, at age fifty-six. *Arena,* March 1896.

The programs of the social reformers were primarily concerned with achieving lower costs for the urban masses from vital public services such as gas, light, and transportation and in redistributing the tax burden equitably. Social reformers recognized that the fight against crime in its commonly understood sense (i.e., rooting out gambling, drinking, and prostitution) was an attempt to treat the symptoms rather than the disease itself. Such campaigns would burn out the energies of a "reform" administration and leave fundamental problems of the urban masses untouched. The interest of social reformers in public baths, parks, playgrounds, and care for the unfortunate was part of a larger effort to humanize the city environment. They hoped within the existing urban framework to redistribute at least in part some of the amenities of middle-class life to the masses. Their programs tended to alienate them from the business classes and invariably drove them to depend upon lower-class constituencies for political power.[12] Although social reform provided the only significant alternative to structural reform nevertheless it was the structural variant that came by the end of the progressive period to dominate municipal reform.

Structural reform was in the process of taking shape among associational reformers within the National Municipal League during the 1890s. This species of reform had not risen *ex nihilo* out of the first Good Government Conference in 1894 nor was it handed down from high council in 1899 with the league's model charter. Like most historical movements and events it had important antecedents. The forerunners and progenitors were many and varied and were found in most large cities during the post–Civil War period and often shared their reform calling with Mugwumps.

During the three decades preceding 1890 the role of municipal reformers had been neither very fruitful nor very instructive. The mayoral model for municipal reform before 1890 had been set by men such as New York's Mayor William F. Havemeyer (1873–74), the first good government victor over corrupt Tammany Hall; Brooklyn's Mayor Seth Low (1882–85), an efficiency-minded theoretician; and Buffalo's rugged and honest "veto" Mayor Grover Cleveland (1882). Mayors of this reform persuasion had attempted to fuse the efficiency of the business world with the Protestant ethic of scrupulous honesty to wipe out graft and corruption in city government. Fiscal integrity and the businesslike exercise of stewardship were important considerations. Implicit within this pattern of reform was an attempt to fasten onto an idealized notion of the business ethic a Mugwump concept of merit and disinterested service to banish the excesses of patronage and spoilsmanship. As vigilant fiscal watchdogs these business-minded reformers struck at what they perceived to be the roots of municipal malaise—loose budgetary controls, poor law enforcement, vote fraud, general peculation, and the venality of the immigrant-based, political machines.[13]

To correct such abuses civic uplifters and good government people launched a broader effort in the 1890s that coalesced in the National Municipal League and aimed at changing the structures and mechanisms of municipal government. Thus began the nationwide movement to revise city charters; the model charter of 1899 drew together the disparate elements of structural reform and crystallized them into a single national program.

These nineteenth-century good government reformers were the intellectual precursors of a new generation of municipal managers and students who rose to prominence during the Progressive Era and who perfected the mechanisms of structural reform. University professors, municipal theorists, businessmen, and the personnel of the new municipal research bureaus formed the nucleus. After much tinkering and experimenting with city charters, these structural reformers advanced a number of proposals to redesign city government: the citywide election, the abolition of the ward system of representation, and the nonpartisan election were important components of a new design that would evolve into the city-commissioner and city-manager systems.[14]

These new urban forms were more than merely an expression of the internal dynamics of the advanced professions and new organizational structures of big business. They also facilitated a fundamental shift of urban political power. The lower classes invariably lost representatives to the business classes and their professional auxiliaries who moved into the centers of municipal power. The retooling of the city made it possible to "change the occupational and class origins of decision-makers." This radical departure from traditional forms caused "a revolution in the theory and practice of city government."[15] The triumph of the structural reform tradition in the movement to city commissioner and finally manager occurred in the closing years of the progressive period and permanently influenced and controlled much of the direction of urban reform in the twentieth century.

The reshaping and redefining of an important dimension of structural reform occurred in the deft and effective transformation of Mugwump morality into scientific efficiency under the aegis of the scientific-management movement. Another important problem that the National Municipal League identified was the moral behavior of urban man, one of the two principal lines of diagnosis that emerged from the information-gathering phase of the league's work. Not only bad systems but bad men corrupted civic virtue. Cities were honeycombed with lazy and slothful workmen, dishonest purchasing agents, malingering work crews and inattentive bosses, and careless leadership that wasted unaccounted material and human resources at high cost to the city. If one pursued the evangelical Christian line that held that men were inherently depraved and could be saved and turned from their evil ways only by a national moral reawakening, then the nostrums of municipal theorists seemed feeble and innocuous palliatives. Human nature in its larger urban collectivity appeared beyond redemption by a few hundred good government zealots. The moral problem posed a crisis of great magnitude that had to be faced and resolved to the satisfaction of good government people before structural reform could be pushed to an advanced stage. The resolution of this problem is an interesting one and has been overlooked. It says much for the ingenuity of structural reformers and shows how they adapted a model from another discipline (in this case the engineering and management sciences) and applied it to the urban political sphere. They redefined dishonesty and immorality in city government in a fashion that made it malleable to the newly developing field of scientific management.

The transformation of the high moral emphasis of nineteenth-century good government reformers into a keen concern for municipal efficiency was one of the principal accomplishments of institutional municipal reform. The doctrine of efficiency expanded from a simple input-output measure of mechanical efficiency to include a wider range of human activity. Municipal theorists and reformers played a key role in enlarging this mechanical paradigm and eventually bringing it into the structural reform tradition.

During the aftermath of the depression of 1893 the word *efficiency* first came into widespread use in municipal circles. Initially, *efficiency* was linked to *economy* and *honesty* and seldom used by itself as a prescription for recovery. The economic crisis shaped the concerns and language of reformers. Good government conferees spoke endlessly about "honest, efficient and economical government" that was "wisely administered" by the "ablest and purest men." "Economical and efficient government" soon emerged as the primary catchwords.[16] This translated into spending less and squeezing maximum benefit out of the city's tax dollar. Efficiency was merely the helpmate to achieving government at lower cost.

Yet almost simultaneously efficiency took on the tone and character of a larger concept. Theodore Roosevelt, an often astute observer of the public mood, recognized early the growing importance of efficiency. In an address to the First National Conference for Good City Government in 1894, he told the delegates: "There are two gospels I always want to preach to reformers. . . . The first is the gospel of morality; the next is the gospel of efficiency. . . . I don't think I have to tell you to be upright, but I do think I have to tell you to be practical and efficient." The "most practical" politician was the "most honest," he added, and practicality and efficiency were two sides of the same winning political equation.[17]

The meaning of *efficiency* during the late 1890s was clearly in its expansive phase and possibly had, as one writer argued, some weak linkages to muscular Christianity. Yet the directional flow at that time was from efficiency to religion and not the other way around. The concept of efficiency had not risen *de novo* from civic uplifters. The systematic aspect of efficiency had derived largely from Frederick Winslow Taylor's scientific-management movement and its great popularizer, Harrington Emerson, who had helped to introduce it to reformers.[18] Even though what both men had to offer was already in practice in some of the most advanced sectors of business, they gave to efficiency a scientific character and a systematic form that made it attractive to the new students of urban government.

Efficiency had its greatest impact on the city during the progressive years. By the turn of the century it was apparent that honesty and morality, while desirable, were not in themselves sufficient to meet the needs of municipal reform. The president of the American League for Civic Improvement, Charles Zueblin, made that clear to the 1901 Conference for Good City Government. Zueblin pointed out that although Chicago had elected many "honest" councilmen, honest councilmen were not enough. "We now want to get some efficient councilmen," he added. The city still had a backlog of needed reforms that would require more than "honest councilmen to accomplish," he continued. Zueblin concluded that it was the realization of how much more could be done with an efficient council and an efficient corp of civil servants that led to the formation of the American League for Civic Improvement.[19] Like other advanced reformers, Zueblin questioned the efficacy of pure and simple honesty and suggested that morality in itself was not sufficient to achieve the larger purposes of municipal reform.

One of the important agencies in helping to transform morality into efficiency was the municipal research bureau. The bureaus played a central role in compressing and directing expressions of umbrage and explosions of outrage into scientific channels of business management and toward finding standardized, scientific, and objectifiable measures for good city government. The first and most important bureau was established in New York City in 1906. No institution was comparable to New York's bureau on the state and national level in bringing modern business methods to the city. Financial and business administration in city after city was modernized through the expertise and advice of the bureau—improved budgeting, new accounting and auditing systems, time and motion studies, inventory controls, unified management, and measures to improve personnel efficiency were all part and parcel of the services exported.[20] The New York Bureau, more than any other single agency, transmitted the doctrine of efficiency to hundreds of American towns and cities.

The bureau stressed the arduous discipline that efficiency required on the uphill road to municipal improvement. As one staff specialist put it in 1907: "To be efficient is more difficult than to be good." Bureau spokesmen also excoriated common and ordinary morality which they obviously saw as an impediment to universalizing efficiency. Dr. William H. Allen, a director and secretary of the New York bureau, argued in 1908 that in only two years "municipal research has proved . . . that public intelligence is more effective than public opinion; that graft and inefficiency fear light more than ballots; that more can be done for good government on budget day than on election day." He added, that penetrating rays of efficiency "can do more good than a moral explosion."[21]

The president of the National Municipal League also pointed out the inadequacy of morality as a measure of the public good. William Dudley Foulke warned that very little progress could be expected against municipal misrule by discussing its morality or immorality and added: "There is many a perfectly moral parasite on the public payrolls that is no less a grafter because protected in his incompetence by a false interpretation of civil service." Foulke soundly condemned what he called "waste-graft" and thundered against the "graft of inefficiency, the graft of a man who is on the payroll and doesn't do a day's work, the graft of a noble-spirited and obstinate man who thinks that because he is virtuous it is all right for him to block progress for five or twenty-five years, or the graft of a body of men on a hospital or school board who limit the future efficiency of school children or patients by their lack of competence or study."[22] This hard-hitting presidential address scored not the immoral but the inefficient. It was not the lack of virtue or a lack of honesty but a lack of efficiency and a lack of competence that wasted scarce municipal resources. The concept of efficiency by 1910 had now become inclusive enough to embrace morality and honesty as they applied to municipal administration.

Efficiency's contribution did not simply end with a new means test of civic worth. Efficiency also had the capacity to shape and reshape occupational behavior and to act as a manipulative agent of social control on the job. The New York bureau, for example, conducted time and motion studies in Chicago and New York and concluded that the average efficiency of municipal labor in large cities did not exceed 50 percent. In 1912 Henry Bruere of the New York bureau asserted that New York City employees as whole had perhaps "been raised from forty per cent to sixty-five per cent efficiency, but hardly more than that." He estimated that "still one-tenth" of a $90 million payroll was "wasted by unnecessary employment, low grade service or misdirected energy." There was hope, however, for slovenly habits could be reformed. Bruere asserted that "where there is method, record and publicity, many incompetent employees cultivate efficiency." Bruere supported his point by relating how boiler room workers "responded almost automatically to the tell-tale of recording devices, showing water and coal used, amount of steam developed, current generated." Supervision, comparison of time reports, cost data, and efficiency records, according to Bruere, proved a "powerful stimuli to the slothful worker" to ungrade himself and an encouraging incentive to the "energetic."[23] Thus work behavior could be revitalized and favorably rehabilitated by the tools of efficiency.

By 1912 it was clear what had happened. Men could then look retrospectively and perceive how a simple moral precept of honesty had evolved into a more scientific concept of efficiency. Mr. Good Government in Chicago, Professor Charles E. Merriam, charted the course of that moral value with his observation: "Until recently public interest has centered around efforts to secure honest councils or honest administrators. Only within the last few years has attention been directed to the importance of efficiency as well as honesty in administration. . . . We are slowly advancing from 'gray wolf' dishonesty to 'dub' honesty, from honest incompetency to business efficiency." Although Merriam's odyssey of efficiency certainly reflected aspects of Chicago's experience, even more important it described a national process that had been unfolding in municipal circles for more than a decade. Indeed more attention had been devoted to the subject of efficiency as a test of good city government during the early years of the new century than in any previous time in the nation's history. Harrington Emerson, an efficiency "expert" and publicist, offered a new doctrine of right and wrong in 1909: "Efficiency is not to be judged from preconceived standards of honesty, of morality, but honesty, morality are perhaps to be reconsidered and revised by the help of the fundamentals of efficiency."[24]

In the palladium of values that informed structural reform, efficiency had won its spurs and edged out good old-fashioned honesty. In the universe of city government, management mechanisms had been found to tame and harness bad systems and bad men for the municipal good. No one suggested that efficiency methods would bring about a total moral regeneration of the urban wayward and of those who violated the city's public trust. But clearly, the proponents of efficiency had few doubts about its capacity to regenerate and redeem wasteful and inefficient municipal operations and reap dividends for the civic renaissance. Indeed, an input-output measure had brought scientific precision to the measure of civic morality.

The rising prestige of technicians in industry and the increasing demand for new municipal services strengthened proposals for efficiency in city government. The city commission plan was an advanced step on the way to the city-manager plan, the ultimate structural reform. Both systems were formulated from business models and both hoped to achieve some of the cost benefits of modern business. The city-manager system was about as close as municipal theorists came to installing the substance of modern corporate management systems while still preserving a modicum of political democracy.

The idea of improving municipal government by consciously imitating some of the main organizational features of private business was applied in the city-commission plan in Galveston in 1901. The central idea of the commission plan abandoned the separation of powers and unified all authority in a small body of commissioners, usually five, who were comparable to corporation directors. Unlike corporation directors, however, they were required to take an active administrative control of various city departments. Policy-making and day-to-day administration were combined. The plan generally abolished ward boundaries and instituted nonpartisan elections. Although begun in Galveston, Texas, the plan was refined in 1908 in Des Moines, Iowa, which became the city that most characteristically and effectively advertised commission government to other American cities. By 1909 the commission plan was in operation in thirty-seven cities, and by 1911 it had spread to 160. The plan reached its peak rate of adoptions in 1917 and receded thereafter.

The principal problem of commission government, according to its critics, was that it scattered administrative functions among several elected officials and failed to bring expert central direction to the city. The appointment of the nation's first city manager in Staunton, Virginia, in 1908 was an attempt to overcome that problem. The effort there was not deemed satisfactory because it incorporated very few other structural changes. The Staunton experiment was modified by Richard S. Childs, who is credited with having "invented" the modern city-manager plan. The Childs program merged the commissioner and manager ideas and concentrated all administrative authority in a single official or manager who was to be appointed by a council or a commission. The plan attracted relatively little attention until Dayton, Ohio, acquired it in 1914, and thereafter the Dayton model became a worthy rival to the Des Moines idea for adoption in small and medium-sized cities.[25]

Commissioner and manager proponents and structural reformers in general had called for business government operated efficiently with less waste and lower taxes and blamed the contrary state of affairs upon unreconstructed politically controlled municipal systems. When the new managers and commissioners took charge of city governments and began their efficient, businesslike operations that promised to end waste and to bring economies and lower taxes to the citizens, these promises proved to be mirages that shimmered only during the heat of political campaigns. Once in office, the capacity of these structural reformers to order change was severely limited. They could shift funds about, sometimes spend them a little more efficiently (or perhaps more efficiently by the lights of their class or occupational groups) but seldom, if ever, could they bring about tax reductions. In fact, during the heyday and bloom of manager-commissioner reform, just the opposite occurred. Taxes and municipal costs increased at unprecedented rates. Not only did the structural reformers fail to cut spending, but their administrations often placed higher "governmental costs" upon the shoulders of the average taxpayer than had the old corrupt patronage machines. The campaign illusions of streamlining and fat trimming vanished when confronted by the sobering and stubborn realities of the escalating costs of urban governance.

During the four years following Dayton's acceptance of the manager system, the plan experienced great popularity and grew rapidly. By 1916 a sufficient number of cities were under the manager plan to permit some statistical measure of its efficacy, especially the claim that it could manage government more efficiently with less waste and lower cost. For those cities for which statistical data is available for the years 1916 through 1919, the per-capita governmental costs were trending upward in a majority of manager cities. These rising costs were translated into a heavier tax burden for the average taxpayer in ten of the thirteen cities during the first full year of manager control. Although the commission system had a head start on the manager system by at least one decade and thus more opportunity to rationalize and control governmental costs, the story was essentially the same. Of the twenty-four commission cities for which comparative data is available, the per capita governmental costs in slightly more than one-half were in control and at or under the average costs for cities of the same size class. The tax picture was less encouraging, for there the per-capita cost tax payments were increasing in twenty of twenty-four cities.[26]

What was happening was in most cases actually beyond the control of either corruptionists or purifiers and, that was inflation and rapidly increasing prices during the climax of the progressive period and during the wartime buildup.[27] Soaring prices in the nation made a mockery of the promises of managers and commissioners. The role of the business or boss-ridden administration in producing any significant difference in city expenditures was ineffectual. Price inflation was an important factor in pushing expenses out of reach of promises of economy.

Other factors appear to be more important in accounting for the greater variation in cost of operation in cities so differently governed as Dayton and Chicago. For example, "corrupt" Chicago's expenses per citizen look large if compared to city-manager Dayton's only if both cities are taken out of their population class and compared indiscriminately. The face of the figures, Chicago $37.10 and Dayton $28.32 in 1917 might suggest that a high level of civic virtue had been attained in Dayton which was run by a flinty-eyed city manager compared to unregenerate Chicago which was under Mayor William "Big Bill" Thompson, the proponent of dubious fiscal morality and the "wide open town." In her size group, Chicago's expenses were reasonable and part of a stepwise progression whereby city-size and per-capita governmental expenses associate very highly and offer a much more convincing explanation of differential costs than civic virtue or its absence. Chicago's higher costs were related to her size. The general pattern indicated that the larger the city, the higher the per capita expense. Group I cities of the 500,000 plus population class on the average registered governmental expenses of $39.43 in 1917 compared to an average of $26.81 for Dayton's Group III population class. Tax rates for the period follow the same profile: the highest per-capita rates are found in the largest cites and the lowest in the smallest. City size seems a far better predictor of urban expenditures and tax rates than does any other single factor.

Businessmen in public office were often treated to a rude shock when they discovered another important shortcoming of the facile business-government analogue. In their businesses they knew that enlarging the scale of operation almost invariably brought economies of scale to bear upon production which resulted in a lower unit cost. Cities, many of them reasoned, should operate the same way. Cities, after all, were corporations; their executive officers could be considered managers, and their councilmen or commissioners were often referred to in reform publications as members of the board of directors. Why should not municipal corporations bring the same economies to bear upon the municipal product or service? The extraordinarily high per-capita cost in big cities, they reasoned, was caused by patronage, waste, inexpertness, and inefficiency. This line of reasoning obviously led many business-minded candidates to proclaim sincerely and with some confidence that they could provide more services for less cost if elected: voters often understood (or perhaps misunderstood) this to mean lower taxes and in most cases reformers did nothing to discourage that thought. Once in power many managers and commissioners discovered that the economies of scale did not work in cities. In fact urban governmental costs operated in just the opposite direction—the larger the scale the higher the unit cost. The smallest cities had the lowest costs and taxes, and the largest had the highest. Every statistical measure from 1908 through 1921, during the zenith of business influence upon progressivism, supports the thesis that city size was the most reliable determinant of governmental cost. The urban boss and the patronage system, though obviously the source of some waste and leakage, were far less the cause of burgeoning city expenses than good government reformers popularly believed.

On the other hand, there does appear to be an important relationship between high governmental costs and the occurrence of successful reform or protest movements in cities during the late progressive period. Three widely separated cities in geography, culture, and ethnic composition—Los Angeles, Seattle, and Boston, for example—suffered exceedingly high governmental costs which were visibly and prominently out of line with those of their sister cities of the same population groups in the years immediately preceding successful protest, structural reform, and recall movements. The figure in 1909 for Seattle was $74.16 and for Los Angeles $43.19, which were astronomical compared to the $26.72 which was the average for their Group II cities. In this category, these two high-cost cities led the list and in fact, if compared out of their class with the highest cost Group I cities, they were outranked only by New York City. The third city, Boston, was also out of cost control in the year immediately preceding her adoption of structural reforms. In 1908 the Hub City registered per capita expenses of $45.06, again outclassed in municipal spending only by New York City, the nation's urban behemoth. In the year following peak taxes, Boston adopted a typical structural reform charter in 1909 calling for nonpartisan councilmen, at-large elections with the abolition of ward representation, and the enhancement of power for the mayor. In Los Angeles and Seattle, protest and recall got underway in both cities in 1909 and 1910 and led to recall campaigns that deposed mayors in both cities. Both cities also passed charter amendments that brought in business government and structural reforms.[28]

The reactions of all three followed closely on the heels of burdensome tax years. On the other hand, cities that had many of the same problems but generally low tax rates, such as Detroit, were relatively quiescent during the stormy years in Los Angeles, Seattle, and Boston. Detroit clearly was not spared examples of flagrant urban misrule, for seventeen of her councilmen were indicted for corruption and bribery in 1912. At the same time, Detroit's governmental cost remained comparatively low from 1909 through 1915 and rose but moderately, remaining below the average for cities of its Group I population class. During the low-cost years, Detroit seemed able to absorb the constant news of bribery, low-grade theft, bad municipal service, and the like. But when Detroit's expenses soared in 1916 and 1917 and exceeded the average for cities of Detroit's size, the structural reform forces of the city gathered strength and moved into high gear. The business-led reform groups moved decisively and pressed through structural reforms which abolished partisan elections, eliminated the ward system, reduced the size of the council, and put in its place at-large elections with a council of nine members. Detroiters also elected as their first charter-reform mayor, the Ford Motor Company's principal cost cutter and business manager, James Couzens.[29]

The coincidence of successful structural reform and high governmental costs is obviously more than an accidental or random relationship. These cost figures seem to behave as triggering factors; once municipal costs pass a threshold—generally the average governmental cost for cities in a given population category—then the probability for structural change and reform movements, or successful protest movements, increases immeasurably. In any event, the study of municipal expenses and tax rates for those cities in which comparable data is available, when linked together with information we have about reform and change, can help to gain new perspectives into hitherto hidden dimensions of progressivism.

7

AMERICAN DIPLOMACY IN THE PROGRESSIVE ERA

The Dictates of Strategy and Defense

WILTON B. FOWLER

In 1917 the progressive journalist Walter Weyl surveyed the history of American foreign policy and concluded that during most of it the United States had enjoyed "Peace Without Effort." Beyond the reach of European armies or of other constraining forces, citizens of the United States had spread their control over the immensely rich North American continent. There, anything they wanted could be taken from "weak peoples, and a nation which fights weak peoples need not be martial, just as a man who robs orphans need not be a thug." Because of their history of unimpeded advance, Americans had learned to think of themselves as peaceful, unmartial, and not needful of the expensive diplomatic and military apparatus of European nations. But with the close of the nineteenth century and especially with the beginning of the First World War, Weyl's Americans discovered that democracy, righteousness, and geographical advantage no longer sheltered them from the squalls of international politics. In the twentieth century, the condition of peace would no longer be as natural and easy as breathing. Their government would now have to work at diplomacy just as other nations must.[1]

Good polemicist that he was, Weyl naturally overstated his case. Nineteenth-century American diplomacy had frequently been calculating and resourceful. Yet Weyl's notice of an acceleration in the movement of American diplomacy, an acceleration amounting to a qualitative change, marked him as a perceptive observer. The Progressive Era constituted the busiest and most seminal period in American foreign policy since the exciting time of James K. Polk. The First World War, at least four other war scares, several military expeditions into other countries, and the mopping-up after the Spanish-American War gave the diplomacy of these years a noticeable cadence. The government departments involved in foreign relations—Navy, War, and State—grew significantly. The combined diplomatic and defense budgets climbed steadily, from less than $200 million in 1900 to more than $300 million in 1914. During the war year of 1917, these budgets exceeded the $1 billion mark, and in 1919 they ascended to the stratospheric peak of $17 billion.[2] The principles underlying this expensive foreign policy emerged in some encapsulated presidential prose: Theodore Roosevelt's Corollary, William Howard Taft's Dollar Diplomacy, Woodrow Wilson's Fourteen Points.

But this new involvement in world politics, beginning at the turn of the century, did not mean American action in every quarter of the globe. Far from it. Until the outbreak of the European war in 1914, American foreign policy confined itself almost entirely to two well-defined geographical areas: the Caribbean and the Far East. A sustained involvement in these two areas developed logically from the "revolutionary consequences," of the Spanish-American War.[3] From that war the United States emerged the owner of Puerto Rico, the Philippines, and Guam, and as the temporary occupier of Cuba. Starting with these altogether tangible interests, a succession of American governments constructed a foreign policy which, though colored by idealism and economic ambition, never lost sight of the fundamental concern of defense or of security. The strategic consideration both located the geographical theaters of American diplomatic activity and set the limits within which any crusading tendency, such as the support of China's territorial integrity, must confine itself.

The Caribbean had been important commercially and strategically to the United States since the nation's beginning. The Spanish-American War, however, forced the United States government to arrange its relationship to the area into a system. The war worked its effect in two ways. First, it caused many persons, in government and out, to think for the first time about the matter of security. For example, in his history published in 1902, Woodrow Wilson noted that the possibility of an attack by a Spanish warship brought home the realization that the long coasts of the United States were barely defended.[4] Second, the run of the USS Oregon from the West Coast around South America to Cuba during the war dramatized the difference that a canal across the Central American isthmus would make. Since 1880, when President Hayes called for a "canal under American control," American officials had fitfully urged action. Now the naval lesson learned from the war was quickly inscribed upon the statute books. In March 1899 Congress empowered the president to establish a commission to select a site for a canal to be built "under the control, management and ownership of the United States."[5]

The process by which the Caribbean would become an American lake was now in motion. For the decision to build a canal brought in its train a number of assumptions, best articulated by Alfred Thayer Mahan and virtually unopposed by anyone. Mahan felt sure that the canal would change the Caribbean beyond recognition. It would no longer be a "comparatively deserted nook of the ocean," but a crossroads of the world[6] As such it would inevitably draw the great powers there, both to protect their commerce and to protect the canal for their own use. In short, the canal would produce an almost miraculous efficiency in maritime communication and also a new object of contention among the powers. When Theodore Roosevelt succeeded to the presidency in 1901 the United States had a chief executive whose desire for a canal was if anything greater than Mahan's and whose subscription to Mahan's associated assumptions was complete.

While plans and negotiations for a canal site moved fitfully ahead, Roosevelt in 1902 observed in the Caribbean an episode which he interpreted as possibly the preparation for a new European foothold in the soon to be enriched sea. The Venezuelan dictatorship had defaulted on its official debts to European bondholders. The German and British governments decided to try to compel payment and informed Washington of their intention to demonstrate in force. While Roosevelt accepted British assurances that the blockade and possible occupation of Venezuelan soil would be temporary, he suspected Germany of desiring a permanent stake. German warships had been sighted making soundings off the Venezuelan coast during the preceding year (1901), and rumors were circulating that German intrigues had persuaded the Danish parliament to reject the treaty selling the Virgin Islands to the United States. Consequently, Roosevelt ordered the navy to assemble at Puerto Rico and, according to his version, then confidentially warned the Kaiser that unless the blockade ended he would have to protest openly and bring the American navy into position along the Venezuelan coast. As it happened, Venezuela requested Roosevelt to arbitrate the dispute. He got all parties to agree to take their case to the Hague tribunal, and so the blockade ended. But the affair left numerous Americans suspicious of Germany. Not the least of these was Admiral George Dewey, who headed the nation's official agency for strategic planning straight through till 1915.[7]

During 1903 Roosevelt broke through the final obstacle to the construction of a canal. Already the United States had freed itself of the fifty-year-old treaty obligation to share equally with Great Britain in the construction and operation of a canal. Next had come negotiations with Colombia for its concession of right-of-way across Panama. Just as a satisfactory conclusion seemed at hand, the Colombian senate balked at the amount of compensation the United States offered and refused to approve the treaty. Roosevelt was furious and resolved that the "Bogotá lot of jack rabbits" should not be allowed to "bar one of the future highways of civilization." Since the consequences of the canal's construction would be felt "centuries hence," the location must be exactly right. Engineers said Panama was the right site, so for Roosevelt Panama it would be, and not Nicaragua, a possible alternative. Panamanians, through their agent Philippe Bunau-Varilla, learned of Roosevelt's private opinion that an independent Panama would be a good thing.[8]

In November 1903 Panama declared independence, and three days later Roosevelt granted diplomatic recognition. Colombia now indicated a willingness to accept the treaty which it had so lately scorned. This change of heart only confirmed Roosevelt in the opinion that the Colombians had earlier acted in bad faith. Now he told them to accept the *fait accompli,* for he felt bound "by the interests of civilization, to see that the peaceable traffic of the world across the Isthmus of Panama shall not longer be disturbed by constant succession of unnecessary and wasteful civil wars." Within days a treaty with the new nation of Panama was completed, and by the beginning of the new year Roosevelt was ready with a defense to Congress of his actions. They had been taken, he reported, because the past five years' history had demonstrated that a canal was a "vital necessity to the United States."[9]

The treaty with Panama granted the United States the right to intervene should Panamanian independence be threatened. With a hostile Colombia next door, the Panamanian secessionists understandably favored the provision, which in other circumstances might have taken the form of a defensive alliance. But alliances were still taboo in the United States, so the precedent chosen was the device invented by Secretary of War Elihu Root, the Platt Amendment (1901). This device, first attached to an appropriations bill and then written into the United States treaty with Cuba, was designed to enable the United States to help Cuba back upon her feet if she should trip and fall on the unaccustomed pathway of independence. There was of course something anomalous in including within a treaty which granted independence a provision allowing a breach of that independence by another country for the purpose of guaranteeing the said independence. In effect, the United States had granted Cuba its independence on probation, and now the device used to formalize that arrangement was applied to Panama as well. These two little countries were protectorates of the United States.[10]

Roosevelt's actions regarding Panama produced some pointed criticism, but he dismissed it as the noises of a "small body of shrill eunuchs" from the Northeast. Neither eunuchs nor "the little wildcat republic of Colombia" slowed his canal preparations, because "the rest of mankind will be all the better because we dig the Panama Canal and keep order in its neighborhood."[11] Throughout the remainder of his presidency, and also during the terms of his two successors, the completion of the canal and the maintenance of order around it served as the premise of Caribbean policy. Bit by bit the neighborhood became, in the slang of a later day, the undisputed turf of Uncle Sam's gang.

Not long after the Panama treaty, Roosevelt began to worry about conditions in the Dominican Republic, which lay between Puerto Rico and Cuba and also across the approach to the canal site. The Dominicans were drifting into chaos, Roosevelt feared, and it seemed to him "inevitable that the United States should assume an attitude of protection and regulation in regard to all these little states in the neighborhood of the Caribbean." After sending an investigatory commission to Santo Domingo, and after talking to representatives of the European countries whose nationals were the Dominicans' creditors, Roosevelt concluded that the Venezuelan situation of 1902 was being repeated. Following consultation with Elihu Root he decided upon a course of action which was announced in language that became familiar as the Roosevelt Corollary to the Monroe Doctrine. The corollary laid claim to a sweeping right of intervention in the Western Hemisphere to prevent or correct "wrongdoing." But clearly the president had not the whole hemisphere but the Caribbean in mind, and the Dominican Republic immediately so. There he soon established an American-managed customs receivership, so that disinterested experts could collect and disburse the republic's revenues. Although the United States Senate initially (1905) refused to approve the receivership treaty, by 1907 it did approve, and the receivership "solution" proved so successful that financial reorganization became the stock prescription for ailing Caribbean states. Washington understood the object of revolutions in these states to be access to the national treasury. With it removed from contention, both revolutions and European interventions would be a thing of the past. So Washington hoped.[12]

As of 1907, Cuba, Panama, and the Dominican Republic had become American protectorates, through the mechanism of a bilateral treaty in each case. Now a new technique of keeping order in the neighborhood came into use in Central America, where a general war among the five neighboring states threatened. Root, now secretary of state, expressed concern, because "the building of the Panama Canal puts these Central American countries in the front yard of the United States and their conduct is important to us." Therefore, when some of the Central Americans called on the American and Mexican governments to supervise a settlement, Root could hardly refuse, although he preferred to have Mexico take the lead. At the Washington Conference (1907), under the avuncular eyes of Mexico and the United States, the Central American states signed accords which, among other things, established (1) the neutrality of much-fought-over Honduras, and (2) the mutual agreement not to extend diplomatic recognition to any government coming to power in Central America by revolutionary means, "so long as the freely elected representatives of the people thereof have not constitutionally reorganized the country." The Central Americans also acted at their Washington meeting to set up the Central American Permanent Court of Justice, to rule on disputes among themselves. A hint from Elihu Root led Andrew Carnegie to contribute the money for the court's building in Costa Rica.[13]

Elihu Root was not one of those Americans who carelessly lumped all Latin American states into the same category. Indeed at the same time that Roosevelt appeared so highhanded in the Caribbean, Root courted the large states of South America and Mexico more earnestly than any previous secretary of state. His efforts bore some fruit. It was during these years that the diplomatic focus for Brazil shifted from London to Washington, chiefly because Brazil was searching for markets in the United States. When Root visited Rio de Janeiro in 1906 as head of the United States delegation to that year's Pan-American Conference, he was given a reception by the Brazilian government said to cost $700,000 and including, among other niceties, conveyance ashore in the sixty-four-oared royal barge left over from Brazil's imperial days. Other stops on Root's goodwill tour were Argentina, Uruguay, and Colombia, where he tried to salve the wound opened three years earlier by Roosevelt's Panama action. In 1907 he traveled to Mexico to pay respects and public praise to the long-time stabilizer of that country, Porfirio Díaz. And in the routine of Washington Root made Latin American diplomats feel, for the first time, that they were on an equal official and social level with their European colleagues.[14]

It is possible that President Taft's perky little secretary of state, Philander Knox, observed the success of Root's Caribbean policy without fully appreciating the rationale or the amount of work behind it. In any case, the State Department under Knox, who was sometimes called the "sawed-off cherub," exhibited an insouciant confidence in its ability to provide the Caribbean with tranquility. From Honduras and Nicaragua came word of revolution and indebtedness, so the State Department responded with the panacea of a Dominican-like arrangement for financial reorganization. But Knox did his homework among senators no better than he did among Latin American diplomats, and the Honduran and Nicaraguan treaties failed of approval. Knox then resorted to executive agreements which amounted to tripartite contracts among the State Department, Honduras (or Nicaragua), and the American banking group providing the loan.[15]

But his substitution of loans for bullets, as Taft liked to describe his "dollar diplomacy"—without specifying which Rooseveltian bullets he had in mind—proved by the summer of 1912 to be an inadequate guarantor of order in Nicaragua. Revolutionary overthrow of the government there was imminent, and in order to prevent it, Assistant Secretary of State Francis Huntington Wilson (acting for Knox, who was frequently absent from his office) asked Taft for permission to send in the marines.

> "We are having so much trouble in Mexico, in Cuba and in Panama," he stated, "and we have had for so long frequently to express 'grave concern' and to lodge protests that . . . the authority of our words seems lessened. We think that if the United States did its duty promptly, thoroughly and impressively in Nicaragua, it would strengthen our hand and lighten our task, not only in Nicaragua itself . . . but throughout Central America and the Caribbean and would even have some moral effect in Mexico."

Taft granted permission. The State Department announced that the United States had a "moral mandate" under the 1907 Washington accords (which of course the United States had not signed) to preserve the peace of Central America. The marines landed—without benefit of congressional authorization—helped stamp out the revolution, and then left behind a small but highly visible legation guard, which functioned as a damper on disorder until the mid-1920s. The episode was an ironic finale to the diplomacy of the administration that had wanted to demilitarize American Caribbean policy.[16]

The Panama Canal opened its locks for business during the same week in August 1914 that the Great War began. With all the powers of Europe at war, one could have been excused for thinking that the canal was safe from attack. But actually the war made American officials more security-conscious than ever. The Joint Army and Navy Board, the body directly responsible for strategy, worried that the winner in Europe, particularly if it were Germany, would next turn on America. Japan and Germany had consistently been at the top of the list of potential enemies since the joint board's creation after the Spanish-American War, and both were suspected of wanting bases near the canal. In 1912 the so-called Lodge Corollary, a resolution passed by the Senate, was meant to prevent an anticipated Japanese leasehold in Mexico. And Secretary of State Robert Lansing clearly had Germany in mind when, more than a year after the world war's beginning, he wrote this lucid statement of the Wilson administration's Caribbean policy:

> The possession of the Panama Canal and its defense have in a measure given to the territories in and about the Carribbean [sic] Sea a new importance from the standpoint of our national safety. It is vital to the interests of this country that European political domination should in no way be extended over these regions. As it happens within this area lie the small republics of America which have been and to an extent still are the prey of revolutionists, of corrupt governments, and of predatory foreigners.
>
> Because of this state of affairs our national safety . . . requires that the United States should intervene and aid in the establishment of a stable and honest government, if no other way seems possible to attain that end.[17]

Lansing's bluff attitude came to bear in 1915 upon Haiti, which had until then escaped protectorate status, and in 1916 upon the Dominican Republic, which had not been fully redeemed by the receivership solution after all. Wilson and Lansing knew that their landing of marines in Haiti was highhanded and extralegal, but the internecine struggle there was so far out of hand that Wilson did not hesitate to act the policeman. The landing in the Dominican Republic took place under color of the 1907 treaty inherited from Theodore Roosevelt. In both cases, the result was American rule and then supervision of elected indigenous governments. The new Haitian government then signed a treaty (1916) with the United States similar to the ones her neighboring republics had negotiated earlier. By its terms Haiti agreed "not to surrender any of the territory of the Republic . . . by sale, lease, or otherwise . . . to any foreign power." One more potential submarine base for Germany was now closed off. And when later in the year Denmark at last sold to the American government the long-sought Virgin Islands, yet another possible German base was preempted.[18]

Roosevelt "under the bamboo tree" celebrates the "taking" of Panama. *Judge,* December 12, 1903.

While the Wilson administration scampered around the Caribbean restoring order and preventing the establishment of influence by a foreign power, Mexico collapsed into civil war. The stance taken by Wilson during the Mexican Revolution exasperated many Mexicans, many Americans, and several European governments. The complications of the question remain exasperating today, but several general observations may be risked. First, it was most unlikely that any American president, even one less didactic than Wilson, could simply ignore an upheaval of such duration and intensity as the Mexican Revolution. Wilson was in the beginning, however, overeager to try his hand at directing the course of the revolution. Second, Wilson's interferences in Mexico were devoid of any attempt at special concessions or favoritism for Americans. Third, throughout the Mexican difficulty Wilson's guiding objective was the institution of what he called a constitutional government. This ideal was, he knew, perhaps impossible, but if attained it would be a lasting solution, for a constitutional government was one that truly represented its constituents and was therefore constantly reforming itself in ways to safeguard their interests.[19]

Wilson's grappling with the Mexican question divides itself into chronological phases. During the first of these, from the time Wilson took office in March 1913 into the autumn of 1914, his immediate objective was to dislodge Victoriano Huerta, the caudillo whose armed force had first overthrown and then assassinated Francisco Madero, the legitimately elected, reformist president. Wilson decided from the outset not to recognize Huerta, whom he called a butcher. When the butcher nevertheless continued to occupy office in defiance of Wilson's preference for a new, freely elected leader of Mexico, Wilson resorted to forceful measures. He took advantage of a petty incident involving alleged disrespect for the American flag to seize the port of Veracruz. It is questionable whether Congress would have authorized Wilson's use of troops if he had told them that his true purpose was to force the resignation of Huerta. But that was his objective, and Huerta, cut off from the revenues of Mexico's chief port, was soon driven out of Mexico City by the followers by Venustiano Carranza.

In the second phase, from the fall of 1914 through the fall of 1915, Wilson hoped to support the man likeliest to carry out the reforms, notably land reform, needed in Mexico. He chose to back not Carranza but one of the latter's promising young commanders, Pancho Villa, who American observers thought would be the choice of the 1914 constitutional convention. But when the convention gave way to war, Wilson retreated from preference for Villa to a position of "watchful waiting" and announced that he would recognize whoever emerged as the undoubted choice of the Mexican people. The fighting continued and became so destructive by the spring of 1915 that Wilson ordered Villa and Carranza to cease fighting or risk the intervention of the United States. In response Carranza, with marvelous irony, used the American Civil War to illustrate his contention that a civil war could not end in compromise. Carranza, every bit as stubborn as Wilson, proceeded to supplement his argument with military victories over Villa, with the result that Wilson granted him recognition as the de facto government of Mexico.

Next followed the third phase of the Mexican problem, from October 1915 through February 1917. In this period of de facto recognition Carranza was supposed to be perfecting the authority of his regime and preparing for the inauguration of the new constitution being written by a representative convention. Pancho Villa, both to keep his own tattered force alive and to embarrass Carranza, now began a series of murderous raids on border towns of the United States. To protect the border and to appease the American public, many of whom had become impatient with the "mess" in Mexico, Wilson stationed the national guard along the border and eventually sent an expedition commanded by General John J. Pershing into Mexico to catch Villa. Not surprisingly, Pershing's men did not capture Villa but did manage to clash with regular Mexican (i.e., Carranzan) troops. For a time war seemed really likely, but fortunately each of the obstinate old schoolmasters, Wilson and Carranza, left the other room to retreat gracefully from the confrontation. Pershing's expedition started home in December 1916, empty-handed but with dignity intact, and early in 1917 a fully empowered American ambassador presented his credentials to President Carranza.

Just before the final measure of diplomatic recognition was extended to Carranza, an adviser urged Wilson to delay until the Mexicans formally guaranteed the security of American property against uncompensated expropriation or other depredation. But Wilson declined to use the means available to him—the grant of recognition or, possibly, the continuation of Pershing in Mexico—to extract promises or concessions. No doubt his motivation was in part expedient: good relations with Mexico were desirable as Wilson's attention turned more and more to the European war. But there is also no reason to doubt the sentiment behind Wilson's publicly stated intention to let the Mexicans devise their own remedies. "Mexico," he said, "can never become a peaceful, law abiding neighbor until she has been permitted to achieve a permanent and basic settlement of her troubles without outside interference."[20]

Woodrow Wilson's close advisor, Colonel Edward M. House (1858–1938). University of Texas Library.

Secretary of State Robert Lansing, at age fifty-one. *World's Work,* August 1915.

Secretary of State Elihu Root in an informal pose, at age sixty. *Review of Reviews,* August 1905.

On the eve of American entry into the First World War, the strategic nerve center, the Caribbean, appeared reasonably secure. Even in troubled Mexico, where so much money was being spent by German espionage, there was now a government which, Wilson could testify, no foreign power could easily manage. And in the remainder of the "neighborhood" of the canal, the protectorate system begun a decade and a half ago by Roosevelt and Root was more firmly in place than ever. In retrospect it appears that the United States overestimated the possibility of the establishment by other powers of bases near the canal. But for American officials who surveyed the world in the early years of this century it was altogether plausible that something which they valued very highly, the Panama Canal, should seem desirable to other powerful nations.

Imposing as were the changes which took place in the Caribbean after 1898, they hardly compared with the upheavals, social and political, taking place simultaneously in East Asia. Nor was American policy in East Asia, or the Far East, as clear in intent, as decisive in effect, or as unopposed in implementation as it was in the almost territorial waters of the Caribbean. In the Far East the United States was decidedly a latecomer to the power struggles attending the drawn-out death of the Chinese empire. Tardiness did not induce bashfulness, however, and the United States became prone to pronouncements of purpose which, to be realized, would have required means far greater than Congress would have supplied. Especially in regard to China, United States Far Eastern policy could have been frequently summed up as, praise the Lord and pass the rhetoric.[21]

The necessity for a Far Eastern policy arose from (1) the possession of the Philippines and (2) a commercial expectation of and sentimental attachment to China, a country with magnetic attraction for American missionaries. Both of these factors forced upon the United States an intercourse with Japan, the nation which strove to control China, and the nation which, especially after its defeat of Russia in 1905, emerged as the strongest power in the Far East, easily capable of taking the Philippines. And, as if by design, California chose these very years to offend Japan by segregating Japanese children in her public schools and by denying the right of land ownership to Japanese farmers. Clearly there were enough complications in the Far Eastern situation to tax the most skilled of diplomats.

The possession of the Philippines was very much military in its instigation. Lieutenant William W. Kimball's war plan, which was the blueprint followed by the U.S. navy in the Spanish-American war, required the retention of Manila Bay as a base of operations during the war, when United States warships, since they were belligerent, would be forbidden to provision in such customarily used neutral ports as Hong Kong. After the war, according to the Kimball projection, Manila would be an item to be returned to Spain for a desired equivalent, such as Cuban independence.[22] In the event, of course, McKinley decided to keep not only Manila but the whole of the Philippines.

Had Kimball rather than McKinley been permitted to dispose of the Philippines, many later worries could have been avoided. One of the first of these was McKinley's obligation, in order to make good on the American possession, to order a force of over 70,000 troops into action against Filipino insurrectionists. And when, a few months later, the American and other foreign legations in Peking were seized by chauvinist Chinese revolutionaries, the Boxers, McKinley found it feasible to order 2,500 troops from the Philippines to assist in the rescue of the legations.[23] Only two years earlier he would not have had troops so conveniently at hand.

Except for a permanently detached legation guard, the American troop contingent left China as soon as the Boxers were repulsed. The somewhat larger Russian contingent did not. Fearful that a new round of dismemberment was in store for China, Secretary of State John Hay issued the second of his Open Door notes (1900). In it, as is well known, he stated the desire to preserve China's territorial and administrative entity and the desire to keep all parts of China open to trade on equal terms with all foreigners, by which he meant especially Americans. Clearly Hay's wish to prop up China as an independent government was not mere altruism. A sovereign China would be one accessible to American merchants. But a China partitioned into leaseholds would probably trade exclusively with the nationals of the governments possessing the leaseholds. And despite one tentative effort the United States government never acquired a leasehold.

While Hay was composing his Open Door circular of 1900 he had the Philippines in mind too. In a memorandum urging Hay to issue the circular, John Bassett Moore pointed out the awkwardness that the ownership of the Philippines caused. "If Russia, or Russia and powers in alliance with her, held China we should be at their mercy in the Philippines."[24] Unless the United States was willing to make the Philippines an impenetrable fortress, strategy required that the power of potential attackers be absorbed in diversions or be kept in check. In 1900 the potential attacker appeared to be Russia, and the means—ineffective, as it developed—of discouragement chosen was the Open Door note. In subsequent years Japan replaced Russia in the strategic calculations, but the connection between the Philippine and Chinese parts of the equation continued.

No one understood the strategic realities more clearly than Theodore Roosevelt. His apprehensions over Russia's ambitions in the Far East, and his appreciation of the vulnerability of the Philippines, made him welcome the Russo-Japanese War (1904–1905) and root for the Japanese. He was glad to sponsor an ending of the war before Russia was utterly defeated, because he wanted the two contenders to remain strong enough to keep each other in check. As it turned out, Japan's ascendancy continued, and therefore the fundamental objective of Roosevelt's Far Eastern policy became that of getting along with Japan.[25]

Getting along with Japan in 1905 meant assuring her that the United States did not object to her control of Korea. In response Japan, in the Taft-Katsura agreement, stated that the Philippines had nothing to fear from Japan. In 1907–1908 getting along meant persuading California to cease the school segregation of Japanese children and coaxing Japan into voluntarily reducing emigration to the United States. In the passion of their objection to American racial discrimination numerous Japanese talked of war. Roosevelt took the war scare seriously. To put more caution in those who entertained the thought of war so lightly—and also because he loved to publicize the expanding navy—he sent the battleship fleet around the world, and especially to Japan.

The record does not reveal much sympathy or concern for China on the part of Roosevelt. In 1905 he did, in one effort to build American influence there, try to dissuade Pierpont Morgan from selling a Hankow railway line to a Belgian firm. But as his term of office moved toward its close, his actions more and more indicated that while he would not publicly disavow the Open Door, neither would he antagonize Japan by any conspicuous defense of it. The Root-Takahira agreement (1908), an affirmation of Japan's and America's respect for each other's Far Eastern holdings, and, incidentally, a reminder of their relative vulnerability, endorsed the Open Door and China's integrity. Roosevelt's understanding that Japan could not be denied control of territories still nominally Chinese was starkly outlined, however, in a letter to his successor:

> Our vital interest is to keep the Japanese out of our country.
> . . . The vital interest of the Japanese . . . is in Manchuria and
> Korea. It is therefore peculiarly our interest not to take any steps
> as regards Manchuria which will give the Japanese cause to feel
> . . . that we are hostile to them. . . . The "open-door" policy in

China was an excellent thing, and will I hope be a good thing in the future, so far as it can be maintained by general displomatic agreement; but as has been proved by the whole history of Manchuria, alike under Russia and under Japan, the "open-door" policy, as a matter of fact, completely disappears as soon as a powerful nation determines to disregard it, and is willing to run the risk of war rather than forego its intention. . . .

Our interests in Manchuria are really unimportant, and not such that the American people would be content to run the slightest risk of collision about them.[26]

Roosevelt's letter was prompted, no doubt, by the heroic muddle into which his own hard-headed policy had been transformed by the administration of William Howard Taft. According to the German ambassador at Washington, the Far East was Taft's *Lieblingsfrage*.[27] And China was the darling country in the darling question. The care, the fastidiousness with which Root treated Japan, as in the Root-Takahira negotiations, now vanished as Taft and Secretary of State Philander Knox succumbed to the vision of a new China, revitalized by transplants of American capital. Unfortunately the vision produced a policy that was half-baked, cheaply and clumsily pursued, and unsuccessful.

One might have expected better performance, for Taft himself and also two crucially important advisors, Francis Huntington Wilson and Willard Straight, possessed considerable first-hand experience of the Far East. Equally at home whether occupying the Far Eastern desk at the State Department or an office on Wall Street, Straight was living proof that love for China and adherence to finance capitalism could be mutually reinforcing sentiments. His experience and views epitomized the peculiar spell that China worked on a number of American idealists. He had gone out to China after his graduation from Cornell, a year after Hay's second Open Door note. He was soon one of numerous Western enthusiasts who talked of the "Chinese Renaissance." John Bassett Moore, Hay's adviser, ridiculed such enthusiasts: "some of our people, mostly students and men unfamiliar with practical affairs, . . . conceived that it would be a good thing if the Powers would take China under their tutelage and reorganize her and transform her." It was fantasy, proceeding from "erroneous principles," Moore thought.[28]

How could a fantasy be turned into a workable plan of action? Straight's solution bore more than a passing resemblance to some economic thought of the 1970s. Straight's premise, which became firmer after the Russo-Japanese War, was that China could not hope to avoid subjugation unless she modernized. While she was modernizing she would need a protector, preferably the United States, to keep the predators at arm's length. But Straight realized that there was very little in the way of a tangible American stake in China. Despite voluminous ballyhoo about commercial opportunity there, the actual China trade of Americans amounted to only 2 to 3 percent of their total foreign trade. How could the trade be increased? By creating consumers in China. How create consumers? By industrializing the country. How industrialize? By pumping in capital. And here was the role for the American government. It could do what a freely operating market mechanism had not yet done—make China attractive to American investors of capital.[29]

Although he failed to win the endorsement of Roosevelt and Root for his project, Straight did apparently find a sympathetic listener in Taft, as early as 1907. When Taft became president, Straight and his likeminded colleague, Huntington Wilson—both of whom were robustly anti-Japanese—had their opportunity. Through a series of diplomatic initiatives, including an extraordinary personal appeal from Taft to the prince regent of China, the State Department secured places for American banking groups in the large international consortiums which were providing the capital for railway-building and public works in China. Despite much hard work, the State Department saw its China project fail. An important reason for the failure was the shortage of capital in the United States. Thus when American bankers went into the European money market to finance a currency loan to China, they found that European banks were not forthcoming until Knox agreed to scrap that part of the arrangement which would have placed an American financial adviser in the Chinese government.[30]

By the end of the Taft administration the American bankers were ready to abandon the complicated China loan business. They did not complain when President Wilson, soon after his inauguration, withdrew the sponsorship of the American government from the scheme.[31]

In his first months in the White House Wilson's attention to Far Eastern matters proceeded along two courses. First, in the question of Japan's protest against California's prohibition of land ownership by aliens, Wilson kept the Japanese talking while he tried, unsuccessfully, to get the California law changed. Unlike many of those around him, Wilson did not think that the vehemence of the Japanese protest meant that war with Japan was likely. And as it happened, Japan in time simply broke off discussion of the question, which declined in importance anyway when the world war began.[32]

Marines on a railroad car in Nicaragua, *World's Work*, March 1916.

Second, Wilson decided to make the United States the first government to recognize the recently declared republic of China. Other governments were apparently waiting for some indication that the republic could prevail against its opponents. Not Wilson. Out of staggering ignorance of the situation in China he and Bryan seized what they took to be the opportunity to promote a trend toward democracy in China.[33] Wilson's action is the more interesting when it is remembered that simultaneously he was denying recognition to Huerta in Mexico. Aside from its obvious meaning, Wilson's response to the superficially similar Mexican and Chinese situations showed an appreciation of the variable strength of the recognition prerogative as a diplomatic lever. In the case of Mexico, American recognition was overwhelmingly important; it could make or break a Mexican government, and therefore its grant must be carefully weighed. In China, however, American recognition was not all decisive and consequently could be employed more recklessly. It might help the republican faction and so was worth a gamble. If the gamble failed, the American government would then be free to take fresh action.

The Far Eastern situation next seriously intruded upon Wilson's attention as the chain reactions of world war rumbled into China. In the first phase of the war, Japan did her part for the European allies by taking possession of Germany's Asian colonies and then sitting back to await additional windfalls. With the European powers increasingly absorbed in the destruction of their own continent, Japan, in 1915, was free to expand onto the Asian continent. When they learned of Japan's infamous Twenty-One Demands upon China, American missionaries and the American minister to China mounted a campaign to make the United States China's protector in her hour of need. Before the crisis reached the point at which Wilson himself became directly involved, Robert Lansing, as the second-ranking official of the State Department, asserted that "it would be quixotic in the extreme to allow the question of China's territorial integrity to entangle the United States in international difficulties." But when a full comprehension of what was happening to China dawned upon the president, he told the State Department to become the champion of China's "sovereign rights."[34]

What could the champion do? The "only means" that Wilson could think of to assist China was anything but imaginative. He reissued, for the information of the powers, the substance of John Hay's endorsement of Chinese territorial and administrative integrity. Meanwhile Japan, under pressure from her British ally, moderated the demands on China. The American effort did not even elicit a reply from Russia or France and apparently made no difference in the agreement as finally signed by China and Japan. As a kind of last word in the dispute, Bryan, at Wilson's direction, stated that the United States did not recognize any changes in its own treaty rights with China which the recent Sino-Japanese agreement might produce. In this way Wilson hoped to warn Japan against any further ravaging of China.[35]

The episode revealed Wilson's understanding both of the utter vulnerability of China and of the slender means available to himself to influence events in the Far East. In the hope of placing some obstacle in Japan's way, Wilson now dusted off the old Knox concept of a financial consortium. The Japanese professed willingness to let American capital into China, but the American bankers first consulted seemed hesitant. Eventually a couple of independent American loans were completed in 1916, and in 1917 an American-Japanese consortium made a series of loans to the Chinese government. Wilson was still afraid that the Chinese might be taken advantage of, but their chances were in his view improved by the provision now of surveillance of the proceedings by the State Department.[36]

In Professor Warren Cohen's excellent phrasing, "the Japanese hoped to draw the Americans into the order they envisaged for China and Wilson hoped to draw the Japanese into the order *he* envisaged for China." But ardent Sinophiles, such as the missionaries, never could bring themselves to admit that the United States, lacking any forceful levers in the Far East, had to cooperate with Japan. They were bitterly distressed when at the Paris Peace Conference (1919) Wilson finally consented to Japan's inheritance of Germany's leasehold of Shantung. A Far Eastern expert in the State Department then wrote, "When I first came here, Secretary Lansing told me that the President would stand right behind China. He did and pushed her over."[37]

Certainly Wilson had no desire to push China over. At Paris he could find no way around conceding Shantung because that was part of Japan's price for agreeing to participate in the League of Nations. The League as the embodiment of Wilson's new strategy of defense must, of course, include so powerful a nation as Japan if it was going to succeed. The championing of China, which Wilson knew from the first had a practical limit, lost out to the accommodation of Japan. Similar appeasement of Japan took place during the war itself.[38] In the autumn of 1917, when the military outlook was very bleak indeed for the European Allies which the United States had so recently joined, Japan hinted that she might desert the Allies and come to a settlement with Germany. Thus warned, Lansing was prepared to humor the special emissary, Viscount Ishii, who came to Washington to "coordinate" Japanese and American war policies. The result of their talks was the public acknowledgment by the American government that Japan by virtue of her geographical location had "special interests" in China. The Wilson administration was in effect repeating Theodore Roosevelt's earlier sentiment: the Open Door is a good thing, but not right now.

The United States did not participate in the negotiations and recriminations which followed the assassination at Sarajevo. The crisis resulting from the assassination aborted the freshly and mistakenly conceived hope of Edward M. House, President Wilson's friend, that the great powers of Europe would allow the United States government to lead them into a general arms reduction. The war foreseen by Colonel House came in August 1914, earlier than he had expected and in supreme disregard of the peaceable counsels which he had recently breathed to the Kaiser and to Sir Edward Grey. Nearly two years later, Wilson suggested that the Europeans in their secret calculations had too casually dismissed the consideration of American policy: "If we ourselves had been afforded some opportunity to apprise the belligerents of the attitude which it would be our duty to take, of the policies and practices against which we would feel bound to use all our moral and economic strength, and in certain circumstances even our physical strength also, our own contribution to the counsel which might have averted the struggle would have been considered worth weighing and regarding."[39]

The reprimand in the president's words is obvious. There is also the implication that, if only asked, the United States might have helped Europe avoid war. Wilson did not mean, however, that the United States had been ready in 1914 to undergo the baptism of total immersion into European politics. Indeed, during the preceding decade of proliferating diplomatic activity in the Caribbean and the Far East, the traditional abstinence from purely European matters continued. It is true that simultaneously the similarity of American and British interests resulted in an important rapprochement, but the separateness of the two national policies was caught in Sir Cecil Spring Rice's summation: "The two vessels sail on parallel courses and should have a common code of signals."[40] Even with British "kinsmen" no common code was put into formal writing, and the wording of the American adherence to the Hague conventions (1899 and 1907) and the Act of Algeciras (1906) stressed the absence of political commitment. The overwhelming reaction of American leaders and people to the European war's outbreak was, not surprisingly, "It's none of our business."

Actually, if the Europeans in 1914 had asked Wilson point-blank what actions he would take in the event of war, he probably could not have told them with any precision. Of course, if the Germans at that point had announced that beginning on February 1, 1917, they would institute unrestricted submarine warfare against all shipping, including American, headed toward the Allies, Wilson could have responded that the United States would be obliged to retaliate. But neither the Germans nor the Allies could foretell the course of the war. Nor, certainly, could Wilson, since as a nonparticipant he would necessarily be in the position of always reacting to the actions of the belligerents. They would call the shots. All he could do was state his government's neutrality and then let the State Department lawyers devise specific applications of the principle as specific cases occurred. For the strategists of the Joint Army and Navy Board, defense planning under the neutrality injunction was even more problematic. The principal contingency they could plan against was the war to follow the current one. This meant securing the Caribbean, always seen as the likeliest point for a future German attack, and relying upon Canada's vulnerability as a hostage to British good behavior.[41]

President Wilson's own attitude to the war usually approached the impartiality that he urged upon the country.[42] Even though he sometimes privately expressed a preference for British institutions over German, he believed that in the circumstance of the war neutrality was both right and expedient. Right, because the United States was not formally or morally committed to either side at the beginning, and because until early 1917 no deliberate and irretrievable violations of American national honor occurred. Right, also, because as 1915 and 1916 passed he became more and more convinced that both sides were wrong in their purposes and therefore uselessly debilitating what he called "white civilization." But if it was right to stay out of such fighting, it was also right to try to stop it. And here the expediency of neutrality appealed to Wilson. If he could command the confidence of both sides then he might bring the ruinous war to a close, just as Theodore Roosevelt, by the credibility of his disinterestedness, had been able to act as the go-between in the conclusion of the Russo-Japanese War. Further, as the great neutral peacemaker, Wilson could be the presiding officer of the peace conference and thus be in position to replace the old international system which had resulted in war with a new one that would not.

Wilson's neutrality underwent considerable contemporary criticism, and not just from those who thought that in his heart he favored the Allies. To a restive American diplomat the neutrality policy was wrong because it prevented Americans from shaping the important events in

Europe, it made them "diplomatic eunuchs."[43] By 1915, the year of the destruction of the *Lusitania,* numerous critics complained of the administration's impotence. Not only did the United States lack the power to influence events across the sea, they said, it did not even have the power to make its pronouncements on neutral rights stick. By the end of the year Wilson himself took the lead of the "preparedness" movement, with the result that in 1916 Congress enacted legislation for impressive expansions of the army and navy.

A glance at the implementation of the Navy Act reveals, in a striking way, the genuineness of the administration's neutrality. The Navy Act gave the strategists vast new materials for building a war machine but it did nothing to change the political vacuum in which they worked. In the absence of presidential guidance, they went forward, as Wilson undoubtedly wished them to, with the objective of building not an immediate defense against Germany but the world's most efficient fleet. This meant, in effect, constructing ships in all categories so that the American navy would be able to defeat any other navy—German, British, or Japanese. Had the navy been instructed instead to prepare for war with Germany, it would have built a concentration of destroyers, to use against the submarine. But in fact the expansion began in capital ships too, at the very time when the German capital ships were immobilized by the British in the North Sea. The result was that when war came in April 1917 the United States had a grave deficiency in the type of ship it required to fight the submarine, the destroyer.[44]

When Germany had at last constructed enough submarines to attempt a knock-out blow against the Allies, she withdrew the assurances given to Wilson not to use the submarine against merchant shipping, and did so in the deliberate expectation that war with the United States would result.[45] This calculated risk by Germany knocked the pins from under Wilson's previous diplomatic successes, such as the Liner and *Sussex* pledges, and made American retaliation against German belligerency only a question of time. But though Wilson reluctantly decided to become a belligerent, he was not willing to become an Ally. Rather than being co-opted by the Allies into the endorsement of their objectives and their claims regarding guilt, he hoped to put the rapidly expanding economic and military power of the United States government behind his own objectives and to bend the Allies to agreement. The trump in his independent diplomacy was the liberty it gave him to threaten a separate peace settlement. Whenever the enemy proved willing to accept his terms, the Allies would have to, too—or fight on on their own.[46]

The formal statement of Wilson's terms came, not by accidental timing, in January 1918. In that darkest of winters for Germany's enemies, the Russians had dropped out of the war, the French and British had bled their manpower reserves dry, and the Americans were discovering that their "bridge of ships" to carry their army to Europe was still only a catchy phrase. Everyone knew that Germany would make a heroic offensive when the weather improved, probably in March. So, Wilson's Fourteen Points, made instantly famous by his propaganda experts, were very much designed in the context of winter 1918: to persuade the Russians that the side they had recently deserted now had objectives worth fighting for, to encourage the Austrians to count the costs before continuing another season of war alongside the Kaiser, to buck up Allied and American morale all along the line. But it was not until the hundred of thousands of American troops appeared on the Western Front in the following summer that the Fourteen Points had their influence upon the course of the war. Then the Germans began to count costs and decided to parley with Wilson rather than continue fighting. Now came Wilson's greatest diplomatic triumph. After tying the Germans to an unconditional acceptance of his terms, he played his trump on the Allies, with the result that they too accepted the Fourteen Points as the basis for an armistice.[47] Ominously, though, it had required Wilson's threat of a separate peace to bring the Allies around, and Britain and France adamantly held out for reservations regarding reparations and freedom of the seas.

The fine words of the Fourteen Points had done their part, a very limited part, in bringing the combat to an end. How now could these principles—open diplomacy, self-determination, freedom of the seas, the reduction of trade barriers and of armaments, and a league of nations—be put into sustaining operation so as to prevent another such war? The league was, of course, the essential starting point, the mechanism by which Wilson hoped to work his reformation of the international system. The league was to be first and foremost a system of security, based upon the mutual guarantee of political independence and territorial integrity. Every nation would be in alliance with every other nation, so there would no longer be the necessity or temptation to form competing power blocs. Second, the league was to be the enforcer of the other standards listed in the Fourteen Points, and it was to be a continuing problem-solver. Although Wilson brought a corps of technical experts with him to the Paris Peace Conference, he was not naive enough to think that permanent solutions to all the disputes over territories, reparations, and the hundreds of other difficulties could be reached in one fell swoop. Items impossible to settle at Paris, as well as unforeseen ones of the future, could be entrusted to the league, which would as a result have real work to do and would thus engage the attention of the nations. Once it proved its capacity, nations would come to rely upon it. Its actual constitution, then, would be a functional one, to be built upon a written charter, or covenant—a constitution that would grow and adapt, in much the fashion of the British constitution.

Since the league was so important to his projected reformation of world politics, Wilson insisted that the peace conference make the writing of the covenant its first business. He had his way, and the document was in large part his actual composition. Then it came the turn of the other victors to make their insistences, and Wilson found that he could not exercise leverage against the Allies—leverage such as the suspension of loans, or the conceivable possibility of withdrawing troops from the occupying force—without destroying the peace conference, and with it, of course, the projected league. So, as the weeks stretched into months Wilson felt forced to compromise in order to get the treaty completed without losing any adherents to the league. The Treaty of Versailles (June 1919), incorporating the compromises, deeply disappointed a number of internationalists who until that point had supported Wilson. The sentence of guilt with a huge reparations bill for Germany, the award of Shantung to Japan, the failure to bring Russia or Germany into the League of Nations—these all had the appearance of a traditional victor's peace to such internationalists as the staff of the *New Republic,* which went into opposition to the treaty. The far more important opposition came from the Republican party, where ultranationalists and idealists united in the feeling that the treaty was not traditional enough, that Wilson had entangled the United States too deeply in European affairs. Ultimately the treaty failed of approval by the Republican-controlled Senate because not enough Republicans would cross over the party line to vote for the treaty unmodified by reservations, and not enough Democrats would defy Wilson by crossing over to vote for the treaty with reservations.[48]

Maybe the result would have been different if Wilson had not lost his health—or if any number of other circumstances had been different. One thing appears certain, though. The high drama surrounding the defeat of the treaty insured that the principles associated with Wilson's name would live on after him. In time, the course he projected struck many as the high road not taken, the opportunity missed. Until at least 1945 the Wilsonian legacy set the terms of public debate over foreign policy.

Alfred Thayer Mahan was once president of the American Historical Association, at the time a "preposterous little organization," according to Theodore Roosevelt. Mahan, in his presidential address to the AHA, expounded the necessity of subordination in the writing of history. He meant that the historian, if he is to impart graspable meaning to a body of data, must, presumably after trial and error, discard or subordinate themes of little or no explanatory value in favor of those which do explain, which do reveal the relatedness of facts and the progression of events. Of course Mahan did not have to inform his learned listeners that he himself had found the concept of seapower to be a theme of considerable explanatory value for the study of the history of the relations among nations.[49]

Is the present essay's emphasis on the defensive or strategic aspect of American foreign policy during 1901–19 warranted? Does it serve as the organizing principle around which the diplomatic actions of the period center, as the interpretive principle to which other themes may be logically subordinated? The answer is no, of course, if we require that in every case considered there be produced from the archives a deposition in which a president or secretary of state swore that he made his particular decision because he was afraid that otherwise the United States would be instantly attacked. Nor will the strategic emphasis seem useful as explanation if we deny it the capacity to subsume economic or reformist motivations, or even on occasion to be overwhelmed by them. But if we mean by strategy the calculation (whether by the statesman or later by the historian) of the barrier(s) across or through which the outward impulses of the United States could not prevail, then we have a starting point for understanding many of the conflicts that occurred— as well as some that did not occur—in the relations of the United States with other countries. Perhaps two Progressive Era cases not yet mentioned will illustrate the point.

Taft's administration is best remembered, so far as its foreign policy is concerned, for its Dollar Diplomacy in the Far East and the Caribbean. Taft himself hoped, however, to make the inclusion of Canada in a kind of North American common market his master stroke in diplomacy.[50] Like virtually all his other diplomatic projects this reciprocity scheme failed, partly because the Canadians feared a complete absorption by the United States. It is important, for our purposes, to notice that in this matter, which in dollars and cents made the Nicaraguan projects appear piddling indeed, it never occurred to Taft to employ his armed forces to salvage the work of the State Department, as he did in Nicaragua. Such an act was no doubt quite literally unthinkable. Even when not thinking, however, Taft knew or sensed, as one senses nature's limitations, that he could not force his will upon the dominion backed by Great Britain. This comparison leads to the conclusion that Taft's employment of force in the one situation and not in the other tells us nothing about his commitment to economic expansion. What the comparison does suggest is that he used force in the Caribbean because he knew he could get away with it, while for unstated conditions of power and respect the use of force in Canada was inconceivable.

The second case in point concerns the American landing in Siberia in 1918. Virtually all who have touched this question—historians, journalists, and politicians—have come away with less than satisfactory answers. Even General William S. Graves, who commanded the expedition, failed to discover a rationale in the operation, and ten years of study apparently only compounded his confusion. For he wrote: "It is more difficult to come to a logical conclusion as to the reasons for intervention in Siberia by the United States, than that of any other nation. I can come to a conclusion, satisfactory to myself, as to why other nations took part, but have never been able to come to any satisfying conclusion as to why the United States ever engaged in such intervention."[51]

A frequently stated explanation, familiar to General Graves and abstractly plausible, represented the American intervention as primarily and largely an effort of American capitalism to defeat the Bolshevik Revolution.[52] A second explanation ascribed to the American government the purpose of heading off the takeover of Siberia by Japan.[53] A third explanation, George F. Kennan's,[54] stressed the sentimental impression made on Wilson, after he had been softened up by Allied demands for the reconstruction of the Eastern Front, by the reports of the danger facing the Czech Legion, soldiers committed to the Allied side and on their way to Vladivostok for embarkation to the Western Front. It was for the stated purpose of escorting this body of men out of Siberia, as well as of assisting the Russian people toward self-government, that General Graves's 7,000 troops went to Siberia. Kennan leveled devastating criticism against Washington officials for acting without bothering really to inform themselves of the circumstances in Russia (including Siberia), for making their decisions upon considerations relating to the conduct of the war rather than upon those relating to the internal conditions of Russia or the future of Russian-American relations.

Kennan's criticism provokes the fundamental question and also implies the answer. What possible business did the United States, whose past relationship with Russia was only moderately important on anybody's scale of measurement, have in the Russian Civil War? The answer is that except for the war, none. When the United States became the newest but nevertheless senior member of the anti-German coalition, her strategic boundaries ballooned to encompass those of her associates. It was out of a concern both to keep the coalition together, for that was necessary in order to defeat Germany, and at the same time to prevent the coalition from engaging in imperialistic expansion, that Wilson at last decided upon the half-measure of the Siberian expedition. It is simply not believable that, in view of the critical manpower shortage at the time, Wilson would have sent a detachment to Siberia for any purpose *not* connected to the war. (If he had been looking for opportunities to impose order or engraft capital, Mexico or China would have offered better prospects.) Not very long after he made the decision for the expedition, Wilson exhibited confusion and exasperation over the state of affairs in Siberia. Clearly he would have preferred to wish the whole problem away. Since he could not do that, he tried the next best thing. At the Paris Peace Conference, during which of course the state of war continued, Wilson indicated that he hoped to keep the Siberian matter anesthetized, or frozen in place, until the war with its necessity of getting along with the Allies was over. He would not rock the boat in Siberia until the treaty was safely signed. After the treaty was signed the State Department tried to delay the withdrawal of the American troops until the Japanese agreed to withdraw their ten times larger force simultaneously. But Secretary of War Newton Baker opposed the State Department's scheme and noted how ridiculous the public justification for the continuation of the intervention had become: 5,000 American troops were ostensibly protecting 72,000 Czech troops. An inter-departmental hassle ensued in the American government, prolonged by the attack on Wilson's health. Finally, in January 1920 the president turned his attention to the troublesome matter for the final time. Graves was instructed to complete his mission, and when in April 1920 a substantial number of the Czechs were embarked on ship the American contingent departed. The freakish extension of the bounds of American strategy into such an untoward place was over.[55]

8

THE PROGRESSIVE LEGACY

THOMAS K. MCCRAW

Few intellectual pastimes are more self-flattering than debunking American reform movements. How easy it is to dismiss the New Deal, because it rescued a system that deserved to perish; to cavil at abolitionism, because blacks remain oppressed more than a century after Emancipation; to indict progressivism, because of its glaring failures. Yet to do so often ignores the American context of reform and the sequential dimension of history. It evades responsibility to measure change not only by ideological ideal, but by contemporary reality; not only by what seems obvious in our time, but by what seemed possible in theirs. Without these standards firmly in mind, judgment is likely to be snobbish.

The progressive legacy, even more than most historical legacies, is steeped in ambiguity. But on balance, and especially in comparison with other generations, the progressives emerge with more credits than debits. They emerge tarnished by their inability to understand that unequivocal change cannot occur quickly without a measure of radicalism and unpleasantness, but bright in their willingness to attempt reforms that, at the time, seemed quite bold and innovative to *them,* not to mention their opponents.

The unadorned record commands respect. Year by year, important reforms accumulated in steady rhythm: the Newlands Reclamation Act and the first Workmen's Compensation Act in 1902, the first mandatory direct primary system in 1903, the Pure Food and Drugs Act and the Hepburn Act in 1906, the first city manager in 1908, the first minimum-wage law in 1912, the Federal Reserve Act and the 16th and 17th amendments in 1913, the Federal Trade Commission Act in 1914, the prohibition amendment in 1919, and the women's suffrage amendment in 1920. The list could be many times longer, of course. It should in-

clude the subtle intellectual shifts that underlay legislation and other
formal change. It should also specify the central trend of the period—
the bureacratization of American life—a trend well served by many
progressive reforms.

Virtually all of the reforms derived from a few basic convictions
probably shared at some point during the era by most thoughtful Americans. Among such convictions, the following were decisive: (1) that the
recent, rapid industrialization and urbanization of society had undermined cherished values and created unacceptably hazardous new conditions; (2) that the task of reform was urgent, but not urgent enough to
require genuine radicalism; (3) that personal morals could improve, and
that Protestant Christianity offered the best model; (4) that some of the
new conditions demanded political remedies absent from existing constitutions and foreign to the extreme partisans of American politics; (5)
that government, particularly state and local, should be more democratic;
(6) that the details of reform should follow "scientific" principles devised by experts devoted to efficiency; (7) that the extraordinarily diverse American population, less than one-half of which in 1900 was
both white and born of two native American parents, must become more
homogeneous; (8) that certain abstractions—"the trusts," "the Negro,"
"the public interest"—closely resembled reality; (9) that the deep uncertainties of life must yield, through the professionalization of key occu-
pations, the application of the insurance principle, and the development
of institutions to manage the new problems on a continuous basis rather
than solving them on an *ad hoc* basis.[1]

The principles could combine with each other in several different
ways, to produce powerful subcultural movements like progressive education, progressive farming, or a progressive way of writing history.
Quite as easily, they could conflict, as was the case in the simultaneous
effort to make American life more efficient and more democratic. And
a too rigorous application of certain principles, such as the quest for
homogeneity and the improvement of morals, could end in illiberal reforms like the restriction of immigration and the prohibition of alcohol.

Among the earliest and clearest articulators of progressive principles
were the writers Theodore Roosevelt called "muckrakers," who in journals like *McClure's* and *Cosmopolitan* exposed astonishing patterns of
corruption in American business and government. Muckraking and reform were not the same thing, though observers at the time, and historians since, sensed an intimate relationship. Occasionally the nexus was
direct, as with Upton Sinclair's novel, *The Jungle,* which nauseated the
nation in 1906, and the Meat Inspection Act of the same year, which

calmed gastric unease even if it did not guarantee safe meat. But most muckrakers, like many other progressives, owed primary allegiance to a profession, in their case journalism. All were superb, exciting writers. All named names. Almost all spoke from the democratic, highly moralistic stance so typical of progressivism.[2]

The tradition of exposure persists in highly potent form, in the work of true professionals like Ralph Nader—a progressive type in more ways than this one—and also in the less responsible work of a host of journalists who inherited the muckrakers' scent for a story minus their passion for the integrity of their facts. The most creditable legacy of Sinclair, Steffens, and company was their proof that journalistic exposure, even for a mass audience, can be done responsibly and professionally. In the end, this demonstration was more important, more genuinely progressive, and more directly their own than was their contribution to political reform.

When Lincoln Steffens unearthed "the shame of the cities," he blamed it mostly on bad morals and venal alliances between political bosses and corporate magnates engaged in providing utility, traction, or other urban services. A more penetrating analyst might also have noted that industrialization made urban government incalculably more important than it had been in the agrarian age, and that much of the corruption followed a simple failure to adapt old methods to the change. Even so, Steffens' use of the word *shame* hit the mark. At the turn of the century, its urban government disgraced the United States.

Accordingly, a major progressive effort focused on the cities.[3] Concentrating their zeal on corrupt bosses and corrupted ethnic voting blocs, many reformers sought salvation through procedural innovations aimed at driving the bosses from power and diminishing the role of "politics" in city administration. An inevitable casualty in this process was the throwing out of the baby with the bath water; the decline of "politics" often meant that immigrants and other minorities lost political power. There were important exceptions. A few progressives (Jane Addams and other newly professionalized social workers) labored directly with the urban poor. Individual mayors mixed a deep concern for social welfare with their programs for economy. But the typical agenda of progressive reform aimed most directly at efficient public administration. Urban progressives upgraded utilities and tried (unsuccessfully) to cut tax rates. They prosecuted vagrants and cleaned up saloons. They reduced the number of elective offices by shortening the ballot and lengthening the appointive lists. Above all, they labored to banish the politicos. One southern newspaperman summed it up well in 1910, noting with approval that reforms in the nearby state capital had brought "the end of politics in the management of municipal affairs."[4]

The favored procedural devices were the commission plan, and its more popular successor, the council-manager plan. The very title of the new professional officer called forth, "city manager," expressed the principle behind the change. This innovation—professionalization of administration through nonpartisan management—remains the chief institutional legacy of urban progressivism. By the end of the 1960s, about one-half of all American cities of between 10,000 and 500,000 population had converted to the manager system.[5] From its inception, the plan has worked better in medium-sized, homogeneous cities than in enormous, ethnically diverse ones, a fact that highlights the appeal the manager system had for progressives. One of their fundamental motivations was intense worry about the heterogeneity of the American people after the entry of immigrant masses. The council-manager plan, in removing administrative decisions from "politics," assumed a homogeneous, citywide, nonpartisan public interest that transcended the divergent interests of particular neighborhoods. Acting on this premise, urban progressives also changed the makeup of the city council. They often combined the new commission or manager plan with a shift from ward election to at-large election, and sometimes simply reduced the size of the city council. These steps frequently abolished the seats of ethnically oriented aldermen, or replaced such incumbents with professional and business types. The new councilmen purported to represent the whole city, which usually meant the white Protestant value system most progressives themselves affirmed.[6]

How the reformers secured the electoral majorities to do these things is not entirely clear. But one obviously successful tactic was a fervid, and mostly sincere, rhetorical appeal to principles of democracy and honesty. They promised to turn out political bosses and return power to "the people." That some of the people experienced a loss of power in the process suggests again the ambiguity of the progressive legacy. In practice, there were important gains and important losses. Urban reform did clean up cities physically, diminish the role of "politics," professionalize administrators, tighten loose budgets, and improve the transportation and utility services vital to commerce. But the same reforms reduced the political power of minorities, replaced the bosses' haphazard welfare system with a vacuum, and preserved the influence of some of the corporate interests formerly allied with the bosses.

A major difference between the old system and the new was a virtual consensus about goals and priorities among city officials and businessmen.

The need for chicanery thus dropped sharply. Businessmen accepted and often promoted efficient administration—including regulation of their own activities—because it was more systematic, more predictable. Sometimes the new city officials were themselves businessmen. Campaigns for reform very often originated within groups like the Chamber of Commerce and the Business League, and planners consciously patterned the council-manager structure after the organization of the business corporation. In the new dispensation efficient government avowedly meant businesslike government.[7]

The movement toward the manager system peaked in 1921, the year of President Harding's inauguration, and remained strong for several years thereafter. It surged forward again in the years after World War II, years which in some ways recalled the business ethos of the 1920s and the progressive urge toward homogeneity. Seen in this light, urban reform exemplifies the persistence of certain major progressive thrusts into the 1920s and beyond.[8]

The erstwhile bosses who had controlled city governments were themselves often cogs in statewide machines. Since the cities were, in the legal sense, creatures of the state, these machines could thwart local reform by invoking limitations on the power of cities to alter their government. Confronted with such roadblocks, urban reformers perforce moved into state politics, urging "home rule" amendments or legislation that would grant cities greater freedom to manage their own affairs.[9] Urban reform thus became one of the forces behind state progressivism. Other forces were at work, too. As industrialization centralized economic life, larger political units had to deal with larger private corporations. Eventually, this process would involve the federal government, but first it challenged the states.

The chief political legacy of state progressivism is probably the cluster of procedural reforms called "direct democracy." Sporadically, there had been such movements in the cities, but the most powerful drives for such innovations as the direct primary, the referendum, the recall, and the initiative came in state politics, because of state jurisdiction over election laws. None of these remedies actually originated in the Progressive Era. The Greek city-states had used the initiative, and the American Articles of Confederation, written in the 1770s, contained a recall provision. The striking aspect about their emergence in the early twentieth century was their simultaneous, rapid adoption in dozens of states, and the high enthusiasm which greeted them as cures for sick democracy. Enormous attention converged on them. Pages of print explained their pros and cons, with advocates predicting magical remedies for democracy's ills, opponents prophesying frenzied mob rule. Their enactment yielded neither of these extremes. In fact, some scholars have detected no tangible results whatever from them, and have dismissed them out of hand. But here, as with so many other progressive legacies, one must consider not only the inflated promises of their proponents, but the system they replaced, what they may have prevented, and their immediate purpose.

A case in point is the direct primary, a device intended to facilitate the nomination of reformers and, secondarily, to bring the process closer to popular control.[10] Originating in the contemporary revulsion from partisan machines, direct-primary laws swept the country, until by 1917 only four states had not enacted them. Like urban progressivism, these laws created new sets of problems: further disfranchisement of southern blacks, intensified factionalism within parties, and victors with tiny pluralities in states without runoff elections. Even so, few could question that primaries cleared much of the smoke from smoke-filled rooms, and made politics a career more open to talent. In presidential politics, the importance of primaries has leaped forward in the recent past, bringing the defects of excessive cost and cumbersomeness, but withal opening the nomination to candidates committed as much to principle as to victory. This was true whether the principle involved was that of the right, as with Barry Goldwater, the left, as with George McGovern, or the disenchanted, as with George Wallace. The progressives would have approved of such nonpartisan operation.

The enthusiastic enactment of the initiative and referendum derived from a well-founded disillusionment with representative government. Many state legislatures had compiled almost incredible records of corruption and obeisance to corporations. The progressive impulse in California, for example, originated as a crusade to banish the Southern Pacific Railroad Company from the state's political life.[11] The same principle applied for other corporations in other states. And to keep the octopuses out of politics, to make legislators less receptive to their siren calls of lucre, reformers like the California progressives wrote laws enabling the electorate to veto offensive acts of the legislature (the referendum),[12] or, if they wished, to legislate on their own motion (the initiative).

Again, unexpected problems arose. Technical or trivial items, such as the definition of Grade A milk or the duration of the fire department's lunch hour, distracted voters from weightier matters.[13] Voter participation, already embarrassingly low in American elections, dropped still further when issues rather than persons appeared on ballots (though for moral issues like prohibition, participation was often high). In some states, a high signature requirement for petitions limited the use of initiatives and referenda. And in California, one of the few states for which there is an authoritative study, the trend after the Progressive Era was toward use of direct democracy more by monied interests than by reform groups.[14]

It is tempting, therefore, to discount these procedural legacies. The same temptation applies to other progressive reforms, such as the direct election of United States senators and the enfranchisement of women, each of which required a long, arduous fight culminating in an amendment to the federal Constitution. In the end, none of the devices of direct democracy in and of themselves accomplished great substantive reforms, except in the sense that the vote for women was itself a substantive reform. But in every case, the new procedures improved on methods past. At the very least, they provided a remedy of last resort against gross corruption and flagrant private government. That these devices do not guarantee freedom from such abuses is not the fault of the progressives, who used them primarily to gain office and protect their other reforms. Rather, the blame lies with subsequent generations, which have often endured abuses few progressives would have tolerated.[15]

In one sense, the direct-democracy movement went against that major stream of progressivism that enthroned the expert and made him the determinant of public policy. In state progressivism, this drive for expertise appeared most clearly in the idea of regulatory commissions. In California, progressives pumped life into the old railroad commission, giving it powers not only over the Southern Pacific, but over all kinds of public utilities. The Wisconsin commission experienced a similar rejuvenation after Governor Robert M. La Follette led a popular crusade to tame the corporations. Like California's Hiram Johnson and Wisconsin's La Follette, determined governors appeared in many other states, in a remarkable demonstration of the growing importance of state government: Woodrow Wilson in New Jersey, James Cox in Ohio, Charles Evans Hughes in New York—each of whom, at one time or other, received a major party's nomination for the presidency.

Most of these governors ardently affirmed progressivism's broad faith in expertise and nonpartisanship, a faith that led straight to the regulatory principle. As ideas, commissions with jurisdiction over corporations were not new in the Progressive Era. As with direct democracy, however, so pronounced was the faith of progressives in regulation that they either created or revitalized many scores of state commissions. Typically, the sequence began with widespread denunciations of corporate political influence and tax evasion. Next the progressives wrote new laws creating commissions or giving teeth to existing ones. Finally the search began for experts to serve as commissioners and staff members. The appointment of so many accountants, lawyers, and engineers not only signified the technical dimension of regulation, but also typified the progressives' faith in the competence of experts to settle controversial economic questions in "the public interest." Like the movement for city managers, commission regulation deliberately aimed to take administration "out of politics."[16] The commissioners and their assistants would be nonpartisan experts, guided by the principles of professionalism, efficiency, and the interests of the public. So went the arguments in their favor.

Later generations, increasingly consumer-conscious, would view these state commissions with much disfavor. Accused of capture by the regulated interests, the commissions would suffer from latter-day muckraking attacks, as would their federal counterparts. Yet in examining more closely this evidently negative progressive legacy, it is necessary again to ask what the commissions replaced, what they may have prevented, and what they in fact accomplished.

They unquestionably performed better than had their predecessors, the legislative committees or (usually) weak railroad commissions of the nineteenth century. At the same time, they clearly did not fulfill the promises of their more extravagant apologists. For one thing, service on commissions tended to attract neither the apolitical expert nor the aggressive, ambitious, prosecutor type so familiar to students of American politics. With an occasional exception, like Public Service Commissioners Huey Long of Louisiana or David Lilienthal of Wisconsin, such officers have been shadowy, bureaucratic, but still political figures who did their work outside the public eye. Secondly, commissions which did pursue the consumer interest against powerful vested interests often confronted immovable obstacles in the state and federal judiciary. The courts, to which regulated interests routinely appealed adverse decisions, frequently undercut or even emasculated state regulation. An element much underestimated in many judgments of the commissions, the courts jealously guarded their own powers against what they regarded as encroachment by a usurping, would-be fourth branch of government.[17] Thirdly, commissions have no more succeeded in taking controversial questions "out of politics" than has any other branch of government. They have not settled fundamental economic questions concerning the relationship of private power to the general welfare. On this last point the progressives committed a serious conceptual error, because grave issues such as those confronting regulatory commissions cannot be taken "out of politics" without also taking them out of public control. If there is no national consensus on such issues, then there is no clear "public interest," and they must therefore remain in politics.[18]

What, then, did the progressive commissions accomplish? Basically, and almost immediately, they brought relative peace to innumerable ancient and bitter controversies, not only between consumers and their corporate enemies, but especially between warring economic interests. The inauguration of progressive railroad regulation, for instance, normally ushered in a period of relative harmony between the railroads and their freight customers. The commissions did not automatically side with the underdog, but instead attempted to work out through compromise questions of rates and valuations—questions highly technical but heavily laden with symbolic significance as well. By providing legitimate and continuously available arenas and procedures for various interests to present their cases, the commissions put an institutional check on the old resort to immediate public debate—debate often uninformed and habitually couched in emotional terms of right and wrong.

The Wisconsin Railroad Commission, reorganized in 1905, is a good example. Instead of sharply cutting rates, as La Follette and other proponents had represented as the purpose of its rebirth, the commission struck a conciliatory posture between shippers and carriers. It pursued a moderate program of piecemeal rate adjustment, and in the end won more admiration from railroad men than from the reformers who had staked so much emotional capital in it. In one sense this was an ironic "betrayal of reform ideals," the more so because La Follette and others ceaselessly puffed Wisconsin as a model of enlightenment.[19]

But in the broader sense, regulation was not, and should not have been, aimed only at fighting capitalists. Most commissions were in no sense antibusiness, nor even always antitrust. Instead, they were pro-peace, and sometimes pro-entrepreneur. They attempted to maximize harmony, minimize friction, and reopen competitive opportunities to those sidetracked by a generation of growing privilege for a shrinking number of corporations.[20] To accomplish these objectives, the commissions often evaded or postponed thorny decisions. They frequently sold out the short-run consumer interest. But they contributed decisively to the winding down of a generation-long warfare, not only between the people and the interests, but between different types of capitalists. The experience of the 1880s, and especially the violent 1890s, suggests that this was a substantial achievement. Thus, insofar as a quest for harmony motivated the creation of commissions (and their enthusiastic promotion by many businessmen indicates that it did, notwithstanding more sinister interpretations of businessmen's motives), they succeeded better than recent folklore would have it. That they are clearly insufficient to the problems of our day does not mean that the progressives erred in creating them, or that they are odious legacies.

Under the progressive impulse, many states also made halting motions toward rectifying social injustice. There were important attacks on child labor and sweatshop exploitation of women. Social work, which remained largely voluntaristic, nonetheless became professionalized. These crusades too are significant legacies of state progressivism. Typically, they were not always well-conceived, seldom totally successful, and often thwarted by the judiciary. For example, many states had strengthened their laws concerning child labor, but the abuse was still widespread on the eve of World War I, causing reformers to seek federal remedies. To remove the judicial roadblock, such remedies ultimately included an attempted constitutional amendment.[21]

The most numerous state laws aimed at social justice, and the ones best illustrating the limitations of progressivism, had to do with industrial accidents. These were the workmen's compensation laws, arising out of the almost unbelievable human toll exacted by industrialism. In the South Chicago plant of United States Steel, for example, forty-six men were killed in the single year 1906. This ghastly byproduct of the constant drive for faster machine production and greater productivity frequently became the target of muckrakers' attacks. So shameful was the situation that former President Theodore Roosevelt, who had given the journalists their name in a spirit of contempt, became a muckraker himself on the subject of industrial maimings. In 1913 the former Rough Rider published in *Collier's* the grisly story of a woman's hand being crushed in the cogwheels of a machine in a hardware factory. Roosevelt's article, "Sarah Knisley's Arm," noted the dreadful inadequacy of common-law remedies in an age of industrialization.[22]

Enactment of compensation laws began in Maryland in 1902, and became epidemic just after 1910. By 1920, more than forty states had written new legislation, in a remarkable demonstration of unanimity. The nature of these laws, the circumstances of their enactment, and their operation afterward make them an ideal case study in progressive reform, as well as a textbook-like instance of the evolution of law under changing social conditions.[23]

"The public interest," so fuzzily abstract in most matters, had special clarity here. The horror of industrial accidents was evident to all, from the workers themselves to the middle-class readers of muckraking periodicals. Corporate managers devoted to efficiency disliked the cumbersome system of settlement through the common law. Most important of all, the absence of a predictable, continuously functioning system of compensation exposed employers to the deep uncertainties of tort litigation. Although corporations usually escaped with treasuries intact, they remained at the mercy of human caprice. There was always the chance that a jury, horrified by an unusually grisly maiming, might set damages so high as to reverse a company's profit and loss statement. Foreseeing these possibilities, many corporations had long since purchased liability insurance. The problem here was an astonishing four-fold disparity between the premiums corporations paid in and the benefits insurance companies paid out to injured employees or their survivors.[24] In short, the existing situation satisfied nobody, creating a pregnant instance for reform in "the public interest."

The new system, a microcosm of the progressive legacy, gained a little for industrial workers, a lot for their employers, and a sufficient (though feeble) reply to the demands of more radical reformers like the socialists. For the employers, workmen's compensation regularized the benefit system, eliminated the courts from most proceedings, and exacted a relatively small, predictable fee. New commissions materialized to administer the laws. For the workers, compensation clearly ameliorated their previous plight but fell far short of a satisfactory solution. The schedules of benefits were well below any compassionate estimate of fairness. Other flaws inhered in the new system as well, flaws rooted in the familiar fear of judicial emasculation and in the traditional American aversion to state-owned insurance enterprises. As a result, the system is very far from satisfactory, even in our own day.[25]

Attenuated as compensation reform was, it represented a limit beyond which legislatures balked in creating welfare programs to meet squarely the problems of industrialization. To the progressive generation, such schemes as unemployment insurance, social security, aid to dependent children, and a host of others seemed too radical or too expensive or not sufficiently in the public interest for ready enactment. In refusing to move beyond workmen's compensation, refusing to listen to the more perceptive progressives, lawmakers of the era defined their sharply limited grasp of the needs of an urban, industrial society. The next important steps would not be taken until the New Deal.

From the standpoint of our own time, this perverse value system of the progressive generation stands out most vividly in their treatment of the race question. In this, the most difficult problem in American history, the progressive contribution was mostly negative and the progressive legacy mostly ominous. Whatever it may have achieved elsewhere, progressive reform exhibited what several historians have called a "blind spot" toward the problems of race.[26]

Evidence of the "blind spot" abounds. The last black congressman departed Washington in 1901, and another did not appear until the late 1920s. Disfranchisement of blacks, begun systematically by Mississippi in 1890, swept the other southern states during the next two decades, taking a multitude of ingenious forms: the poll tax; the white primary of the Democratic party; the "understanding," "grandfather," and "good character" clauses in state constitutions. In Louisiana, to take one statistically remarkable example, such policies reduced the state's 130,334 registered black voters of 1896 to 1,342 by 1904.[27] Jim Crow laws multiplied rapidly. Begun tentatively in the 1880s and accepted by the Supreme Court in 1896, legal segregation moved inexorably forward during the Progressive Era in state after state. It applied not only to street and railway cars, but to hotels, restaurants, schools, and urban residential sections. In isolated fits of purism, a state or city would require segregated telephone booths, courtroom Bibles, or prostitutes.[28]

As the South divided itself into separate and unequal cubicles, the North either applauded or acquiesced. From the national government blacks received the occasional gesture of a black man's appointment to some post in the minor bureaucracy. Once Booker T. Washington dined at the White House, but this elicited such noise from white supremacists that presidents began to avoid any sort of contact with Negroes at all, except to court their diminishing votes at election time. By the time Woodrow Wilson entered the White House, with his entourage of southern cabinet members, the white people of the United States had reached a consensus about their black countrymen. When several of Wilson's subordinates instituted segregation in their departments, the few loud protests which arose soon drowned in a sea of general silence.[29] Surely, here was an anomaly, a generation of whites ostensibly devoted to reform, but actually making things worse for American blacks. A riddle? Surely. A blind spot? Only partly.

A clue to the riddle appears in the "Brownsville affair," perhaps the most shameful incident involving blacks and the federal government during the progressive years.[30] In 1906, three companies of black United States Army soldiers took up their new duty station at Fort Brown, Texas, near the mouth of the Rio Grande. Shortly afterward, a group of unidentified men shot up the town in a ten-minute rampage, leaving a bartender dead and a policeman wounded. A slipshod army investigation accepted the townspeople's unproved allegation that the black soldiers had perpetrated the "raid." Following the recommendation of the officer in charge of the investigation, President Theodore Roosevelt ordered all 167 of the troops discharged without honor. The president reasoned that some of the troops were certainly involved, and since they themselves declined to identify the guilty few, then all must suffer.

A minor political turmoil ensued, and the affair was later the subject of merry satire at the annual Gridiron Dinner in Washington. In an exchange with Senator Joseph Benson Foraker of Ohio, the leading defender of the black soldiers, President Roosevelt was heard to say, "There may have been but two companies of that regiment engaged in that unwholesome business [he had discharged all three companies], but 'all coons look alike to me.' "[31]

Roosevelt did not invent the sentence. Planners of the Gridiron Dinner had inserted it into the evening's program, as part of a dialect verse to be spoken by Foraker. The planners themselves may have borrowed it from a popular song of the same title. There were many such songs abroad in white America at the time. Still, that the president of the United States would utter such words in public is deeply suggestive of white attitudes.

In truth, all blacks did look alike to Theodore Roosevelt.[32] Like most whites of his generation, he customarily thought not of black individuals or groups, but abstractly of "the Negro." Contemporary titles suggest the abstraction's characteristics: *"The Negro a Beast,"* "The [small] Negro Brain," *The American Negro as a Dependent, Defective, and Delinquent.*[33] Many blacks, schooled in white thought and anxious to accommodate, construed themselves as "the Negro." The letters of Booker T. Washington contain frequent references to "the Negro," and more militant blacks also used the term frequently. But blacks registered their objection to the principle involved whenever they called attention to the custom whereby white Americans blamed "the Negro" for any crime committed by a black.[34] The apex of stereotyping arrived in 1915, with D. W. Griffith's cinematic masterpiece "The Birth of a Nation," which depicted the happy-go-lucky, childlike, but very corruptible plantation Negro of white American folklore.

The timing could hardly have been worse. However rural and southern most blacks had been before the twentieth century, they were rapidly becoming urban and northern as well. The Great Migration out of the South had already begun. The Garvey movement and the Harlem Renaissance were soon to come. Thus, "the Negro," an abstraction even in slavery times, bore rapidly diminishing resemblance to reality. Yet few seemed able to pierce the streotype. Reformers were generally no more racist than others of the period, but they were in the forefront of those worried about the profound heterogeneity of the American people after the entry of the immigrants. Hence the Americanization movement, an intensive program to acculturate the immigrants, to make them more like the "old American stock," to restore the vanished homogeneity of the people of the United States. Progressives were conspicuous participants in this effort.[35]

Sometimes it was hard to conceive of Italian Catholics or Polish Jews becoming fully Americanized. As for "the Negro," the imagination —progressive or not—found it impossible to make the leap. In the South, the leading progressives were often the leading disfranchisers. And in the North, a man like Charles Francis Adams, descendant of presidents and erstwhile friend to blacks, could reflect in 1906 on the lessons of his recent trip to Africa. "Equality results not from law, but exists because things are in essentials like; and a political system which works admirably when applied to homogeneous equals results only in chaos when generalized into a nostrum to be administered universally."[36]

Southern progressives were ready to act on such conclusions. To them, reform and disfranchisement were two sides of the same coin. They viewed segregation not as a denial of human rights, but as a necessary precondition of the economic and social reform which the South so badly needed. As long as blacks participated in politics, and with their votes tempted competing white factions, so long would the white race remain divided against itself, impotent to secure essential change. Thus arose the otherwise baffling connection between progressivism and racism in the South. The spokesmen for the one were the spokesmen for the other: Tom Watson, James Kimble Vardaman, Benjamin Tillman, Josephus Daniels.[37] Southerners spoke confidently of disfranchisement as "electoral reform," with little evident sense of paradox. For southern progressivism, therefore, segregation was not properly a "blind spot" at all. It was a choice made with open eyes—a conscious, deliberate, even bold decision that at the time seemed consummately logical.[38] Northerners, quiescent on the subject of civil rights since the end of Reconstruction and myopic with abstracted visions of "the Negro," could only assent. For these reasons, the progressives, who typically were no more and no less racist than other whites (including Europeans, who at the time were eagerly shouldering the white man's burden), bequeathed to subsequent generations a race problem not merely as bad as the one they themselves inherited, but one even worse; not merely a dream deferred, but a time bomb.

Theodore Roosevelt's unilateral dismissal of the 167 black soldiers was symptomatic of another progressive tendency. This was the movement toward a strong executive. Partly a function of the centralizing forces of the age, partly of the activist personalities of Roosevelt and Woodrow Wilson, the emergence of the White House as the focus of national life was one of progressivism's major legacies. Roosevelt—so young, so exuberant, so fascinating an executive—created the same sort of image later projected by Franklin D. Roosevelt and John F. Kennedy, and did it without their access to electronic media. Sometimes the image of dynamism obscured dangerous departures from the sober responsibility of the McKinley era. In particular, the adventurous foreign policy thrusts of both Roosevelt and Wilson (the corollary to the Monroe Doctrine, the taking of Panama, the intervention in Mexico) presaged some unfortunate tendencies. Here the image of an active executive disguised dangerous trends.

But it helped enormously in maximizing the public impact of symbolic presidential actions, such as Roosevelt's unprecedented intervention on behalf of the miners in the anthracite coal strike of 1902. It also helped to galvanize the American people behind specific crusades, such as the remarkable progressive conservation movement.[39] When Roosevelt called his conference on conservation in 1908, he embraced the modern imperative of blending scientific substance with promotional hoopla. He left few dramatic possibilities unpublicized. All state governors received invitations to the conference. Seventy national organizations sent representatives. And, as surrogates for the public, Roosevelt named five additional delegates, men of the stature of Andrew Carnegie and William Jennings Bryan.

This ostentation aimed not only at awakening public interest but at wresting control of resources policy from a jealous Congress lately grown uneasy over the initiatives of Roosevelt and Chief Forester Gifford Pinchot. The result was a running feud between the executive and the legislature and an almost incomprehensible public debate over conservation, a debate evidently permanent. But throughout the struggle the substance of progressive conservationism remained its scientific dimension. This legacy, though often ignored and sometimes betrayed, persisted in many different forms. It persisted in the Forest Service's practice of allowing commercial lumbering on public lands, so long as annual cutting did not exceed annual growth (the "sustained yield" philosophy); and in other policies that emphasize management for efficient use rather than for esthetic preservation.

The gospel of efficiency reached one of its highest refinements in the doctrine of multiple-purpose water projects. An idea thoroughly worked out during the progressive years, it did not receive its major practical application until the 1930s and Franklin D. Roosevelt's New Deal. One of the New Deal's showcase agencies, the Tennessee Valley Authority, took as its bible the progressive principle that water is a resource of many uses, and a given development should exploit every such use. For the Tennessee River, this meant not only that shining new dams should be built to contain floods but that a series of inland lakes should materialize behind the dams, providing facilities for public recreation and a 650-mile waterway for commercial barge traffic. The installation of hydroelectric generators within the dams completed the circle of efficiency, by providing electricity to residents and industries of the Tennessee Valley. This electric power would sell at very low prices but still yield revenues sufficient to pay for a major part of the entire project. The central point of the multiple-purpose idea often disappeared behind the public uproar over the government's entry into the power business, but the TVA's remarkable success confirmed the wisdom of a major progressive legacy.

The Tennessee Valley Authority was preeminently a creature of the president, not of Congress. Its close identification with Franklin D. Roosevelt again pointed up the tendency of many progressive ideas to enhance executive power and extend executive discretion. The same point emerged with the numerous federal boards and commissions which seemed to blossom during the administrations of Theodore Roosevelt and Woodrow Wilson. Roosevelt's appointments to the Inland Waterways Commission, for example, strengthened his influence over conservation policy. And the birth of such extremely important new agencies as the Federal Reserve Board and the Federal Trade Commission signified not only the steady growth of presidential appointment powers but also the extending reach of the government itself.

The career of the Federal Trade Commission illuminates especially well the evolving progressive legacy.[40] Created in 1914 with the hope that it represented, at long last, a solution to the trust problem, the commission had an erratic and troubled history in its first half-century. By the late 1960s, the modern muckraker Ralph Nader was ready with a stinging verdict: "The 'little old lady on Pennsylvania Avenue' was a self-parody of bureaucracy, fat with cronyism, torpid through an inbreeding unusual even for Washington, manipulated by the agents of commercial predators, impervious to governmental and citizen monitoring."[41] Considering its source, such a denunciation had a double irony. Not only was Nader a muckraker squarely in the progressive mold; he was in addition a public-interest lawyer, a role with no clearer precedent than the career of Louis D. Brandeis, the progressive "People's Lawyer," who himself played a significant part in the birth of the Federal Trade Commission.[42]

One reason for the commission's departure from Brandeis' hopes lay in the legislation creating it. The FTC Act states: "Unfair methods of competition in commerce are hereby declared unlawful."[43] The vagueness of this key passage was deliberate, representing not buck-passing but candid acknowledgment that Congress itself was too busy, too inexpert, too unwieldy to decide precisely what business practices were unfair. The authors of the act exhibited a modern conception of the regulation of business as a continuous process, not an *ad hoc* emergency action. The commission would provide the expert precision in individual cases. This was the point not only of the FTC, but of the commission idea itself.

In its first years, from 1914 into the early 1920s, the Federal Trade Commission occasionally fulfilled the expectations of the progressives. It pursued serious tasks with some energy and under heavy handicaps. The first of these handicaps, World War I, shifted economic priorities from fair competition to massive production, thereby shifting the FTC's role from overseer of business to collector of production data. Once the war ended, the commission attempted to return to its original function by concentrating on its first really major case, an investigation of the meat-packing industry. The packers had been a target of progressives for many years, not only because of the filth recorded by Upton Sinclair, but also because of their status as a despised trust.

What happened to the FTC when it challenged the packers well illustrated the difficulties of "independent" regulation. After much research, the Federal Trade Commission found that the five largest meat packers (Swift, Armour, Morris, Wilson, and Cudahy) were all engaging in unlawful combinations and unfair trade practices. As a remedy the commission suggested changes in the industry's structure, including public ownership of certain parts of it. The response was immediate and semi-hysterical. Legislators friendly to the packers denounced the commission for promoting socialism, and called for a new investigation, this time of the Federal Trade Commission itself. The furor ended with Congress neatly withdrawing most of the meat-packing industry from the FTC's jurisdiction and placing it under the more cordial Department of Agriculture, where it still remains.

Simultaneously, the commission was absorbing heavy blows from the federal judiciary. In much the same fashion as with state commissions, the courts countered progressives' attempts at federal regulation with sharp assertions of judicial supremacy. In 1920, the Supreme Court ruled (over the dissent of people's lawyer Brandeis, now an associate justice) that "The words 'unfair methods of competition' are not defined by the [FTC] statute and their exact meaning is in dispute. It is for the courts, not the Commission, ultimately to determine as matter of law what they include."[44] Thus the deliberate and essential latitude of the statute's language became its Achilles heel, and until the Court reversed its ruling in 1934, the commission could do little more than function as a fact-finding agency.

Such a role coincided with the wishes of new members appointed by Presidents Harding and Coolidge. In particular, the arrival of Commissioner William E. Humphrey in 1925 completed the subversion of the intent of 1914. Personally detested by many progressives, Humphrey was a former congressman and lumber lobbyist who believed and energetically asserted that the commission's job was to help businessmen do what they wanted to do. For the old friends of the commission, Humphrey represented the last straw. The aged progressive Robert M. La Follette lamented the irony of it all, not long before his death: "The last of the Commissions at Washington to be taken over by the forces it was intended to regulate, the Federal Trade Commission has been packed with its worst enemies, its rules have been perverted, the law under which it was created has been emasculated, and its usefulness has been destroyed." Soon progressives were calling for the commission's abolition.[45]

It would be wrong, however, to judge the progressive legacy by the current status of the Federal Trade Commission, or any other commission. That status changes repeatedly, in response to shifting appointments and shifting public attitudes toward business practices. The record is full of inconsistency. The New Deal, for example, gave the Federal Trade Commission a new lease on life, and even in the Humphrey period the agency pursued a painstaking investigation of utility corporations, which led directly to the Public Utility Holding Company Act of 1935. The question is not only whether regulatory commissions have done their work well, or whether they should be abolished, but precisely what happened to limit their effectiveness. The answer lies partly with the judiciary, but in the broad sense with the American people, who have never made up their minds whether they really wished to end oligopoly and "unfair methods of competition."

The progressives share this responsibility only because they erred in their conception of "the public interest," and in both meanings of that elusive term. First, they did have an exaggerated sense of the attention span of the public, imagining that their children would remain as interested in public affairs as they themselves were. In this they were mistaken. Secondly, "the public interest" in its usual sense is an abstraction, even more in their era than in ours. In our own period, plagued with environmental pollution and preoccupied with mass consumption of standardized products, the public interest has a clearer, more immediate meaning than it had during the progressive years. Yet it is still essentially abstract, an inadequate guide for concrete decisions by regulatory agencies. Contending parties at typical commission hearings (even some rate hearings) bear little resemblance to the "public." Instead, they are highly paid advocates for sharply focused private interests, battling each other over some commercial advantage. More often than not, the commissions' decisions favor one private interest over the other, not the public interest over both. Many times the public interest seems insufficiently clear, or even irrelevant. Seldom is a given problem as one-dimensional as that which produced the workmen's compensation laws, a rare situation in which virtually all parties agreed on a specific response toward a self-evident public interest.

It would be a serious mistake to assert that regulation in the progressive pattern has entirely failed. That it has even largely failed is debatable, without a careful definition of *failure*. But insofar as it has failed, the fault lies less with the idea itself than with the American context in which the idea materialized—a context that pays high tribute to individualism, private property, and personal success. And the alternatives to commission regulation invariably seem less appealing to the American electorate than the commissions are now or ever were. Even with decades of experience the progressives did not have, policy-makers have failed to move conclusively beyond their solutions to the problems of fair competition, oligopoly, and corporate power. In time, some of the progressives' key failures have become our failures as well.

This is one reason why the progressive legacy seems so distinctly ambiguous. In their limited understanding of the transcendence of the twentieth century, the progressives seem rudimentary, naive versions of ourselves, addressing problems clearly modern but offering solutions clearly inadequate. With one foot stuck firmly in the nineteenth century, the other striding overconfidently into the twentieth, they were certain to react in a manner that would strike us as ambiguous. Habituated to outmoded patterns of thought, they nonetheless sensed that the impersonal, cosmopolitan, ultimately post-industrial twentieth century was, without question, a new type of world.

They were the first to have this essential insight. To their credit, they accepted the responsibility it implied and acted on it: hence their meticulous rearrangement of the procedures, forms, and institutions of American life. Yet this very procedural emphasis tended to preclude a full comprehension of the surpassing modernity of the new century: hence they usually stopped just short of the real substance of social justice. If, on occasion, the glimmer of understanding did grow into perception bright to the point of pain, then the substance could be stereotyped, abstracted, made impervious to rigorous analysis, and thus evaded, as with "the trusts," "the Negro," and "the public interest." One way or other, the most severe problems could be taken "out of politics," entrusted to an elite of professional experts. But in a democratic society, this too was evasion, since by definition it meant removal from popular control.

Indeed professionalism itself—a central value of progressive thought —could as easily inhibit reform as promote it. For the organized bar, and its lawyers who drafted progressive legislation and served on regulatory commissions, the dominance of procedure over substance was not merely an occupational hazard but a source of potential paralysis, of inability to strike at a whole range of problems that simply would not yield to institutional tinkering, as experience over time showed. For muckraking journalists, obedience to the canons of their profession could lead, after reform ceased to be news and became old hat, to an easy support of American intervention in World War I, and from there to a partial defense and celebration of the business culture of the 1920s. Like other journalists, they followed popular taste more than they led it. Like the lawyers, they could not transcend the limitations of a narrow professional code.

In constructing a broader perspective for progressivism, one might indulge in the ahistorical and risky enterprise of "attempting to name the generation that accomplished more."[46] Only two come readily to mind: the Founding Fathers, who organized the United States; and the New Dealers, who held it together through a perilous time, partly by relying on reforms developed by the progressives. The progressives themselves come in third, an impressive showing.

Rankings and reputations, however, are less central to the study of history than are processes. The process of reform, for the progressives or any other generation so oriented, nearly always exhibits a marked disparity between the energy expended and the permanent results achieved. In securing their limited list of reforms, the progressives worked very hard—not so much to leave a legacy, of course, as to fulfill their own lives. That so many of them succeeded was progressivism's chief legacy for them, and one of its many meanings for the future. In the larger sense, progressivism "failed," insofar as it was no final solution to anything. But that is merely a historical truism, applicable to all times and all places. Between doing nothing and solving nothing lies the long, finely graded scale of the American experience. It is along this scale that one might measure the process of progressivism and understand its legacy.[47]

CONTRIBUTORS

JOHN J. BROESAMLE is associate professor of History at California State University, Northridge, and the author of *William Gibbs McAdoo: A Passion for Change, 1863–1917* (Port Washington, N.Y.: Kennikat Press, 1973).

STANLEY P. CAINE is associate professor of History at DePauw University. He has written *The Myth of a Progressive Reform: Railroad Regulation in Wisconsin, 1903–1910* (Madison, Wisc.: State Historical Society of Wisconsin, 1970).

WILTON B. FOWLER is associate professor of History at the University of Washington. He is the author of *British-American Relations, 1917–1918: The Role of Sir William Wiseman* (Princeton, N.J.: Princeton University Press, 1969).

LEWIS L. GOULD is associate professor of History at the University of Texas at Austin. He has written *Wyoming: A Political History, 1868–1896* (New Haven, Conn.: Yale University Press, 1968), and *Progressives and Prohibitionists: Texas Democrats in the Wilson Era* (Austin, Tex.: University of Texas Press, 1973).

MELVIN G. HOLLI is associate professor of History and director of the Urban Historical Collection at the University of Illinois at Chicago Circle. He is the author of *Reform in Detroit: Hazen S. Pingree and Urban Politics* (New York: Oxford University Press, 1969).

THOMAS K. McCRAW is assistant professor of History at the University of Texas at Austin. He has written *Morgan vs. Lilienthal: The Feud Within the TVA* (Chicago: Loyola University Press, 1970), and *TVA and the Power Fight, 1933–1939* (Philadelphia, Pa.: Lippincott, 1971).

R. LAURENCE MOORE is assistant professor of History at Cornell University. He is the author of *European Socialists and the American Promised Land* (New York: Oxford University Press, 1970).

JAMES PENICK, JR., is professor of History at Loyola University of Chicago and is the author of *Progressive Politics and Conservation: The Ballinger-Pinchot Affair* (Chicago: University of Chicago Press, 1968).

NOTES TO THE CHAPTERS

1. The Origins of Progressivism

1. Henry George, *Progress and Poverty* (New York: Robert Schalkenback Foundation, 1949), p. 7. See Daniel Aaron, *Men of Good Hope* (New York: Oxford University Press, 1960), Chapter 3, for a perceptive analysis of George's life and work. The definitive biography of George is Charles A. Barker, *Henry George* (New York: Oxford University Press, 1955). See also David P. Thelen, "Progressivism as a Radical Movement," in Howard Quint, Milton Cantor, and Dean Albertson, eds. *Main Problems in American History* (Homewood, Ill.: Dorsey, 1972), II, 150–53.

2. See Barker, *Henry George,* pp. 265–304, for an analysis of the major ideas in *Progress and Poverty.* Quotations on pp. 289–90, 297.

3. As quoted in Eric Goldman, *Rendezvous with Destiny* (New York: Vintage, 1952), p. 28. See also Hamlin Garland, "The Single Tax in Actual Application," *The Arena* 10(June 1894):52–58.

4. Henry F. May, *Protestant Churches and Industrial America* (New York: Harper, 1949), p. 154; Barker, *Henry George,* pp. 270–71.

5. Henry Ward Beecher, *Plymouth Pulpit* (New York: Fords, Howard and Hulbert, 1874–75), II, 209, as quoted in Sidney Mead, *The Lively Experiment* (New York: Harper, 1963), p. 163.

6. Charles Sheldon, *In His Steps* (Chicago: Advance, 1897). See also May, *Protestant Churches,* 210.

7. Jane Addams, *Twenty Years at Hull House* (New York: Signet, 1961), pp. 97, 98. See Robert H. Bremner, *From the Depths* (New York: New York University Press, 1956), pp. 27–28: Allen F. Davis, *Spearheads of Reform* (New York: Oxford University Press, 1967), pp. 27–29, 35–36, 12; and Aaron I. Abell, *The Urban Impact on American Protestantism, 1865–1900* (Cambridge, Mass.: Harvard University Press, 1943).

8. May, *Protestant Churches,* pp. 174–75; Davis, *Spearheads for Reform,* pp. 57, 123–25.

9. Walter Rauschenbusch, in Baptist Congress for the Discussion of Current Questions, *Proceedings,* 1893, p. 11, as quoted in May, *Protestant Churches,* p. 192.

10. May, *Protestant Churches,* pp. 226–29; Willard H. Smith, "William Jennings Bryan and the Social Gospel," *Journal of American History* 53(June 1966):41–60.

11. May, *Protestant Churches,* pp. 138–40; Benjamin G. Rader, "Richard T. Ely: Lay Spokesman for the Social Gospel," *Journal of American History* 53 (June 1966):61–74.

12. Richard T. Ely, *Studies in the Evolution of an Industrial Society* (New York: Macmillan, 1903), p. 427.

13. May, *Protestant Churches,* p. 195.

14. Davis, *Spearheads for Reform,* p. 38; Frederick C. Howe, *The Confessions of a Reformer* (New York: Scribner's, 1925), p. 1.

15. See Samuel Haber, *Efficiency and Uplift: Scientific Management in the Progressive Era, 1890–1920* (Chicago: University of Chicago Press, 1964), for an analysis of the efficiency theme in progressive thought.

16. Arthur Mann, "British Social Thought and American Reformers of the Progressive Era," *Mississippi Valley Historical Review* 42(March 1956):672–92; May, *Protestant Churches,* p. 186; Davis, *Spearheads for Reform,* p. 8.

17. See John D. Hicks, *The Populist Revolt* (Lincoln: University of Nebraska Press, 1961), pp. 439–44, for platform. In addition to Hicks, see H. Wayne Morgan, "Populism and the Decline of Agriculture," in H. Wayne Morgan, ed., *The Gilded Age* (Syracuse: Syracuse University Press, 1970).

18. See Samuel P. Hays, *The Response to Industrialism* (Chicago: University of Chicago Press, 1957), pp. 44–45; and Robert H. Wiebe, *The Search for Order* (New York: Hill and Wang, 1967), pp. 84–90.

19. Haber, *Efficiency and Uplift,* p. 99. John G. Sproat, *"The Best Men"* (New York: Oxford University Press, 1968), is the most comprehensive treatment of the Mugwumps. See also Geoffrey Blodgett, "Reform Thought and the Genteel Tradition," in H. Wayne Morgan, ed., *The Gilded Age* (Syracuse: Syracuse University Press, 1970).

20. Haber, *Efficiency and Uplift,* pp. 99–103. See also Ari Hoogenboom, *Outlawing the Spoils* (Urbana, Ill.: University of Illinois Press, 1961); and Ari Hoogenboom, "Civil Service Reform and Public Morality," in H. Wayne Morgan, ed., *The Gilded Age* (Syracuse: Syracuse University Press, 1970).

21. David P. Thelen, *The New Citizenship* (Columbia, Mo.: University of Missouri Press, 1972), p. 45.

22. May, *Protestant Churches,* p. 128. For a description of the process of change from Mugwumpery to progressivism in Wisconsin see Thelen, *The New Citizenship,* Chapter 6 and 10.

23. Charles Eliot Norton, "Some Aspects of Civilization in America," *The Forum* 20(February 1896):644; E. L. Godkin, "Who Will Pay the Bills of Socialism," *The Forum* 17(June 1894):400.

24. Samuel Resneck, "Unemployment, Unrest, and Relief in the United States During the Depression of 1893–97," *Journal of Political Economy* 31(August 1953):328–29, 333–35.

25. See Walter LaFeber, *The New Empire* (Ithaca, N.Y.: Cornell University Press, 1963), especially Chapters IV and V; and David F. Healy, *US Expansionism* (Madison, Wisc.: University of Wisconsin Press, 1970).

26. Theodore Roosevelt to Cecil Spring Rice, August 5, 1896, in Elting E. Morison, ed., *The Letters of Theodore Roosevelt* (Cambridge, Mass.: Harvard University Press, 1951), I, 556; Wiebe, *The Search for Order,* p. 96; John Braeman, *Albert J. Beveridge* (Chicago: University of Chicago Press, 1971), p. 21. See also John Braeman, "Seven Progressives," *Business History Review* 35 (Winter 1961):581–92.

27. Ray Stannard Baker, *American Chronicle: The Autobiography of Ray Stannard Baker* (New York: Scribner's, 1945), pp. 18–19; Roy Lubove, *The Progressives and the Slums: Tenement House Reform in New York City, 1890–1917* (Pittsburgh: University of Pittsburgh Press, 1962), p. 127; and Addams, *Hull House,* p. 123.

28. Lubove, *Progressives and Slums,* p. 40.

29. Resneck, "Depression of 1893," *Journal of Political Economy* 334. See Douglas W. Steeples, "The Panic of 1893: Contemporary Reflections and Reactions," *Mid-America* 47(July 1965):155–75, for a summary of popular reactions to the depression of the 1890s. Also G. Emil Richter, "Monopolism and Militarism in the City of Churches—A Review of the Brooklyn Street Railway Strike," *The Arena* 13(July 1895):98–117; Albion Small, "Private Business is a Public Trust," *Public Opinion* 19(December 26, 1895): 848–49; Lester F. Ward, "Plutocracy and Paternalism," *The Forum* 20(November 1895):300–10; "Trusts and Monopolies the Prime Evil," *Public Opinion* 18(March 7, 1895):223; Henry Frank, "The Crusade of the Unemployed," *The Arena* 10(July 1894): 239–44; and James G. Clark, "The Coming Industrial Order," *The Arena* 11(January 1895):238–49.

30. Healy, *US Expansionism,* p. 232.

31. The *Autobiography of Lincoln Steffens* (New York: Harcourt, Brace, 1931), p. 193. See Harold S. Wilson, *McClure's Magazine and the Muckrakers* (Princeton, N. J.: Princeton University Press, 1970), especially chapters VI and VII for a description of the development of a muckraking journal.

32. Thelen, *The New Citizenship,* p. 67; Tom L. Johnson, *My Story* (New York: Huebsch, 1913), pp. 82–84; Lubove, *Progressives and Slums,* pp. 122–24; and Davis, *Spearheads for Reform,* p. 69.

33. Lubove, *Progressives and Slums,* pp. 88, 114, 140–41.

34. Ibid., p. 217; Frank Parson, "Chicago's Message to Uncle Sam," *The Arena* 10(September 1894):494–96; Baker, *American Chronicle,* pp. 1–2.

35. Lubove, *Progressives and Slums,* pp. 140–42; Bremner, *From the Depths,* p. 209.

36. Lubove, *Progressives and Slums,* pp. 117–18, 140.

37. Walter T. Trattner, *Crusade for the Children* (Chicago: Quadrangle, 1970), p. 35.

38. Ibid., pp. 34–35.

39. Lubove, *Progressives and Slums,* pp. 206, 208.

40. Bremner, *From the Depths,* p. 124. See also Roy Lubove, *The Professional Altruist* (Cambridge, Mass.: Harvard University Press, 1965).

41. Davis, *Spearheads for Reform,* pp. 148–155, 163–65, 173–74, 176, 182–85. Quotation on p. 173.

42. See Melvin G. Holli, *Reform in Detroit* (New York: Oxford University Press, 1969).

43. Baker, *American Chronicle,* p. 29.

44. Sidney I. Roberts, "Portrait of a Robber Baron: Charles T. Yerkes, *Business History Review* 35(Autumn 1961):344–53.

45. Ibid., pp. 354–71; and Joel A. Tarr, "William Kent to Lincoln Steffens: Origins of Progressive Reform in Chicago," *Mid-America* 47(January 1965): 48–57.

46. See Thelen, *The New Citizenship,* especially pp. 156–289.

47. Richard M. Abrams, *Conservatism in the Progressive Era* (Cambridge, Mass.: Harvard University Press, 1964), pp. 62–65.

48. Wiebe, *The Search for Order,* pp. 105–106; May, *Protestant Churches,* p. 201; Addams, *Hull House,* p. 133; and Baker, *American Chronicle,* p. 183.

49. For conference resolutions, see Thelen, "Progressivism as a Radical Movement," in *Main Problems in American History*, pp. 159–61.

50. See Thelen, *The New Citizenship*, pp. 156–57, 220–21, 290–308. La Follette's *Autobiography* (Madison, Wisc.: La Follette, 1913), though marred by factual errors and biased interpretations, is one of the best expressions of the progressive frame of mind.

51. Herbert Croly, *The Promise of American Life* (New York: Macmillan, 1909), p. 168.

52. See Robert H. Wiebe, *Businessmen and Reform* (Cambridge, Mass.: Harvard University Press, 1962), especially Chapter II. Also Wiebe, *The Search for Order*, Chapter 5; James Weinstein, *The Corporate Ideal in the Liberal State* (Boston: Beacon Press, 1908), pp. 8 ff; Samuel P. Hays, "The Social Analysis of American Political History, 1880–1920," *Political Science Quarterly* 80(September 1965):373–94; and Louis Galambos, "The Emerging Organizational Synthesis in Modern American History," *Business History Review* 44(Autumn 1970): 279–90.

53. B. O. Flower, "Union for Practical Progress," *The Arena* 8(June 1893): 78–91.

54. Wiebe, *Businessmen and Reform*, p. 16. See also Hays, *The Response to Industrialism*, pp. 72–73.

55. Hays, "The Social Analysis," *Political Science Quarterly* 80(September 1965):382–83; Wiebe, *Businessmen and Reform*, pp. 42–67; Gabriel Kolko, *The Triumph of Conservatism* (New York: Macmillan, 1963); and Gabriel Kolko, *Railroads and Regulation* (Princeton: N.J.: Princeton University Press, 1965), pp. 84–230. For an example at the state level, see Stanley P. Caine, *The Myth of a Progressive Reform* (Madison, Wisc.: The State Historical Society of Wisconsin Press, 1970), pp. 137–203.

56. Samuel P. Hays, "The Politics of Reform in Municipal Government in the Progressive Era," *Pacific Northwest Quarterly* 60(October 1964):157–69. Haber, *Efficiency and Uplift*.

2. Directions of Thought in Progressive America

1. Henry Adams, *The Education of Henry Adams* (Washington: privately printed, 1907); Henry Adams, *The Degradation of the Democratic Dogma* (New York: Macmillan, 1920).

2. William James, *Pragmatism, A New Name for Some Old Ways of Thinking* (New York: Longmans, Green, 1907).

3. William Allen White, *The Autobiography of William Allen White* (New York: Macmillan, 1946), pp. 107–108, 280–83, 429.

4. William James, "The Will to Believe," *New World* 5(June 1896), 327–47.

5. Jane Addams, *Twenty Years at Hull House* (New York: Macmillan, 1910), p. 452. For a general account of the settlement house movement, see Allen F. Davis, *Spearheads for Reform: The Social Settlements and the Progressive Movement, 1890–1914* (New York: Oxford University Press, 1967).

6. Herbert Croly, *The Promise of American Life* (Cambridge, Mass.: Harvard University Press, 1965; first printed in 1909), p. 400.

7. For background on tenement and school reform in this period consult Roy Lubove, *The Progressives and the Slums: Tenement House Reform in New York City, 1890–1917* (Pittsburgh, Pa.: University of Pittsburgh Press, 1962), and Lawrence A. Cremin, *The Transformation of the School, Progressivism in American Education, 1876–1957* (New York: Knopf, 1961).

8. Thomas Mott Osborne to Mrs. L. F. Deland, April 11, 1900, quoted in Jack M. Holl, *Juvenile Reform in the Progressive Era: William R. George and the Junior Republic Movement* (Ithaca, N.Y.: Cornell University Press, 1971), p. 29.

9. John Dewey, *The Influence of Darwin on Philosophy and Other Essays in Contemporary Thought* (New York: Holt, 1910).

10. James Timberlake, *Prohibition and the Progressive Movement, 1900–1920* (Cambridge, Mass.: Harvard University Press, 1963); Mark Haller, *Eugenics: Hereditarian Attitudes in American Thought* (New Brunswick, N.J.: Rutgers University Press, 1963); Donald K. Pickens, *Eugenics and the Progressives* (Nashville, Tenn.: Vanderbilt University Press, 1968).

11. Lincoln Steffens, *The Shame of the Cities* (New York: McClure, Phillips, 1904), pp. 3–26; Lincoln Steffens, *The Autobiography of Lincoln Steffens* (New York: Harcourt, Brace, 1931), esp. Part 3.

12. Arthur Bentley, *The Process of Government* (Cambridge, Mass.: Harvard University Press, 1967; first printed in 1908), pp. 27, 30, 90.

13. Charles Cooley, *Human Nature and the Social Order* (New York: Scribner's, 1902), pp. 257–58.

14. Charles Beard, *An Economic Interpretation of the Constitution of the United States* (New York: Macmillan, 1913); Charles Beard, "Written History as an Act of Faith," *American Historical Review* 39(1934): 219–27.

15. Walter Lippmann, *A Preface to Politics* (New York: Kennerley, 1913), p. 16.

16. Ibid., pp. 46, 50.

17. Harold Lasswell, *Psychopathology and Politics* (Chicago: University of Chicago Press, 1930); Walter Lippmann, *Public Opinion* (New York: Harcourt, Brace, 1922).

18. Lippmann, *Preface to Politics,* p. 318.

19. Thorstein Veblen, *The Engineers and the Price System* (New York: Viking, 1921).

20. Frederick W. Taylor, *The Principles of Scientific Management* (New York: Harper, 1911). See also Samuel Haber, *Efficiency and Uplift: Scientific Management in the Progressive Era, 1890–1920* (Chicago: University of Chicago Press, 1964), and Samuel P. Hays, *Conservation and the Gospel of Efficiency, The Progressive Conservation Movement, 1890–1920* (Cambridge, Mass.: Harvard University Press, 1959).

21. John Broadus Watson, *The Ways of Behaviorism* (New York: Harper, 1928), pp. 35–36.

22. Croly, *The Promise of American Life,* p. 454.

23. Thorstein Veblen, *The Theory of Business Enterprise* (New York: Scribner's, 1904), pp. 302–73.

24. Mabel Dodge Luhan, *Movers and Shakers* (New York: Harcourt, Brace, 1936), p. 39.

25. John Dewey, "The Future of Pacifism," *New Republic* 11(July 28, 1917):

358–60; John Dewey, "What America Will Fight For," *New Republic* 12(August 18, 1917): 68–69.

26. Randolph Bourne, "The War and the Intellectuals," *Seven Arts* 2(June 1917): 136.

27. Randolph Bourne, "A War Diary," *Seven Arts* 2(September 1917): 545; Randolph Bourne, "Twilight of the Idols," *Seven Arts* 2(October 1917): 692.

28. Bourne, "Twilight of the Idols," *Seven Arts* 2(October 1917): 697, 702.

29. Gabriel Kolko, *The Triumph of Conservatism* (New York: Free Press of Glencoe, 1963); Robert H. Wiebe, *Businessmen and Reform* (Cambridge, Mass.: Harvard University Press, 1962); Paul W. Glad, "Progressives and the Business Culture of the 1920's," *Journal of American History* 53(June 1966): 75–89.

30. Luhan, *Movers and Shakers,* p. 303.

31. Peter G. Filene, "An Obituary for 'The Progressive Movement,' " *American Quarterly* 22(Spring 1970): 20–34.

32. Major works that cover American thought in this period are Morton White, *Social Thought in America: The Revolt Against Formalism* (New York: Viking, 1949); David Noble, *The Paradox of Progressive Thought* (Minneapolis, Minn.: University of Minnesota Press, 1958); Henry May, *The End of American Innocence* (New York: Knopf, 1959); Robert H. Wiebe, *The Search for Order, 1877–1920* (New York: Hill and Wang, 1967); Charles Forcey, *The Crossroads of Liberalism* (New York: Oxford University Press, 1961); Richard Hofstadter, *The Progressive Historians* (New York: Knopf, 1968); Jean B. Quandt, *From the Small Town to the Great Community: The Social Thought of Progressive Intellectuals* (New Brunswick, N.J.: Rutgers University Press, 1970); Christopher Lasch, *The New Radicalism in America, 1889–1963, The Intellectual as a Social Type* (New York: Knopf, 1965).

3. The Republicans Under Roosevelt and Taft

1. Henry Adams to Elizabeth Cameron, March 4, 1901, in Worthington C. Ford, ed., *Letters of Henry Adams, 1892–1918* (Boston: Houghton Mifflin, 1938), p. 320; John Hay, *Addresses of John Hay* (New York: Century, 1906), p. 300; Brand Witlock, *Forty Years of It* (New York: Appleton, 1914), p. 27.

2. Carl Degler, "The Nineteenth Century," in William N. Nelson, ed., *Theory and Practice in American Politics* (Chicago: University of Chicago Press, 1964), p. 38.

3. H. Wayne Morgan, *William McKinley and His America* (Syracuse, N.Y.: Syracuse University Press, 1963); Richard Jensen, *The Winning of the Midwest: Social and Political Conflict, 1888–1896* (Chicago: University of Chicago Press, 1971), pp. 283–92.

4. Walter Dean Burnham, *Critical Elections and the Mainsprings of American Politics* (New York: Norton, 1970), pp. 52–54. On the Democrats, David Burner, *The Politics of Provincialism: The Democratic Party in Transition, 1918–1932* (New York: Knopf, 1968), and J. Rogers Hollingsworth, *The Whirligig of Politics: The Democracy of Cleveland and Bryan* (Chicago: University of Chicago Press, 1963), pp. 156–241. Paul T. David, *Party Strength in the United States, 1872–1970* (Charlottesville, Va.: University Press of Virginia, 1972), p. 39.

5. *The Statistical History of the United States From Colonial Times to the Present* (Stamford, Conn.: Fairfield, 1965), p. 691. Horace Samuel Merrill and Marion Galbraith Merrill, *The Republican Command, 1897–1913* (Lexington, Ky.: The University Press of Kentucky, 1971), takes a critical look at Republican congressional leaders.

6. Henry L. West, "The Present Session of Congress," *The Forum* 32(December 1901): 428. Frank W. Taussig, *The Tariff History of the United States* (New York: Putnam's, 1931), and Richard C. Baker, *The Tariff Under Roosevelt and Taft* (Hastings, Neb.: Democratic, 1941), indicate the importance of the tariff but do not exhaust the subject.

7. For Lodge's remark, *Official Proceedings of the Twelfth Republican National Convention, 1900* (Philadelphia, Pa.: Press of Dunlap Printing, 1900), p. 86. Henry L. West, "American Politics," *The Forum* 35(July 1903): 11–12; Jesse Macy, *Party Organization and Machinery* (New York: Century, 1912), p. 258; George C. Perkins to William E. Chandler, September 20, 1900, William E. Chandler Papers, New Hampshire Historical Society.

8. Baker, *The Tariff Under Roosevelt and Taft*, passim, reviews the party's tariff debate in the early twentieth century. See also Richard M. Abrams, *Conservatism in a Progressive Era: Massachusetts Politics, 1900–1912* (Cambridge, Mass.: Harvard University Press, 1964), pp. 90–95, 110–19, 121–23, passim.

9. Baker, *Tariff Under Roosevelt and Taft*, pp. 74–75. For the impact of the Iowa Idea, Leland Sage, *William Boyd Allison: A Study in Practical Politics* (Iowa City, Ia.: State Historical Society of Iowa, 1956), pp. 282–93; Thomas Richard Ross, *Jonathan Prentiss Dolliver* (Iowa City, Ia.: State Historical Society of Iowa, 1958), pp. 168–71, 181–86.

10. McKinley's efforts for reciprocity are traced in Morgan, *William McKinley and His America*, pp. 461–63, 517–18.

11. Herbert F. Margulies, *The Decline of the Progressive Movement in Wisconsin, 1890–1920* (Madison, Wisc.: State Historical Society of Wisconsin, 1968), pp. 3–50; David P. Thelen, *The New Citizenship: Origins of Progressivism in Wisconsin* (Columbia, Mo.: University of Missouri Press, 1972), pp. 290–308. Ralph M. Sayre, "Albert Baird Cummins and the Progressive Movement in Iowa," Ph.D dissertation, Columbia University, 1958, p. 138; John Braeman, *Albert J. Beveridge: American Nationalist* (Chicago: University of Chicago Press, 1971), pp. 68–81.

12. Brand Whitlock, "The Party Fetich," *Saturday Evening Post* 179 (October 13, 1906): 17–20. William N. Chambers and Walter Dean Burnham, eds., *The American Party Systems* (New York: Oxford University Press, 1967), pp. 165–73; Jensen, *Winning of the Midwest*, pp. 306–308.

13. For studies of Roosevelt, William H. Harbaugh, *Power and Responsibility: The Life and Times of Theodore Roosevelt* (New York: Farrar, Straus and Cudahy, 1961); Henry F. Pringle, *Theodore Roosevelt: A Biography* (New York: Harcourt, Brace, 1931); and John M. Blum, *The Republican Roosevelt* (Cambridge, Mass.: Harvard University Press, 1954).

14. *Taft and Roosevelt: The Intimate Letters of Archie Butt* (Garden City: Doubleday, Doran, 1930), II, 441. For expressions of reserve about Roosevelt, see Albert Clarke to John D. Long, June 27, 1900, John D. Long Papers, Massa-

chusetts Historical Society, and Herbert Croly, *Marcus Alonzo Hanna: His Life and Work* (New York: Macmillan, 1912), pp. 310–11.

15. Henry L. West, "The Growing Powers of the President," *The Forum* 31 (March 1901): 23–29. For Roosevelt's mastery of the press, Oscar King Davis, *Released for Publication* (Boston: Houghton Mifflin, 1925), pp. 123–24; Harry H. Stein, "Theodore Roosevelt and the Press: Lincoln Steffens," *Mid-America* 54 (April 1972): 94–107.

16. Pringle, *Roosevelt,* p. 370.

17. Theodore Roosevelt to Sidney Brooks, November 20, 1908, Elting Morison, ed., *The Letters of Theodore Roosevelt* (Cambridge, Mass.: Harvard University Press, 1951–54), VI, 1369. "The Distance From the White House to the Capitol," *The World's Work* 7(December 1903): 4165–66; Shelby M. Cullom, *Fifty Years of Public Service* (Chicago: McClurg, 1911), p. 294; Willard B. Gatewood, *Theodore Roosevelt and the Art of Controversy* (Baton Rouge, La.: Louisiana State University Press, 1970), pp. 236–87.

18. Pringle, *Roosevelt,* p. 233.

19. *Official Proceedings of the Twelfth Republican National Convention,* pp. 107, 161; *The Works of Theodore Roosevelt: State Papers as Governor and President* (New York: Scribner's, 1926), XV, 91; Arthur M. Johnson, "Theodore Roosevelt and the Bureau of Corporations," *Mississippi Valley Historical Review* 45(March 1959): 571–90. On the continuity between McKinley and Roosevelt, see James O. Wheaton, "The Genius and the Jurist: The Presidential Campaign of 1904," Ph.D dissertation, Stanford University, 1964, pp. 33–34.

20. *Addresses and Presidential Messages of Theodore Roosevelt, 1902–1904* (New York: Putnam's, 1904), p. 15. Harbaugh, *Power and Responsibility,* pp. 155–65.

21. John J. Jenkins to Roosevelt, October 6, 1902, Theodore Roosevelt Papers, Manuscripts Division, Library of Congress; George E. Mowry, *The Era of Theodore Roosevelt, 1900–1912* (New York: Harper, 1958), pp. 130–34.

22. Henry Cabot Lodge to George von Lengerke Meyer, October 27, 1902, Henry Cabot Lodge Papers, Massachusetts Historical Society; Robert H. Wiebe, "The Anthracite Coal Strike of 1902: A Record of Confusion," *Mississippi Valley Historical Review* 48(September 1961): 229–51.

23. Roosevelt to Oscar S. Straus, October 15, 1904, in Oscar S. Straus, *Under Four Administrations: From Cleveland to Taft* (Boston: Houghton Mifflin, 1922), p. 182; J. Hampton Moore, *Theodore Roosevelt and the Old Guard* (Philadelphia, Pa.: MacRae Smith, 1925), p. 130; Frank T. Reuter, *Catholic Influence on American Colonial Policies, 1898–1904* (Austin, Tex.: University of Texas Press, 1967), pp. 123–25; Wheaton, "The Genius and the Jurist," pp. 427–29, 437–42.

24. Mowry, *Era of Theodore Roosevelt,* pp. 143–64; Harbaugh, *Power and Responsibility,* pp. 182–211; Gatewood, *Theodore Roosevelt and the Art of Controversy,* pp. 135–74.

25. Roosevelt to Joseph B. Bishop, April 27, 1903, Morison, *Letters of Theodore Roosevelt,* III, 471.

26. Joseph Wharton to William Boyd Allison, October 30, 1901, November 4, 1901, Allison to Wharton, November 2, 1901, James Wilson to Allison, September 28, 1901, October 4, 1901, William Boyd Allison Papers, Iowa State Department

of History and Archives; Nathaniel W. Stephenson, *Nelson W. Aldrich: A Leader in American Politics* (New York: Scribner's, 1930), pp. 176–83.

27. Moore, *Theodore Roosevelt and the Old Guard*, p. 172; Mowry, *Era of Theodore Roosevelt*, p. 129; Wheaton, "The Genius and the Jurist," p. 36.

28. Wheaton, "The Genius and the Jurist," pp. 70–78.

29. Thomas R. Cripps, "The Lily White Republicans: The Negro, the Party, and the South in the Progressive Era," Ph.D dissertation, University of Maryland, 1967, pp. 102, 111, 137, 160–68, 182; Willard B. Gatewood, "Theodore Roosevelt and Southern Republicans: The Case of South Carolina, 1901–1904," *The South Carolina Historical Magazine* 70(October 1969): 251–66.

30. Mark Hanna to Roosevelt, April 8, 1902, with enclosed article, Roosevelt Papers. Croly, *Marcus Alonzo Hanna*, pp. 411–46; Blum, *Republican Roosevelt*, pp. 37–50.

31. Blum, *Republican Roosevelt*, pp. 50–54; Mowry, *Era of Theodore Roosevelt*, pp. 171–74; Wheaton, "The Genius and the Jurist," pp. 172–211.

32. *Official Proceedings of the Thirteenth Republican National Convention, 1904* (Minneapolis, Minn.: Harrison & Smith, 1904), pp. 132–37. Wheaton, "The Genius and the Jurist," pp. 258–99.

33. Roosevelt to Kermit Roosevelt, November 10, 1904, in Morison, *Letters of Theodore Roosevelt*, IV, 1024. Harbaugh, *Power and Responsibility*, pp. 212–32; Mowry, *Era of Theodore Roosevelt*, pp. 176–80.

34. Orville H. Platt to Nelson Aldrich, November 12, 1904, Orville H. Platt Papers, Connecticut State Library. George H. Mayer, *The Republican Party, 1854–1966* (New York: Oxford University Press, 1967), p. 287; David, *Party Strength in the United States*, pp. 288, 290, 294, 296, 300; Burnham, *Critical Elections and the Mainsprings of American Politics*, p. 26.

35. Morton Albaugh to Chester I. Long, March 18, 1905, Chester I. Long Papers, Kansas State Historical Society. "The Indignant Awakening of the People," *The World's Work* 11(April 1906): 7360; Robert H. Wiebe, *Businessmen and Reform: A Study of the Progressive Movement* (Cambridge, Mass.: Harvard University Press, 1962), pp. 42–69.

36. Roosevelt to Richard Watson Gilder, June 26, 1906, Morison, *Letters of Theodore Roosevelt*, V, 317; John M. Blum, "Theodore Roosevelt and the Legislative Process: Tariff Revision and Railroad Regulation, 1904–1906," Morison, *Letters of Theodore Roosevelt*, IV, 1333–1342.

37. *The Works of Theodore Roosevelt: State Papers as Governor and President*, XV, 282; Blum, *Republican Roosevelt*, pp. 75–92.

38. Roosevelt to Lyman Abbott, July 1, 1906, Morison, *Letters of Theodore Roosevelt*, V, 328; Blum, *Republican Roosevelt*, pp. 93–105. On the Hepburn Bill, see also Gabriel Kolko, *Railroads and Regulation, 1877–1916* (Princeton, N.J.: Princeton University Press, 1965), pp. 127–54, and Albro Martin, *Enterprise Denied: Origins of the Decline of American Railroads, 1897–1917* (New York: Columbia University Press, 1971), pp. 111–20. Braeman, *Beveridge*, pp. 98–111, discusses the meat inspection measure.

39. Roosevelt to Alice Roosevelt Longworth, November 7, 1906, Morison, *Letters of Theodore Roosevelt*, V, 488–89; James A. Tawney to John C. Spooner, September 25, 1906, John C. Spooner Papers, Manuscripts Division, Library of Congress; Mowry, *Era of Theodore Roosevelt*, pp. 208–209.

40. Spooner to Henry Fink, June 5, 1906, Spooner to W. M. Spooner, June 11, 1906, Spooner Papers; Henry L. West, "American Politics," *The Forum* 38(January 1908): 315; Johnson, "Theodore Roosevelt and the Bureau of Corporations," pp. 580–89.

41. Braeman, *Beveridge,* pp. 109–33; Abrams, *Conservatism in a Progressive Era,* pp. 130–33; James F. Holt, *Congressional Insurgents and the Party System, 1909–1916* (Cambridge, Mass.: Harvard University Press, 1967), pp. 8–15.

42. *The Works of Theodore Roosevelt: State Papers as Governor and President,* XV, 363–71, 410–24; Morison, *Letters of Theodore Roosevelt,* VI, 1572–1591.

43. Henry L. Higginson to George von Lengerke Meyer, August 13, 1907, George von Lengerke Meyer Papers, Massachusetts Historical Society; Myron T. Herrick to Higginson, October 2, 1907, Henry L. Higginson Papers, Baker Library, Harvard Business School; Moore, *Roosevelt and the Old Guard,* pp. 163–83.

44. "The Claims of the Candidates," *North American Review* 187(May 1908): 641–83; Alfred D. Sumberg, "William Howard Taft and the Ohio Endorsement Issue, 1906–1908," in Daniel R. Beaver, ed., *Some Pathways in Twentieth Century History* (Detroit, Mich.: Wayne State University Press, 1969), pp. 67–93.

45. Roosevelt to George O. Trevelyan, June 19, 1908, Morison, *Letters of Theodore Roosevelt,* VI, 1085; Henry F. Pringle, *The Life and Times of William Howard Taft* (New York: Farrar and Rinehart, 1939), I, 339.

46. Pringle, *Taft,* I, 311–33; Stanley D. Solvick, "The Pre-Presidential Political and Economic Thought of William Howard Taft," *Northwest Ohio Quarterly* (Fall 1971): 87–97.

47. Joseph L. Bristow to Samuel J. Robert, August 13, 1908, Joseph L. Bristow Papers, Kansas State Historical Society; Pringle, *Taft,* I, 337–53; Mowry, *Era of Theodore Roosevelt,* pp. 228–29.

48. Pringle, *Taft,* I, 369; Howard F. McMains, "The Road to George Ade's Farm: Origins of Taft's First Campaign Rally, September, 1908," *Indiana Magazine of History* 67(December 1971): 317; Edgar A. Hornig, "The Indefatigable Mr. Bryan in 1908," *Nebraska History* 37(June 1956): 183–99, and Hornig, "The Religious Issue in the Taft-Bryan Duel of 1908," *Proceedings of the American Philosophical Society* 105(December 15, 1961): 530–37.

49. Fred W. Upham to William Kent, October 19, 1908, William Kent Papers, Yale University Library. Emma Lou Thornbrough, "The Brownsville Episode and the Negro Vote," *Mississippi Valley Historical Review* 44(December 1957): 469–93; Pringle, *Taft,* I, 366–76; Roosevelt to Taft, September 19, 21, 24, 1908, Morison, *Letters of Theodore Roosevelt,* VI, 1243–44, 1247–48, 1255–56.

50. Joseph L. Bristow to J. R. Harrison, February 4, 1909, Bristow Papers; Taft to Chester I. Long, November 21, 1908, Long Papers; Pringle, *Taft,* I, 377–78.

51. On the cabinet, Francis E. Warren to Willis Van Devanter, March 14, 1909, Francis E. Warren Papers, University of Wyoming. Henry Cabot Lodge to Roosevelt, December 27, 1909, Lodge Papers; *Springfield Daily Republican,* August 17, 1909; Oscar King Davis, *Released For Publication,* p. 99.

52. Henry L. Higginson to Lodge, April 20, 1910, William Wood to Lodge, February 16, 1910, Lodge Papers; E. H. Gary to Henry L. Higginson, March 9, 1910, Higginson Papers; Chauncey Depew to J. R. Joslyn, March 10, 1910, Joslyn to Depew, April 11, 1910, Chauncey Depew Papers, Yale University Library.

53. George E. Mowry, *Theodore Roosevelt and the Progressive Movement* (Madison, Wisc.: University of Wisconsin Press, 1946), pp. 40–44; Holt, *Congressional Insurgents*, pp. 16–18.

54. David W. Detzer, "The Politics of the Payne-Aldrich Tariff of 1909," Ph.D dissertation, University of Connecticut, 1970; Stanley Solvick, "William Howard Taft and the Payne-Aldrich Tariff," *Mississippi Valley Historical Review* 50(December 1963): 424–42. Lewis L. Gould, "Western Range Senators and the Payne-Aldrich Tariff," *Pacific Northwest Quarterly* 64(April 1973): 49–56.

55. James S. Clarkson to Grenville M. Dodge, April 11, 1910, Grenville M. Dodge Papers, Iowa State Department of History and Archives; William Howard Taft, *Presidential Addresses and State Papers* (New York: Doubleday, Page, 1910), p. 226; Mowry, *Theodore Roosevelt and the Progressive Movement*, pp. 68–73.

56. William Manners, *TR and Will: A Friendship That Split the Republican Party* (New York: Harcourt, Brace and World, 1969), pp. 63–88.

57. James L. Penick, *Progressive Politics and Conservation: The Ballinger-Pinchot Affair* (Chicago: University of Chicago Press, 1968).

58. Mowry, *Theodore Roosevelt and the Progressive Movement*, pp. 106–16, 126–30.

59. *The Works of Theodore Roosevelt: Social Justice and Popular Rule*, XVII, 12, 19; Robert S. La Forte, "Theodore Roosevelt's Osawatomie Speech," *Kansas Historical Quarterly* 32(1966): 187–200.

60. "A Review of the World," *Current Literature* 49(December 1910): 587–88; William Kent to Amos Pinchot, October 21, 1910, Kent Papers; Mowry, *Roosevelt and the Progressive Movement*, pp. 120–56.

61. Joseph L. Bristow to Moses E. Clapp, November 10, 1910, Bristow Papers; Roger E. Wyman, "Insurgency and the Election of 1910 in the Middle West," M.A. thesis, University of Wisconsin, 1964; Mayer, *The Republican Party*, p. 318.

62. L. Ethan Ellis, *Reciprocity 1911: A Study in Canadian-American Relations* (New Haven, Conn.: Yale University Press, 1939); Norman M. Wilensky, *Conservatives in the Progressive Era: The Taft Republicans of 1912* (Gainesville, Fla.: Florida State University Press, 1965).

63. Charles D. Hilles to Louis H. Paine, January 18, 1912, Charles D. Hilles Papers, Yale University Library; Holt, *Congressional Insurgents*, pp. 49–52; Mowry, *Roosevelt and the Progressive Movement*, pp. 172–74, 185–88; Helene M. Hooker, ed., Amos R. E. Pinchot, *History of the Progressive Party, 1912–1916* (New York: New York University Press, 1958).

64. James C. German, Jr., "Taft, Roosevelt and United States Steel," *The Historian* 34 (August 1972): 598–613; John P. Campbell, "Taft, Roosevelt, and the Arbitration Treaties of 1911," *Journal of American History* 53 (September 1966): 279–98; Elting E. Morison, *Turmoil and Tradition: A Study of the Life and Times of Henry L. Stimson* (Boston: Houghton Mifflin, 1960), pp. 178–90.

65. Lodge to Brooks Adams, March 5, 1912, Lodge Papers; Abrams, *Conservatism in a Progressive Era*, pp. 277–78; Mowry, *Roosevelt and the Progressive Movement*, pp. 207–19.

66. Mowry, *Roosevelt and the Progressive Movement*, pp. 220–55.

67. For varying appraisals of the Progressive Party, Baker, *The Tariff Under Roosevelt and Taft*, pp. 197–98; Holt, *Congressional Insurgents*, pp. 63–71;

Mowry, *Roosevelt and the Progressive Movement,* pp. 256–83; Blum, *Republican Roosevelt,* pp. 149–50.

68. Taft to Philander Knox, September 30, 1912, Charles D. Hilles to C. Sidney Shepard, October 15, 1912, Hilles to Frederick H. Howland, November 9, 1912, Hilles to Mrs. B. A. Wallingford, November 20, 1912, Hilles Papers; Pringle, *Taft,* II, 815–42; Mayer, *The Republican Party,* pp. 331–32.

4. The Democrats from Bryan to Wilson

1. Carl N. Degler, "American Political Parties and the Rise of the City: An Interpretation," *The Journal of American History* 51(June 1964):48–49; V. O. Key, Jr., *Politics, Parties, & Pressure Groups,* 5th ed. (New York: Crowell, 1967), p. 172; Paul W. Glad, *McKinley, Bryan, and the People* (Philadelphia, Pa.: Lippincott, 1964), p. 204; J. Rogers Hollingsworth, *The Whirligig of Politics; The Democracy of Cleveland and Bryan* (Chicago: University of Chicago Press, 1963), pp. 94, 103; Paul Kleppner, *The Cross of Culture: A Social Analysis of Midwestern Politics, 1850–1900* (New York: The Free Press, 1970), *passim.*

2. E. E. Schattschneider, *The Semisovereign People; A Realist's View of Democracy in America* (New York: Holt, Rinehart and Winston, 1960), pp. 78–79, 83, 85 (quoted), 91; Louis H. Bean, *How to Predict Elections* (New York: Knopf, 1948), p. 181; Vincent De Santis, "American Politics in the Gilded Age," *The Review of Politics* 25(October 1963): 555; Robert D. Marcus, *Grand Old Party; Political Structure in the Gilded Age 1880–1896* (New York: Oxford University Press, 1971), p. 254; Paul T. David, *Party Strength in the United States: 1872–1970* (Charlottesville, Va.: University Press of Virginia, 1972), pp. 35–38, 44. Arizona joined the Democratic phalanx of eleven former Confederate states when it gained statehood in 1912.

3. Walter Dean Burnham, "Party Systems and the Political Process," William Nisbet Chambers and Walter Dean Burnham, eds., *The American Party Systems; Stages of Political Development* (New York: Oxford University Press, 1967), p. 300; Glad, *McKinley,* p. 199; Robert H. Wiebe, *The Search for Order: 1877–1920* (New York: Hill and Wang, 1968), pp. 106, 216; Hollingsworth, *Whirligig,* pp. 119, 208. The degree of Republican dominance in this period can be overestimated. See David, *Party Strength,* p. 59.

4. Walter LaFeber, "Election of 1900," Arthur M. Schlesinger, Jr., et. al., eds., *History of American Presidential Elections: 1789–1968* (New York: Chelsea House, 1971), III, 1878; Walter Dean Burnham, "The Changing Shape of the American Political Universe," *The American Political Science Review* 59(March 1965):23; Walter Dean Burnham, *Critical Elections and the Mainsprings of American Politics* (New York: Norton, 1970), pp. 74–76; James MacGregor Burns, *The Deadlock of Democracy; Four-Party Politics in America,* rev. ed. (Englewood Cliffs, N.J.: Prentice-Hall, 1964), p. 90. Robert D. Marcus presents the disfranchisement hypothesis in *Grand Old Party,* pp. 253–55.

5. Eric F. Goldman, *Rendezvous With Destiny; A History of Modern American Reform* (New York: Knopf, 1958), p. 63.

6. For appraisals of Bryan: Paolo E. Coletta, *William Jennings Bryan,* 3 vols. (Lincoln: University of Nebraska Press, 1964–69); Paul W. Glad, *The Trumpet*

Soundeth: William Jennings Bryan and His Democracy, 1896–1912 (Lincoln, Neb.: University of Nebraska Press, 1960); and Lawrence W. Levine, *Defender of the Faith; William Jennings Bryan: The Last Decade, 1915–1925* (New York: Oxford University Press, 1965).

7. Burnham, "Party Systems," 284; Hollingsworth, *Whirligig,* pp. 209, 239–41; William Nisbet Chambers, *The Democrats 1789–1964; A Short History of a Popular Party* (Princeton, N.J.: Van Nostrand, 1964), p. 65.

8. Harold Zink, *City Bosses in the United States; A Study of Twenty Municipal Bosses* (Durham, N. C.: Duke University Press, 1930), p. 40; Hollingsworth, *Whirligig,* p. 99; Irwin Yellowitz, *Labor and the Progressive Movement in New York State, 1897–1916* (Ithaca, N.Y.: Cornell University Press, 1965), p. 182; Bruce M. Stave, *The New Deal and the Last Hurrah: Pittsburgh Machine Politics* (Pittsburgh, Pa.: University of Pittsburgh Press, 1970), p. 3; James C. Scott, "Corruption, Machine Politics, and Political Change," *The American Political Science Review* 63(December 1969):1142–58; Robert K. Merton, *Social Theory and Social Structure,* rev. ed. (New York: The Free Press of Glencoe, 1964), pp. 71–82.

9. Merton, *Social Theory,* p. 81; Zink, *City Bosses,* p. 40; Stave, *New Deal,* pp. 5–6; Otis L. Graham, Jr., *The Great Campaigns: Reform and War in America, 1900–1928* (Englewood Cliffs, N.J.: Prentice-Hall, 1971), pp. 27–30; William L. Riordon, *Plunkitt of Tammany Hall* (New York: Dutton, 1963), p. 17.

10. C. Vann Woodward, *Origins of the New South: 1877–1913* (Baton Rouge, La.: Louisiana State University Press, 1951), pp. 371–72; George B. Tindall, *The Emergence of the New South: 1913–1945* (Baton Rouge, La.: Louisiana State University Press, 1967), pp. 5–7, 31–32; Dewey W. Grantham, Jr., *The Democratic South* (Athens, Ga.: University of Georgia Press, 1963), pp. 51–56; Sheldon Hackney, *Populism to Progressivism in Alabama* (Princeton, N.J.: Princeton University Press, 1969), pp. 328–29.

11. John B. Wiseman, "Racism in Democratic Politics, 1904–1912," *Mid-America* 51(January 1969): 38–58. In the heavily Bryanized, anti–Wall Street territory west of the Mississippi, the Democracy slipped into decline after 1896. See John B. Wiseman, "Dilemmas of a Party Out of Power: The Democracy, 1904–1912," Ph.D. dissertation, University of Maryland, 1967, p. 11.

12. Edgar Eugene Robinson, *The Presidential Vote: 1896–1932* (Stanford, Calif.: Stanford University Press, 1934), pp. 7–9 and *passim;* Arthur Wallace Dunn, *From Harrison to Harding; A Personal Narrative, Covering a Third of a Century, 1888–1921* (New York: Putnam's, 1922), I, 282–83; Hollingsworth, *Whirligig,* pp. 134–37, 151–53, 178–85, 207, 233; William Jennings Bryan and Mary Baird Bryan, *The Memoirs of William Jennings Bryan* (Philadelphia, Pa.: United Publishers of America, 1925), pp. 123–25; Bean, *Elections,* p. 181; Eugene H. Roseboom, *A History of Presidential Elections* (New York: Macmillan, 1957), p. 332; Key, *Politics,* p. 527; LaFeber, "Election of 1900," 1913–16; Glad, *Trumpet,* pp. 72–73.

13. For a somewhat different view of the reorganization impulse, see James Otis Wheaton, "The Genius and the Jurist: A Study of the Presidential Campaign of 1904," Ph.D. dissertation, Stanford University, 1964, pp. 91–96.

14. W. A. Swanberg, *Citizen Hearst; A Biography of William Randolph Hearst* (New York: Scribner's, 1961), pp. 209, 216 (quoted); Hollingsworth, *Whirligig,*

pp. 211–13; Paolo E. Coletta, "Election of 1908," *History of American Presidential Elections*, III, 2068.

15. Swanberg, *Hearst*, pp. 209, 213; Hollingsworth, *Whirligig*, p. 212; Yellowitz, *Labor and the Progressive Movement*, pp. 201–205, 215, and *passim*.

16. Hollingsworth, *Whirligig*, pp. 210, 218–19, 225, 228–30; George E. Mowry, *The Era of Theodore Roosevelt: 1900–1912* (New York: Harper and Row, 1958), pp. 177–79; Roseboom, *Presidential Elections*, p. 342.

17. Robinson, *The Presidential Vote*, pp. 9–13 and *passim;* Wiseman, "Racism in Democratic Politics," 44; Key, *Politics*, p. 175; Bean, *Elections*, p. 181; Hollingsworth, *Whirligig*, pp. 233–34; William H. Harbaugh, "Election of 1904," *History of American Presidential Elections*, III, 1993–94; Coletta, "Election of 1908," 2070; Wheaton, "The Genius and the Jurist," 418–19, 526–61.

18. Samuel P. Hays, "The Social Analysis of American Political History, 1880–1920," *Political Science Quarterly* 80(September 1965):386; Hollingsworth, *Whirligig*, pp. viii–ix, 191–92, 234–35, 240–41; Hoyt Landon Warner, *Progressivism in Ohio: 1897–1917* (Columbus, O.: Ohio State University Press, 1964), pp. 184–85.

19. Wiseman, "Dilemmas," 108; Paolo E. Coletta, *William Jennings Bryan. I. Political Evangelist: 1860–1908* (Lincoln, Neb.: University of Nebraska Press, 1964), pp. 353, 369, 377–78.

20. Robinson, *The Presidential Vote*, pp. 13–14, 402–403 and *passim;* Bean, *Elections*, p. 181; Coletta, "Election of 1908," 2087–88, 2090.

21. Coletta, "Election of 1908," 2087, 2090; Robinson, *The Presidential Vote*, p. 13; David, *Party Strength*.

22. Marc Karson, *American Labor Unions and Politics: 1900–1918* (Boston: Beacon Press, 1965), pp. 59, 64; Yellowitz, *Labor and the Progressive Movement* pp. 220–23; Wiebe, *Search for Order*, p. 205.

23. James Holt, *Congressional Insurgents and the Party System, 1909–1916* (Cambridge, Mass.: Harvard University Press, 1967), pp. 24, 41–42; Mowry, *Era of Theodore Roosevelt*, pp. 272–73.

24. Randall B. Ripley, *Majority Party Leadership in Congress* (Boston: Little, Brown, 1969), pp. 140–41; Karson, *Labor Unions and Politics*, p. 70.

25. Arthur S. Link, *Wilson: The Road to the White House* (Princeton, N.J.: Princeton University Press, 1947), pp. 431–65; the Clark incident is related in Paolo E. Coletta, *William Jennings Bryan. II. Progressive Politician and Moral Statesman, 1909–1915* (Lincoln, Neb.: University of Nebraska Press, 1969), pp. 70–71.

26. *New York Herald*, August 25, 1912; *New York Sun*, September 8, 1912; *New York Times*, August 13, September 13, 1912; Chambers, *The Democrats*, p. 68; *A Crossroads of Freedom: The 1912 Campaign Speeches of Woodrow Wilson*, ed. by John Wells Davidson (New Haven, Conn.: Yale University Press, 1956), p. 345.

27. The following assessment of New Freedom ideology is largely based on an analysis of Wilson's speeches as printed in the Davidson collection, cited in n. 26. Only quotations will be specified by page.

28. *Crossroads of Freedom*, pp. 156, 314.

29. Ibid., p. 399.

30. Ibid., p. 491.

31. Robinson, *The Presidential Vote*, pp. 14–17 and *passim;* Bean, *Elections*,

pp. 68–69, 177, 181; Karson, *Labor Unions and Politics*, p. 72; Key, *Politics*, pp. 263–64; George E. Mowry, "Election of 1912," *History of American Presidential Elections*, III, 2163, 2165–66.

32. "Interview with Albert Sidney Burleson," n.d., Ray Stannard Baker Papers, Library of Congress; notes for autobiography, William G. McAdoo Papers, Library of Congress; Austin Ranney, *The Doctrine of Responsible Party Government; Its Origins and Present State* (Urbana, Ill.: University of Illinois Press, 1962), pp. 25, 27, 45, 47; Burns, *Deadlock of Democracy*, pp. 131–32, 146–47; John Morton Blum, *Woodrow Wilson and the Politics of Morality* (Boston: Little, Brown, 1956), p. 66; Arthur S. Link, *Wilson: The New Freedom* (Princeton, N.J.: Princeton University Press, 1956), pp. 157–64; James MacGregor Burns, *Presidential Government: The Crucible of Leadership* (New York: Avon Books, 1967), p. 165.

33. Quoted in Coletta, *Progressive Politician*, p. 139.

34. Woodward, *Origins of the New South*, pp. 460, 480–81; Tindall, *Emergence of the New South*, pp. 2–3, 8; Seward W. Livermore, *Politics is Adjourned; Woodrow Wilson and the War Congress, 1916–1918* (Middletown, Conn.: Wesleyan University Press, 1966), p. 9. The "sectional" issue provided the GOP with an important campaign theme in 1916.

35. Randall B. Ripley, *Power in the Senate* (New York: St. Martin's, 1969), pp. 30–31; Ripley, *Majority Party Leadership*, pp. 52, 64–66, 86; Holt, *Congressional Insurgents*, p. 85; Arthur S. Link, *Woodrow Wilson and the Progressive Era: 1910–1917* (New York: Harper and Brothers, 1954), pp. 35, 43; Wiebe, *Search for Order*, pp. 218–19.

36. On Wilson's role in the legislative process, see Ripley, *Majority Party Leadership*, especially pp. 52–69, 86; Holt, *Congressional Insurgents*, pp. 81–89; and Link, *Wilson: The New Freedom*, pp. 145–56 and *passim*.

37. David Burner, *The Politics of Provincialism; The Democratic Party in Transition, 1918–1932* (New York: Knopf, 1968), p. 94 (quoted); Grantham, *The Democratic South*, p. 56.

38. Excised material from the autobiography of Oswald Garrison Villard, enclosed in —— White to —— Wilkins, October 4, 1938, National Association for the Advancement of Colored People Papers, Library of Congress; Oswald Garrison Villard to "Dear Friend," August 18, 1913, Archibald H. Grimké Papers, Howard University Library; J. Milton Waldron to Woodrow Wilson, July 11, 1912, Woodrow Wilson Papers, Library of Congress; W. E. Burghardt DuBois, *Dusk of Dawn: An Essay Toward an Autobiography of a Race Concept* (New York: Harcourt, Brace, 1940), p. 234; *The Cabinet Diaries of Josephus Daniels, 1913–1921*, ed. by E. David Cronon (Lincoln: University of Nebraska Press, 1963), pp. 32–33; Arthur S. Link, "The Negro as a Factor in the Campaign of 1912," *The Journal of Negro History* 32(January 1947):84–86; Link, *Wilson: The New Freedom*, p. 246.

39. Arthur S. Link, "The South and the 'New Freedom': An Interpretation," in Arthur S. Link, ed., *The Higher Realism of Woodrow Wilson and Other Essays* (Nashville, Tenn.: Vanderbilt University Press, 1971), pp. 300–301.

40. Nancy Joan Weiss, *Charles Francis Murphy, 1858–1924: Respectability and Responsibility in Tammany Politics* (Northampton, Mass.: Smith College,

1968), pp. 82–83, 86–87, 89–92; Yellowitz, *Labor and the Progressive Movement,* pp. 127, 157, 159, 166–67.

41. Diary of Edward M. House, I, 130; IV, 14; V, 216; William G. McAdoo to Edward M. House, Feb. 22, 1914, Edward M. House Papers, Yale University Library; Weiss, *Murphy,* pp. 50, 71; Link, *Wilson: The New Freedom,* pp. 168–69; Edwin R. Lewinson, *John Purroy Mitchel: The Boy Mayor of New York* (New York: Astra Books, 1965), pp. 208–209. The highly suggestive imagery concerning what should be done in New York is House's, the terse comment on the upshot McAdoo's.

42. Arthur S. Link, "Woodrow Wilson and the Democratic Party," *The Review of Politics* 18(April 1956):154.

43. Link, "South and the 'New Freedom,'" 305. "The summer of 1916," Arthur S. Link and William M. Leary, Jr., argue, "marked Wilson's final transition from the New Freedom to the New Nationalism, that is, from the philosophy of the Federal Government as an impartial mediator in the nation's affairs to the concept of the Government as an active promoter of social justice," "Election of 1916," *History of American Presidential Elections,* III, 2259. For an important recent statement on the issue, see Melvin I. Urofsky, *Big Steel and the Wilson Administration: A Study in Business-Government Relations* (Columbus, O.: Ohio State University Press, 1969), pp. xii, 76–78.

44. John J. Broesamle, "William Gibbs McAdoo: Businessman in Politics, 1863–1917," Ph.D. dissertation, Columbia University, 1970, *passim,* and John J. Broesamle, "The Struggle for Control of the Federal Reserve System, 1914–1917," *Mid-America* 52(October 1970):280–97.

45. Broesamle, "McAdoo," pp. 208–491.

46. Henry F. Pringle, *The Life and Times of William Howard Taft; A Biography* (New York: Farrar and Rinehart, 1939), II, 887; John S. Smith, "Organized Labor and Government in the Wilson Era; 1913–1921: Some Conclusions," *Labor History* 3(Fall 1962):265–67; Burns, *Deadlock of Democracy,* p. 145.

47. *Crossroads of Freedom,* pp. 80, 264–65. See also Martin J. Sklar, "Woodrow Wilson and the Political Economy of Modern United States Liberalism," James Weinstein and David W. Eakins, eds., *For a New America: Essays in History and Politics from Studies on the Left, 1959–1967* (New York: Random House, 1970), pp. 57–60 and *passim.*

48. *Crossroads of Freedom,* p. 47; Carl P. Parrini, *Heir to Empire: United States Economic Diplomacy, 1916–1923* (Pittsburgh, Pa.: University of Pittsburgh Press, 1969), pp. 1–2, 10, 15–16, 20; Urofsky, *Big Steel,* p. 150; Richard M. Abrams, "Woodrow Wilson and the Southern Congressmen, 1913–1916," *The Journal of Southern History,* 22(November 1956):434–35; Burton I. Kaufman, "United States Trade and Latin America: The Wilson Years," *The Journal of American History* 58(September 1971):342–63; Broesamle, "McAdoo," pp. 463–553.

49. William G. McAdoo to Robert L. Henry, February 16, 1916, McAdoo Papers.

50. Claude Kitchin to A. L. Brooks, November 3, 1915, Claude Kitchin Papers, University of North Carolina Library; "Bryan's Resignation," May 15, 1931, McAdoo Papers; Arthur S. Link, *Wilson: Confusions and Crises 1915–1916*

(Princeton, N.J.: Princeton University Press, 1964), pp. 23–28; Levine, *Defender of the Faith*, pp. 21–22, 58; Coletta, *Progressive Politician*, p. 360.

51. Ripley, *Majority Party Leadership*, p. 55; Link and Leary, "Election of 1916," 2246.

52. Dunn, *Harrison to Harding*, II, 343–44; Karson, *Labor Unions and Politics*, p. 85; Link and Leary, "Election of 1916," 2269; Burner, *Politics of Provincialism*, p. 32. On the question of 1916 as a turning point in the voting behavior of labor, see especially Michael Paul Rogin and John L. Shover, *Political Change in California; Critical Elections and Social Movements, 1890–1966* (Westport, Conn.: Greenwood, 1970); John M. Allswang, *A House for all Peoples: Ethnic Politics in Chicago 1890–1936* (Lexington, Ky.: University Press of Kentucky, 1971), p. 29.

53. John H. M. Laslett, *Labor and the Left; A Study of Socialist and Radical Influences in the American Labor Movement, 1881–1924* (New York: Basic Books, 1970), p. 302; Link, *Woodrow Wilson and the Progressive Era*, p. 250; Roseboom, *Presidential Elections*, p. 387.

54. On the nature of the Wilson coalition, see Arthur S. Link, *Wilson: Campaigns for Progressivism and Peace 1916–1917* (Princeton, N. J.: Princeton University Press, 1965), pp. 124–64; Link and Leary, "Election of 1916," 2245–70; Burner, *Politics of Provincialism*, pp. 28 ff; and Robinson, *The Presidential Vote*, pp. 17–19. The statistics on percentage turnout come from Key, *Politics*, p. 591. Wilson also benefited, apparently, from a switch in voting behavior among Mormons in the West.

55. Burner, *Politics of Provincialism*, pp. 20–22, 31; Blum, *Woodrow Wilson and the Politics of Morality*, p. 114; Link, *Woodrow Wilson and the Progressive Era*, pp. 249, 251; Link and Leary, "Election of 1916," 2269; Samuel Lubell, *The Future of American Politics*, 3rd ed. rev. (New York: Harper Colophon Books, 1965), p. 136.

56. Bean, *Elections*, p. 181; Herbert Agar, *The Price of Union* (Boston: Houghton Mifflin, Sentry Edition, 1966), p. 669; Livermore, *Politics is Adjourned*, pp. 10–11.

57. Quoted in Levine, *Defender of the Faith*, pp. 80–81.

5. The Progressives and the Environment

1. Theodore Roosevelt, "Rural Life," *Outlook* 95(August 27, 1910):919.

2. Ibid., p. 920.

3. Horace Plunkett, "Better Farming, Better Business, Better Living," *Outlook* 94(February 19, 1910):397.

4. *Report of the Commission on Country Life* (New York: Sturgis and Walton, 1911), pp. 30–31.

5. Liberty Hyde Bailey, *The Country Life Movement* (New York: Macmillan, 1913), p. 19.

6. John W. Bookwalter, *Rural Versus Urban: Their Conflict and Its Causes* (New York: Knickerbocker Press, 1911), p. 292.

7. *Official Proceedings of the Seventeenth National Irrigation Congress held at Spokane, Washington* (Spokane, Wash.: Shaw and Borden, 1909), p. 231.

8. *Report of the Commission on Country Life*, p. 148.

9. *Official Proceedings of the Seventeenth National Irrigation Congress*, p. 231.

10. *Official Proceedings of the Thirteenth National Irrigation Congress* (Portland, Ore., 1905), p. 254.

11. E. Louise Peffer, *The Closing of the Public Domain: Disposal and Reservation Policies, 1900–1950* (Stanford, Calif.: Stanford University Press, 1951), p. 21.

12. Ibid., pp. 3–4.

13. Samuel P. Hays, *Conservation and the Gospel of Efficiency: The Progressive Conservation Movement, 1890–1920* (Cambridge, Mass.: Harvard University Press, 1959), pp. 9–11; James Penick, Jr., "The Resource Revolution," in Melvin Kranzberg and Carroll Pursell, Jr., eds., *Technology in Western Civilization* (New York: Oxford University Press, 1967), II, 434; William Lilley III and Lewis L. Gould, "The Western Irrigation Movement 1878–1902: A Reappraisal," in Gene M. Gressley, ed., *The American West: A Reorientation* (Laramie, Wy.: University of Wyoming, 1966), pp. 57–74.

14. Edwin T. Layton, Jr., *The Revolt of the Engineers: Social Responsibility and the American Engineering Profession* (Cleveland, O.: Press of Case Western Reserve University, 1971), p. 213; Layton, "Frederick Haynes Newell and the Revolt of the Engineers," *Journal of the Mid-continent American Studies Association* III(1962):18.

15. Penick, "The Resource Revolution," p. 437.

16. Gifford Pinchot, *Breaking New Ground* (Seattle, Wash.: University of Washington Press, 1972), p. xxiii. His autobiography remains the best source for his career as a forester, but two excellent scholarly studies should be read with it: M. Nelson McGeary, *Gifford Pinchot: Forester-Politician* (Princeton, N.J.: Princeton University Press, 1960); and Harold T. Pinkett, *Gifford Pinchot: Private and Public Forester* (Urbana, Ill.: University of Illinois Press, 1970). Finally, Hays, *Conservation and the Gospel of Efficiency* is indispensable. Unless otherwise cited, material in subsequent pages is drawn from these sources.

17. For a magisterial judgment by a prominent historian see the review in *American Historical Review* 67(October 1961):162–63.

18. Quoted in Penick, "The Resource Revolution," p. 44.

19. For a detailed study of the celebrated controversy, see James Penick, Jr., *Progressive Politics and Conservation: The Ballinger-Pinchot Affair* (Chicago: University of Chicago Press, 1968).

20. He formed a close alliance with many former Powell associates, but Pinchot had little admiration for Powell himself, who was no longer director of the Geological Survey after 1893. His influential voice was never raised in defense of Pinchot's brand of commercial forestry; quite the contrary. Consequently, Pinchot's single mention of Powell in his autobiography pictures him maniacally setting fire to a tree "just to see it burn." Pinchot, *Breaking New Ground*, p. 24.

21. William H. Goetzmann, *Exploration and Empire: The Explorer and the Scientist in the Winning of the West* (New York: Knopf, 1966), p. 388.

22. Robert C. Nesbit, *"He Built Seattle": A Biography of Judge Thomas Burke* (Seattle, Wash.: University of Washington Press, 1961), provides an excellent introduction to the intellectual history of Seattle's early years.

23. Quoted in Penick, *Progressive Politics and Conservation*, pp. 38–39.

24. Pinchot, *Breaking New Ground*, p. 32.

25. Roderick Nash, *Wilderness and the American Mind* (New Haven, Conn.: Yale University Press, 1967), pp. 122–40.

26. Elmo R. Richardson, "The Struggle for the Valley: California's Hetch Hetchy Controversy, 1905–1913," *California Historical Society Quarterly* 38 (September 1959):249–58; Richardson, *The Politics of Conservation: Crusades and Controversies, 1897–1913* (Berkeley, Calif.: University of California Press, 1962).

27. Hays, *Conservation and the Gospel of Efficiency*, p. 143; Hans Huth, *Nature and the American* (Berkeley, Calif.: University of California Press, 1957), p. 184.

28. Peter J. Schmitt, *Back to Nature: The Arcadian Myth in Urban America* (New York: Oxford University Press, 1969), p. 14.

29. Nash, *Wilderness and the American Mind*, pp. 174–75.

30. Donald C. Swain, "The Passage of the National Park Service Act of 1916," *Wisconsin Magazine of History* 50(Autumn 1966):4–17; Hays, *Conservation and the Gospel of Efficiency*, p. 196.

31. Madison Grant, "In Re Van Ames Land," undated memorandum, John C. Merriam Papers, Manuscripts Division, Library of Congress.

32. For a masterful elaboration of this argument, see Hays, *Conservation and the Gospel of Efficiency*.

33. With fine impartiality the Muir syndrome pervades both the utilitarian and esthetic wings among conservationists. For a recent example of this peculiar genre in historical literature, see Frank Graham, Jr., *Man's Dominion: The Story of Conservation in America* (New York: Evans, 1971).

6. Urban Reform in the Progressive Era

1. James Bryce, *The American Commonwealth* (New York: Macmillan, 1888), I, 608–13, 614. My thanks to Peter d'A. Jones for a critical reading of this study.

2. Andrew Dickson White, "The Government of American Cities," *Forum* 10(December 1890):25.

3. *Proceedings of the National Conference for Good City Government, 1894* (Philadelphia: National Municipal League, 1894); William H. Tolman, *Municipal Reform Movements in the United States* (New York: Fleming H. Revell, 1895), pp. 47–129. For the influence of the depression, see Ernest S. Griffith, *The Modern Development of City Government* (London: Oxford University Press, 1927), p. 146, and David P. Thelen, *The New Citizenship: Origins of Progressivism in Wisconsin, 1885–1900* (Columbia, Mo.: University of Missouri Press, 1972), p. 309.

4. Melvin G. Holli, *Reform in Detroit: Hazen S. Pingree and Urban Politics* (New York: Oxford University Press, 1969), pp. 157–81.

5. Clinton R. Woodruff, "Progress of Municipal Reform, 1894–1895," *Proceedings of the National Conference for Good City Government, 1895* (Philadelphia, Pa.: National Municipal League, 1895), p. 304; *Proceedings of the National Conference for Good City Government, 1900* (Philadelphia, Pa.: National Municipal League, 1900), pp. 55, 67.

6. *Proceedings of the National Conference for Good City Government, 1894,* p. 263.

7. William A. Giles, "Social Conditions in Chicago," ibid., p. 234; Charles J. Bonaparte, "Municipal Government of Baltimore," ibid., p. 91; *Proceedings of the National Conference for Good City Government, 1895,* p. 412.

8. J. Richard Freud, "Civic Service of the Merchants' Association of San Francisco," *Municipal Affairs* 1(December 1897):707; Robert C. Brooks, "Business Men in Civic Service: The Merchants Municipal Committee of Boston," ibid., p. 491.

9. Frank Mann Stewart, *A Half Century of Municipal Reform: The History of the National Municipal League* (Berkeley, Calif.: University of California Press, 1950), p. 27.

10. L. S. Rowe, "A Summary of the Program," *Municipal Program of the National Municipal League* (New York: Macmillan, 1900), pp. 157–73.

11. Holli, *Reform in Detroit,* pp. 161, 169–71.

12. Ibid., pp. 157–61, 169–71.

13. Ibid., pp. 161, 169–71.

14. Ibid., pp. 171–81.

15. Samuel P. Hays, "The Politics of Reform in Municipal Government in the Progressive Era," *Pacific Northwest Quarterly* 55(October 1964):157–69.

16. See especially the *Proceedings* of the first three conferences for Good City Government, 1894–96, and the early issues of *Municipal Affairs* (1897–99).

17. Theodore Roosevelt, "Practical Work in Politics," *Proceedings of the National Conference for Good City Government, 1894,* p. 298.

18. Dwight Waldo, *The Administrative State* (New York: Ronald Press, 1948), p. 193; Samuel Haber, *Efficiency and Uplift: Scientific Management in the Progressive Era, 1890–1902* (Chicago: University of Chicago Press, 1964), pp. ix, x, xii, 116.

19. Charles Zueblin, "American League for Civic Improvement," *Proceedings of the National Conference for Good City Government, 1901* (Philadelphia, Pa.: National Municipal League, 1901), pp. 264–65.

20. Clinton Rogers Woodruff, "The New Municipal Idea," ibid., pp. 40–43; Rufus E. Miles, "Municipal Research—A New Instrument of Democracy," *Proceedings of the National Conference for Good City Government, 1909* (Philadelphia, Pa.: National Municipal League, 1909), pp. 284–90; Norman N. Gill, *Municipal Research Bureaus* (Washington, D.C.: American Council on Public Affairs, 1944), p. 16.

21. Waldo, *The Administrative State,* p. 193; William H. Allen, "The Municipal Research Idea," *Proceedings of the National Conference for Good City Government, 1908* (Philadelphia, Pa.: National Municipal League, 1908), p. 127.

22. William Dudley Foulke, "Address," *Proceedings of the National Conference for Good City Government, 1910* (Philadelphia, Pa.: National Municipal League, 1910), pp. 499–500.

23. Benjamin F. Welton, "The Problem of Securing Efficiency in Municipal Labor," *Annals of the American Academy of Political and Social Science* 41(May 1912):103–104; Henry Bruere, "Efficiency in City Government," ibid., p. 16.

24. Charles E. Merriam, "Investigations as a Means of Securing Administrative

Efficiency," ibid., p. 281; Harrington Emerson, *Efficiency as a Basis for Operation and Wages* (New York: Engineering Magazine, 1909), p. 157.

25. Harold A. Stone, Don K. Price, Kathryn H. Stone, *City Manager Government in the United States* (Chicago: Public Administrative Service, 1940), pp. 9–13, 29, 30; Austin F. Macdonald, *American City Government and Administration* (New York: Crowell, 1936), pp. 210–13.

26. For a list of commission and manager cities and dates of adoption, see Clinton R. Woodruff, *City Government by Commission* (New York: Appleton, 1911), pp. 289–94, and Leonard D. White, *The City Manager* (Chicago: University of Chicago Press, 1927), pp. 307–15. All governmental cost and tax data throughout this section is derived from *Financial Statistics of U.S. Cities Having a Population Over 30,000* (Washington, D.C.: U.S. Government Printing Office, 1908–22).

27. Paul H. Douglas, *Real Wages in the United States, 1890–1926* (New York: Houghton, Mifflin, 1930, 1966), p. 60.

28. For Boston reforms, see *Proceedings of the National Conference for Good City Government, 1909*, pp. 87–89: for Los Angeles, ibid., pp. 108–109; F. J. Stilson, "The Recall in Los Angeles," ibid., p. 330; Harvey N. Shepard, "The Boston Finance Commission," ibid., pp. 207, 212; Warren B. Johnson, "Muckraking in the Northwest: Joe Smith and Seattle Reform," *Pacific Northwest Quarterly* 60(November 1971):488–90.

29. William P. Lovett, "Detroit Progressives Win," *National Municipal Review* 8(January 1919):101–103; Jack D. Elenbaas, "The Excesses of Reform: The Day the Detroit Mayor Arrested the City Council," *Michigan History* 54(Spring 1970:3, 8, 17.

7. American Diplomacy in the Progressive Era

1. Walter E. Weyl, *American World Policies* (New York: Macmillan, 1917), especially Chapter 3.

2. U.S. Bureau of the Census, *Historical Statistics of the United States, Colonial Times to 1957* (Washington, D.C.: U.S. Government Printing Office, 1960), pp. 711, 718, 720.

3. Quoted in Frank Freidel, *America in the Twentieth Century* (New York: Knopf, 1965), p. 121.

4. Woodrow Wilson, *A History of the American People* (New York: Harper, 1902), V, 286–87.

5. Dwight Carroll Miner, *The Fight for the Panama Route: The Story of the Spooner Act and the Hay-Herran Treaty* (New York: Columbia University Press, 1940), pp. 20, 90.

6. Alfred Thayer Mahan, *The Interest of America in Sea Power* (Boston: Little, Brown, 1897), p. 12. See also William E. Livezey, *Mahan on Seapower* (Norman, Okla.: University of Oklahoma Press, 1947), and John A. S. Grenville and George Berkeley Young, *Politics, Strategy, and American Diplomacy: Studies in Foreign Policy 1873–1917* (New Haven, Conn.: Yale University Press, 1968).

7. Dana G. Munro, *Intervention and Dollar Diplomacy in the Caribbean 1900–*

1921 (Princeton, N.J.: Princeton University Press, 1964), p. 66 ff. Grenville and Young, *Politics,* Chapter 11.

8. Elting E. Morison, et al., eds., *The Letters of Theodore Roosevelt* (Cambridge, Mass.: Harvard University Press, 1951–54), III, 567; Miner, *Panama Route,* p. 333 ff.

9. Munro, *Intervention,* p. 56.

10. On Root, see David Healy, *US Expansionism: The Imperialist Urge in the 1890s* (Madison, Wisc.: University of Wisconsin Press), Chapter 8. Richard W. Leopold, *The Growth of American Foreign Policy: A History* (New York: Knopf, 1962), is a superb general account of many of the developments touched upon in this essay. See, for instance, pp. 255–58 regarding the protectorate policy.

11. Morison, *Letters of Roosevelt,* III, pp. 644, 663.

12. Ibid., IV, p. 724; Munro, *Intervention,* p. 65 ff.

13. Munro, *Intervention,* pp. 151–55.

14. Wilfrid Hardy Callcott, *The Western Hemisphere: Its Influence on United States Policies to the End of World War II* (Austin, Tex.: University of Texas Press, 1968), pp. 191–95; Munro, *Intervention,* pp. 158–59.

15. Walter V. Scholes and Marie V. Scholes, *The Foreign Policies of the Taft Administration* (Columbia, Mo.: University of Missouri Press, 1970), p. 8 and Chapters 3 and 4; Munro, *Intervention,* Chapter 5.

16. Scholes and Scholes, *Taft,* pp. 65–66; Munro, *Intervention,* pp. 208–16.

17. Grenville and Young, *Politics,* p. 325 ff; *Papers Relating to the Foreign Relations of the United States: The Lansing Papers 1914–1920* (Washington, D.C.: U.S. Government Printing Office, 1940), II, 466–67.

18. Arthur S. Link, *Wilson* (Princeton, N.J.: Princeton University Press, 1947–65), III, 520–50; Rayford W. Logan, *Haiti and the Dominican Republic* (New York: Oxford University Press, 1968), pp. 61–62, 127–41; Charles Callan Tansill, *The Purchase of the Danish West Indies* (Baltimore, Md.: The Johns Hopkins Press, 1932).

19. The chronology of the Mexican problem may be followed through the volumes of Link's *Wilson.* A convenient summary is in his *Woodrow Wilson and the Progressive Era, 1910–1917* (New York: Harper, 1954), Chapter 5.

20. Link, *Wilson,* V, 338.

21. A. Whitney Griswold, *The Far Eastern Policy of the United States* (New York: Harcourt, Brace, 1938), is still the most readable general account, but recent scholarship has produced important corrections. See, for instance, Paul A. Varg, *The Making of a Myth: The United States and China, 1897–1912* (East Lansing, Mich.: Michigan State University Press, 1968); Warren I. Cohen, *America's Response to China: An Interpretive History of Sino-American Relations* (New York: Wiley, 1971); and Raymond A. Esthus, *Theodore Roosevelt and Japan,* (Seattle, Wash.: University of Washington Press, 1966).

22. Grenville and Young, *Politics,* pp. 269–74.

23. Leopold, *Growth of American Foreign Policy,* pp. 215–18.

24. Paul A. Varg, "The United States a World Power, 1900–1917: Myth or Reality," in John Braeman, Robert H. Bremner, and David Brody, eds., *Twentieth-Century American Foreign Policy* (Columbus, O.: Ohio State University Press, 1971), p. 216.

25. This paragraph and the next owe much to Esthus, *Roosevelt and Japan.*

26. Morison, *Letters of Roosevelt,* V, 30; VII, 189–90.

27. Scholes and Scholes, *Taft,* p. 109.

28. Ibid., pp. 18–19; Varg, "United States a World Power," pp. 216–17.

28. See Cohen, *America's Response to China,* pp. 76–82. Herbert Croly's *Willard Straight* (New York: Macmillan, 1924), and Jerry Israel, *Progressivism and the Open Door: America and China, 1905–1921* (Pittsburgh, Pa.: University of Pittsburgh Press, 1971), are useful on Straight.

30. See the important and recent analysis in Scholes and Scholes, *Taft,* Chapter 12.

31. Ibid., p. 246.

32. Link, *Wilson,* II, 283–304.

33. See E. David Cronon, ed., *The Cabinet Diaries of Josephus Daniels, 1913–1921* (Lincoln, Neb.: University of Nebraska Press, 1963), pp. 8 ff.

34. *Foreign Relations, 1914, Supplement* (Washington, D.C.: U.S. Government Printing Office, 1922), pp. 189–90; Link, *Wilson,* III, 307.

35. *Foreign Relations: The Lansing Papers,* II, 418; Link, *Wilson,* III, 307.

36. Roy Watson Curry, *Woodrow Wilson and Far Eastern Policy 1913–1921* (New York: Bookman Associates, 1957), Chapter 7.

37. Cohen, *America's Response to China,* p. 95; Israel, *Progressivism and the Open Door,* p. 150.

38. Curry, *Woodrow Wilson and Far Eastern Policy,* Chapter 6.

39. Ray Stannard Baker and William E. Dodd, eds., *The Public Papers of Woodrow Wilson* (New York: Harper, 1925–27), IV, 185.

40. Raymond A. Esthus, *Theodore Roosevelt and the International Rivalries* (Waltham, Mass.: Ginn-Blaisdell, 1970), p. 52.

41. Grenville and Young, *Politics,* pp. 326–27.

42. See Link, *Wilson,* III, Chapter 1.

43. James Bishop Peabody, ed., *The Holmes-Einstein Letters: Correspondence of Mr. Justice Holmes and Lewis Einstein 1903–1935* (New York: St. Martin's, 1964), p. 115.

44. Harold and Margaret Sprout, *The Rise of American Naval Power 1776–1918* (Princeton, N.J.: Princeton University Press, 1939), pp. 322–46.

45. Link, *Wilson,* V, 246.

46. For development of this theme, see W. B. Fowler, *British-American Relations, 1917–1918: The Role of Sir William Wiseman* (Princeton, N.J.: Princeton University Press, 1969).

47. Ibid., pp. 222–27.

48. Thomas A. Bailey's two volumes, *Woodrow Wilson and the Lost Peace* (New York: Macmillan, 1944), and *Woodrow Wilson and the Great Betrayal* (New York: Macmillan, 1945), remain useful as general accounts of the developments at Paris and in the Senate, but see also the able analysis by Ralph Stone, *The Irreconcilables: The Fight Against the League of Nations* (Lexington, Ky.: University Press of Kentucky, 1970). Charles Forcey, *The Crossroads of Liberalism: Croly, Weyl, Lippmann and the Progressive Era 1900–1925* (New York: Oxford University Press, 1961), is very full on the disappointment of the *New Republic* group.

49. Alfred Thayer Mahan, "Subordination in Historical Treatment," in *Ameri-*

can Historical Association Annual Report, 1902 (Washington, D.C.: American Historical Association, 1903), pp. 47–63. Morison, *Letters of Roosevelt,* III, 707.

50. L. Ethan Ellis, *Reciprocity 1911* (New Haven, Conn.: Yale University Press, 1939); Scholes and Scholes, *Taft,* p. 9 n.16.

51. William S. Graves, *America's Siberian Adventure 1918–1920* (New York: Cape and Smith, 1931), p. 343.

52. Ibid., p. 350; William A. Williams, "American Intervention in Russia, 1917–1920," *Studies on the Left* III(No. 4, 1963):24–40, and IV(No. 1, 1964):39–56.

53. Betty Miller Unterberger, *America's Siberian Expedition, 1918–1920: A Study of National Policy* (Durham, N.C.: Duke University Press, 1956).

54. George F. Kennan, *The Decision to Intervene* (vol. 2 of *Soviet-American Relations, 1917–1920*) (Princeton, N.J.: Princeton University Press, 1958).

55. Fowler, *British-American Relations,* Chapter 7; N. Gordon Levin, Jr., *Woodrow Wilson and World Politics: America's Response to War and Revolution* (New York: Oxford University Press, 1968), Chapter 3; Unterberger, *America's Siberian Expedition,* Chapter 10; *Foreign Relations: The Paris Peace Conference 1919* (Washington, D.C.: U.S. Government Printing Office, 1942–47), V, 529; *Foreign Relations: The Lansing Papers,* II, 392.

8. The Progressive Legacy

1. Discussions of many of these progressive ideas are scattered throughout general works on the subject. Some of the best such works are Samuel P. Hays, *The Response to Industrialism: 1885–1914* (Chicago: University of Chicago Press, 1957); Richard Hofstadter, *The Age of Reform: From Bryan to F.D.R.* (New York: Knopf, 1955); Robert H. Wiebe, *The Search for Order 1877–1920* (New York: Hill and Wang, 1967); George E. Mowry, *The Era of Theodore Roosevelt and the Birth of Modern America, 1900–1912* (New York: Harper & Row, 1958); Arthur S. Link, *Woodrow Wilson and the Progressive Era, 1910–1917* (New York: Harper & Row, 1954); Otis L. Graham, Jr., *The Great Campaigns: Reform and War in America, 1900–1928* (Englewood Cliffs, N.J.: Prentice-Hall, 1971).

2. Stanley K. Schultz, "The Morality of Politics: The Muckrakers' Vision of Democracy," *Journal of American History* LII(December 1965):527–47; Louis Filler, *Crusaders for American Liberalism* (New York: Harcourt, Brace, 1939).

3. Occasionally a movement would begin in the 1890s, as in Detroit, where reform went further than urban progressives elsewhere usually wished to take it; see Melvin G. Holli, *Reform in Detroit: Hazen S. Pingree and Urban Politics* (New York: Oxford University Press, 1969), especially Chapter 8.

4. *San Antonio Light and Gazette,* March 13, 1910. See also Samuel P. Hays, "The Politics of Reform in Municipal Government in the Progressive Era," *Pacific Northwest Quarterly* LV(October 1964):157–69.

5. *The Municipal Year Book 1968* (Washington, D.C.: International City Managers' Association, 1968), pp. 132–34. About one-fourth of the American people live in manager cities. The standard work on the subject is Leonard D. White, *The City Manager* (Chicago: University of Chicago Press, 1927); see also, John Porter East, *Council-Manager Government: The Political Thought of Its*

Founder, Richard S. Childs (Chapel Hill, N.C.: University of North Carolina Press, 1965).

6. East, *Council-Manager Government,* p. 153; Edward C. Banfield and James Q. Wilson, *City Politics* (Cambridge, Mass.: Harvard University Press, 1963), p. 171.

7. James Weinstein, "Organized Business and the City Commission and Manager Movements," *Journal of Southern History* XXVIII(May 1962): 168–75; East, *Council-Manager Government,* Chapter III.

8. White, *The City Manager,* p. 126; George B. Tindall, *The Emergence of the New South 1913–1945* (Baton Rouge, La.: Louisiana State University Press, 1967), Chapter VII.

9. Hoyt Landon Warner, *Progressivism in Ohio 1897–1917* (Columbus, O.: Ohio State University Press, 1964), especially Chapters Five and Sixteen; David P. Thelen, *The New Citizenship: Origins of Progressivism in Wisconsin 1885–1900* (Columbia, Mo.: University of Missouri Press, 1972), pp. 132–33, 244–46.

10. Charles Edward Merriam and Louise Overacker, *Primary Elections* (Chicago: University of Chicago Press, 1928).

11. George E. Mowry, *The California Progressives* (Berkeley, Calif.: University of California Press, 1951), Chapter 1; Spencer C. Olin, Jr., *California's Prodigal Sons: Hiram Johnson and the Progressives, 1911–1917* (Berkeley, Calif.: University of California Press, 1968), Chapter 1; V. O. Key, Jr., and Winston W. Crouch, *The Initiative and the Referendum in California* (Berkeley, Calif.: University of California Press, 1939), p. 423. Direct democracy in general is ably discussed in Harold F. Gosnell, *Democracy—the Threshold of Freedom* (New York: Ronald Press, 1948), Chapter 14.

12. Arthur N. Holcombe, *State Government in the United States* (New York: Macmillan, 1926), Chapter XV.

13. Ibid.; William B. Munro, "Initiative and Referendum," in Edwin R. A. Seligman, ed., *Encyclopedia of the Social Sciences* (New York: Macmillan, 1932), VIII, 50–52.

14. Key and Crouch, *The Initiative and the Referendum in California,* p. 565.

15. Thelen, *The New Citizenship,* p. 304. A particularly strong defense of progressives' use of direct democracy is in Arthur S. Link, *American Epoch* (New York: Knopf, 1955), p. 90.

16. Robert S. Maxwell, *La Follette and the Rise of the Progressives in Wisconsin* (Madison, Wisc.: State Historical Society of Wisconsin, 1956), p. 79; Marver H. Bernstein, *Regulating Business by Independent Commission* (Princeton, N.J.: Princeton University Press, 1955), pp. 36–37, 61–62.

17. The restriction imposed on commission regulation by the courts is well known to all close students of the subject. Eli Winston Clemens, *Economics and Public Utilities* (New York: Appleton-Century-Crofts, 1950), pp. 48–71.

18. Bernstein, *Regulating Business by Independent Commission,* pp. 36–37; E. Pendleton Herring, *Public Administration and the Public Interest* (New York: McGraw-Hill, 1936), Part III (Herring here discusses federal commissions, but the same principles apply to state regulation as well).

19. Stanley P. Caine, *The Myth of a Progressive Reform: Railroad Regulation in Wisconsin 1903–1910* (Madison, Wisc.: State Historical Society of Wisconsin, 1970); the quoted phrase is the title of Chapter 10.

20. Raymond H. Pulley, *Old Virginia Restored: An Interpretation of the Progressive Impulse 1870–1939* (Charlottesville, Va.: University Press of Virginia, 1968), pp. 105–107; Maxwell, *La Follette and the Rise of the Progressives in Wisconsin*, pp. 76–79; Olin, *California's Prodigal Sons*, pp. 37–41; Caine, *Myth of a Progressive Reform*, p. 186; C. Vann Woodward, *Origins of the New South 1877–1913* (Baton Rouge, La.: Louisiana State University Press, 1951), pp. 379–83.

21. Stephen B. Wood, *Constitutional Politics in the Progressive Era: Child Labor and the Law* (Chicago: University of Chicago Press, 1968), Chapter 2. The amendment passed Congress, but was not ratified by a sufficient number of states.

22. Roy Lubove, *The Struggle for Social Security 1900–1935* (Cambridge, Mass.: Harvard University Press, 1968), Chapter III; James Weinstein, "Big Business and the Origins of Workmen's Compensation," *Labor History* VIII(Spring 1967):156–74; Theodore Roosevelt, "Sarah Knisley's Arm," *Collier's*, L(January 25, 1913):9.

23. In fact, a law school textbook has taken the evolution of workmen's compensation as its principal illustration of *The Legal Process: An Introduction to Decision-making by Judicial, Legislative, Executive, and Administrative Agencies*, by Carl A. Auerbach, Lloyd K. Garrison, Willard Hurst, and Samuel Mermin (San Francsico, Calif.: Chandler Publishing Company, 1961).

24. Lubove, *The Struggle for Social Security*, p. 54. Some corporations, notably U.S. Steel, instituted their own voluntary programs for workmen's compensation, without involving the state.

25. The schedule of benefits is still too low in most states. Profits for the underwriting companies are high, and the system itself does little to encourage prevention of accidents, as Ralph Nader has repeatedly noted. On the issue of state-owned enterprise, see Robert Asher, "Radicalism and Reform: State Insurance of Workmen's Compensation in Minnesota, 1910–1933," *Labor History* XIV(Winter 1973):19–41.

26. Dewey W. Grantham, Jr., "The Progressive Movement and the Negro," *South Atlantic Quarterly* LIV(October 1955):473; David W. Southern, *The Malignant Heritage: Yankee Progressives and the Negro Question 1901–1914* (Chicago: Loyola University Press, 1968), p. 85; C. Vann Woodward, *The Strange Career of Jim Crow* (New York: Oxford University Press, 1957), p. 75.

27. Woodward, *Origins of the New South*, p. 321; Woodward, *Strange Career of Jim Crow*, pp. 66–68.

28. Woodward, *Strange Career of Jim Crow*, pp. 81–87; Jack Temple Kirby, *Darkness at the Dawning: Race and Reform in the Progressive South* (Philadelphia, Pa.: Lippincott, 1972), Chapter I.

29. Arthus S. Link, *Woodrow Wilson and the Progressive Era*, pp. 65–66, emphasizes the protests to official segregation.

30. John D. Weaver, *The Brownsville Raid* (New York: Norton, 1970); and Ann J. Lane, *The Brownsville Affair: National Crisis and Black Reaction* (Port Washington, N.Y.: Kennikat Press, 1971).

31. Weaver, *Brownsville Raid*, p. 140; partly owing to the efforts of author Weaver, in 1972 the secretary of the army revoked the dismissal of the 167 black soldiers.

32. Seth M. Scheiner, "Theodore Roosevelt and the Negro, 1901–1908," *Journal of Negro History* XLVII(July 1962):169–82.

33. Charles Carroll, *"The Negro a Beast"; or, "In the Image of God"* (St. Louis, Mo.: American Book and Bible House, 1900); Robert Bennett Bean, M.D., "The Negro Brain," *The Century Magazine* LXXII(September 1906):778–84; Charles H. McCord, *The American Negro as a Dependent, Defective, and Delinquent* (Nashville, Tenn.: Press of Benson Printing Co., 1914). See George M. Frederickson, *The Black Image in the White Mind: The Debate on Afro-American Character and Destiny, 1817–1914* (New York: Harper & Row, 1971), Chapters Nine and Ten.

34. See the comment by Roosevelt quoted in Lane, *Brownsville Affair,* p. 104.

35. Hofstadter, *Age of Reform,* pp. 8–9, 174–86; John Higham, *Strangers in the Land: Patterns of American Nativism 1860–1925* (New York: Atheneum, 1968), pp. 116–23 and Chapter Nine.

36. Adams, "Reflex Light from Africa," *The Century Magazine* LXXII(May 1906):107.

37. Woodward, *Origins of the New South,* pp. 275, 321–28; Woodward, *Strange Career of Jim Crow,* pp. 65–77; the point is even more fully developed in Kirby, *Darkness at the Dawning,* especially Chapter I.

38. This combination of equalitarianism for whites with persecution of blacks was not entirely new in American history, as Frederickson shows in his discussion of *"Herrenvolk* democracy," in *The Black Image in the White Mind,* pp. 61, 68, 93–94, 190, 267.

39. The standard work is Samuel P. Hays, *Conservation and the Gospel of Efficiency: The Progressive Conservation Movement, 1890–1920* (Cambridge, Mass.: Harvard University Press, 1959).

40. On the FTC see Susan Wagner, *The Federal Trade Commission* (New York: Praeger, 1971); Gerard C. Henderson, *The Federal Trade Commission: A Study in Administrative Law and Procedure* (New Haven, Conn.: Yale University Press, 1925); Robert E. Cushman, *The Independent Regulatory Commissions* (New York: Oxford University Press, 1941), pp. 177–228; and G. Cullom Davis, "The Transformation of the Federal Trade Commission, 1914–1929," *Mississippi Valley Historical Review* XLIX(December 1962):437–55.

41. Edward F. Cox, et al., *"The Nader Report" on the Federal Trade Commission* (New York: Baron, 1969), p. vii.

42. Melvin I. Urofsky, "Wilson, Brandeis and the Trust Issue, 1912–1914," *Mid-America* XLIX(January 1967):3–28.

43. 38 Stat. 719.

44. *Federal Trade Commission* v. *Gratz,* 253 U.S. 427 (1920).

45. Davis, "Transformation of the FTC," pp. 452–53.

46. Graham, *The Great Campaigns,* p. 168.

47. The theme of the progressive legacy might be pursued further in the following works: Paul W. Glad, "Progressives and the Business Culture of the 1920s," *Journal of American History* LIII(June 1966):75–89; Arthur S. Link, "What Happened to the Progressive Movement in the 1920's?" *American Historical Review* LXIV(July 1959):833–51; "Legacies of the Progressive Era," Chapter I of Robert M. Crunden, *From Self to Society 1919–1941* (Englewood Cliffs, N.J.: Prentice-Hall, 1972); "The Progressive Legacy," Chapter 2 of Grant McConnell, *Private Power and American Democracy* (New York: Knopf, 1966). On the relationship of progressivism and the New Deal, see Otis L. Graham, Jr., *An Encore*

for Reform: The Old Progressives and the New Deal (New York: Oxford University Press, 1967). An especially challenging critique is Richard M. Abrams, "The Failure of Progressivism," in Abrams and Lawrence W. Levine, eds., *The Shaping of Twentieth-Century America,* 2nd ed. (Boston: Little, Brown, 1971), pp. 207–24.

INDEX